THE VIOLENCE **WITHIN**
THE VIOLENCE **WITHOUT**

Jacqueline Vaught Brogan

THE VIOLENCE **WITHIN**

THE VIOLENCE **WITHOUT**

Wallace Stevens and the Emergence

of a Revolutionary Poetics

The University of Georgia Press | Athens and London

© 2003 by the University of Georgia Press
Athens, Georgia 30602
All rights reserved
Designed by Mindy Basinger Hill
Set in Electra and Trade Gothic by Bookcomp,
Inc.
Printed and bound by Thompson-Shore, Inc.
The paper in this book meets the guidelines for
permanence and durability of the Committee
on Production Guidelines for Book Longevity of
the Council on Library Resources.

Printed in the United States of America
07 06 05 04 03 C 5 4 3 2 1

Library of Congress Cataloging-in-Publication
Data

Brogan, Jacqueline Vaught, 1952–
    The violence within/the violence without :
Wallace Stevens and the emergence of a
revolutionary poetics / Jacqueline Vaught
Brogan.
        p. cm.
Includes bibliographical references and index.
    ISBN 0-8203-2519-8 (hardcover : alk. paper)
1. Stevens, Wallace, 1879–1955—Criticism and
interpretation.   2. Stevens, Wallace,
1879–1955—Political and social views.   3. World
War, 1939–1945—United States—Literature and
the war.   4. Revolutionary poetry,
American—History and criticism.   5. Violence
in literature.   6. War in literature.   I. Title.
    PS3537.T4753 Z619 2003
    811'.52—dc21   2003000795

British Library Cataloging-in-Publication Data
available

"The Sick Man" by Wallace Stevens, from
Opus Posthumous by Wallace Stevens, edited
by Milton J. Bates. Copyright © 1957 by Elsie
Stevens and Holly Stevens, copyright renewed
1985 by Holly Stevens. Copyright © 1989 by
Holly Stevens. Used by permission of Vintage
Books, a division of Random House, Inc. All
other excerpts of Wallace Stevens's poetry,
from The Collected Poems of Wallace Stevens
by Wallace Stevens, copyright 1954 by Wallace
Stevens and renewed 1982 by Holly Stevens.
Used by permission of Alfred A. Knopf, a
division of Random House, Inc. "Nantucket"
by William Carlos Williams, from Collected
Poems: 1909–1939, Volume 1, copyright © 1938
by New Directions Publishing Corp. Used
by permission of New Directions Publishing
Corporation. Wightman Williams's illustrations
for Esthétique du Mal and the title spread
illustration of Notes toward a Supreme Fiction are
reproduced courtesy of the Cummington Press.
Paul Klee's Suicide on the Bridge was originally
published in 1922 in the journal Broom.

CONTENTS

PREFACE

Despite the sustained efforts of several well-known critics over the last two decades to uncover a politically charged Stevens, for most readers Wallace Stevens remains an aesthete—an accomplished one, for sure, but essentially a poet whose work is divorced from the real world. And despite the sustained efforts of many critics to expose a Stevens sensitive to feminist concerns, he also remains for most readers excessively patriarchal, rigidly focused on that "virile" and "masculine poet" he describes in his essays as well as in his poetry. In fact, some major feminist poets have explicitly denounced Stevens precisely for being sexist. Others have also rejected him for being racist. Nonetheless, Stevens remains today one of the leading poets of the early to mid–twentieth century, influencing a wide range of poets writing today.

I have been among those critics who, over the last decade, have described Stevens as an ethically responsible poet, especially in relationship to the political climate of World War II, as well as to feminist concerns. As a consequence, this book draws upon earlier work I have done, though with significant modifications. As I see it, Stevens changes drastically over his career, becoming increasingly responsive to the world rather than remaining the politically distanced poet many other scholars and critics have described. At the same time, however, certain aspects of his work clearly do remain

ironically constant, particularly the continued vacillation between his privileging of or disgust at the world of reality or the world of the imagination, a
vacillation that remains recurrent from his earliest to latest poems. Because
of this ongoing debate in his poetry, it has been difficult for many critics to
hear (or to "see") the important changes in Stevens's "revolutionary poetics"
that I describe in this book.[1] Moreover, the critical changes in his poetry that
interest me here are very complicated and intertwined, once again obscuring
his fundamental changes in perception and poetics over time, particularly
when, as opposed to Dante's commitment to the particulars of his time in
The Divine Comedy, especially in the *Inferno,* Stevens remains committed
to the idea that "It Must Be Abstract" for poetry not only to endure but
to be understood over the long ravages of time (a concern, actually, that
haunted Dante as well). I argue that we can trace Stevens's evolving poetic
practices along three major lines of development: an initial aesthetic battle
(pitted most clearly against William Carlos Williams); a secondary reaction
to the "pressures of reality" in the form of actual war (most specifically, World
War II), within which there are discrete stages ranging from aesthetic "resistance," to the necessity of witnessing, to the call for poetic responsibility in
describing our future world; and a subsequent, almost feminist vision that,
aligned with these first two lines of development, allows for a new kind of
poetry in Stevens's work that readily speaks to women. In essence, what began
in Stevens as a "violence within" (to alter his own phrase)—or an aesthetic
position designed to withstand a "violence without" (most specifically in the
form of social unrest and actual war)—rapidly evolved during his middle
years into one increasingly responsive to his actual times, including in his
later years a critique of the unfortunate remnants and prevalence of racism
in actual American life, despite that earlier "violence" in the form of the
Civil War.

Because I am addressing separately in the following chapters Stevens's
relationship to aesthetics, politics, feminism, and racism as being "critical
stages" in his career when they are actually concurrent developments inter-
secting with each other in fascinating ways, there are occasional overlapping
discussions in the argument of this book. For example, "Description without
Place," among many other poems, offers various entrances and insights into
these braided concerns and changes in Stevens's career. What follows, then,
is my attempt to describe these major lines of development in Stevens's
evolving aesthetics and politics—"words, war, and women"—as well as to
suggest how these separate lines are ultimately intertwined in the canon of

an increasingly ethically concerned poet we have not fully recognized before. The concluding chapter of this work addresses Stevens and racism not as a "critical stage" but as an important current of his work that runs throughout his career, a current we do not readily see without the insights gleaned from the preceding chapters. My conclusion is that despite his continued focus on the "imagination" and "reality," this extraordinarily gifted poet not only changed but matured over time and that the poetic strategies he evolved to accommodate these changes remain relevant—actually important—to many contemporary "revolutionary poets" writing today.

ACKNOWLEDGMENTS

Although this final project is ultimately quite different from my initial proposal, I would like to thank the National Endowment of the Humanities for the fellowship that supported the earliest stages of this work. In addition, I am grateful to the Institute for Scholarship in the Liberal Arts at the University of Notre Dame for sponsoring this work with financial support. I am deeply grateful.

In addition, I owe the inspiration and completion of this work to altogether too many scholars and colleagues to list here. Of special note, however, are Professor Louis Mackey of the University of Texas, who first shared his love of Wallace Stevens and language with me, and the distinguished Professor James Robinson, who read the earliest drafts of this work and whose continued support and friendship were unwavering. I also wish to thank the late Professor Margaret Dickie, whose scholarship and collegial support were inspirational, as well as Albert Gelpi, Eleanor Cook, Charles Altieri, and John Serio for their faith in me all these years.

Other friends and colleagues have influenced this work in many and very different ways. Although a full elaboration of my gratitude would prove far too lengthy, let me name the following people with sincere thanks: Dolores

Frese, Jerry Frese, John Fisher, Alicia Ostriker, Marjorie Perloff, Roy Harvey Pearce, Don Costello, Cynthia Hogue, Kathy Psomiades, Charles Berger, Abby Werlock, Drucilla Cornell, and Cyraina Johnson-Roullier.

Special thanks goes to Imogene Pilcher and to Fred Moramarco, both of whom made invaluable suggestions in the late stages of this work; to Mary M. Hill for her careful copyediting; to Sarah McKee at the University of Georgia Press; to Daniele Paulding, whose meticulous work at the very end of this project saved my sanity; and particularly to Cheryl Reed, whose diligence and cheer allowed the completion of this work and without whom I could not have managed. I also owe special thanks to my children, Jessica and Evan, for their continual patience and poise. And, finally, I must thank Wallace Stevens himself, whose changing visions and creative words have inspired me, professionally and personally, for nearly two decades.

Parts of the following chapters repeat, often in very different forms, sections taken from previously published essays: "Wallace Stevens: Poems against His Climate," *Wallace Stevens Journal* 11, no. 2 (1987): 75–93; "Sister of the Minotaur: Sexism and Stevens," *Wallace Stevens Journal* 12, no. 2 (1988): 102–18; "Stevens in History and Not in History: The Poet and the Second World War," *Wallace Stevens Journal* 13, no. 2 (1989): 168–90; "Planets on the Table: From Wallace Stevens and Elizabeth Bishop to Adrienne Rich and June Jordan," *Wallace Stevens Journal* 19, no. 2 (1995): 255–78; "Wrestling with Those 'Rotted Names': Wallace Stevens' and Adrienne Rich's 'Revolutionary Poetics,' " *Wallace Stevens Journal* 25, no. 1 (2001): 19–39; and "It Must Be 'Re-Named': Dante's *Comedy* and Stevens's 'Notes toward a Supreme Fiction,' " *Lectura Dantis* 7 (fall 1990): 122–32.

ABBREVIATIONS

CP	Stevens, *Collected Poems*
L	Stevens, *Letters of Wallace Stevens*
NA	Stevens, *The Necessary Angel: Essays on Reality and the Imagination*
OP	Stevens, *Opus Posthumous*
PR	*Partisan Review*
WCP	William Carlos Williams, *Collected Poems: 1921–1931*

INTRODUCTION

The artist is not the aesthetician, not the psychologist, not the art historian; as the need arises, he could, of course be all these, and more.
HENRI FOCILLON, *The Life of Forms in Art*

In the relatively late poem "Prologues to What Is Possible," Wallace Stevens writes, "He belonged to the far-foreign departure of his vessel and was part of it" (CP, 516). The difficulties involved in interpreting these lines could well stand as an exemplum for the difficulties facing this book. If, for example, we regard "He" as a fictional character within the poem, simply riding in a "boat carried forward by waves resembling the bright backs of rowers," the chief issues in interpreting the lines become sheer plot (with attention to the almost mythic fear "He" feels about voyaging out alone) or perhaps the hermeneutic and theoretic complications of things beyond "resemblance." But we can also regard the "He" as a mask for Wallace Stevens, poet par excellence, making a barely veiled statement about his relation to poetry, in particular, to modern poetry. From this perspective, the "stones" comprising his "vessel" are poetic traditions that have "lost their weight." Here, we might wish to discuss Stevens's relation to other modern poets, such as William Carlos Williams and Ezra Pound, and his relation to previous poetic periods, such as those "[r]omantic tenements of rose and ice" (CP, 239) he dismisses

1

elsewhere. Additionally, given the "hereditary lights" that appear later in the poem and the actual climatic shift from South to North that occurs toward the end of the second section, we might be tempted to regard the "He" as Wallace Stevens, a person in reality, meditating upon his relation to the actual world, which includes not only his personal heredity but the larger climatic shifts of the world as he continues in his "vessel" to move through the relentless passage of time. Here biographical, psychological, or even New Historicist approaches would provide crucial contexts to be explored in fully understanding this poem.

As should be obvious enough, any number of other critical approaches are "possible" for "Prologues to What Is Possible." I can think, for example, of a particular "Freudian" reading about his belonging to his "vessel" and its "departure" that instantly undoes the actual power of this lyric. However, among the variety of critical approaches taken with Wallace Stevens, what proves most revealing, as a number of recent Stevens specialists have shown, is the possibility that Stevens's poetry—his aesthetics—is actually politically responsive to his times, particularly to the violence that so dominated the first half of this century, first with World War I and then, most acutely, with World War II. Here, as in the remainder of this book, "He" of "Prologues to What Is Possible" can be understood to be Stevens as both poet and person, taking his "vessel" or aesthetics on a voyage that at once responds to but also systematically "resists" (to adapt his own word) the violence and chaos of his larger climate, most specifically, that surrounding and constituting the Second World War.

However, I would like to clarify that, given the violence that continued to characterize the twentieth century, what I have to say about Stevens's poetry in relation to World War II could easily be extended backward to poetry responding to the disillusionment surrounding World War I. My arguments could also be projected forward to the cultural angst surrounding subsequent military crises, most notably the Vietnam War, but also the various ethnic wars across the globe over the last decade as well as our current situation after terrorist attacks and the accompanying escalations of rhetoric. My primary purpose, nonetheless, is to adjust our understanding of Stevens as a poet and as a person and to demonstrate that far from being an aesthete, removed either by inclination or by economic position from any involvement with the political realities of his time, Stevens was in fact deeply responsive to his times and evolved rapidly over the course of World War II into one of the most compelling and ethical poets of the twentieth century. One salutary consequence of such an understanding would be the continued unsettling of what I and others regard as a fallacious division between "modernism" (in particular, that highly selected poetry termed "high modernism") and what is loosely called "postmodernism," especially if the work of women poets such as Gertrude Stein, Mina Loy, H.D., and even Marianne Moore were genuinely factored into the so-called modernist period.[1]

With regard to the larger issue of modernism and postmodernism, it is fair to say that an almost overwhelming number of recent works have upset the traditional distinction between the two periods as well as other corollary distinctions such as "structuralism," "poststructuralism," "New Criticism," and the subsequent proliferation of various "new" criticisms. In a variety of different ways, theorists and critics everywhere are reminding us that both literature and our understanding of that literature are inevitably political and *contextual*. As Joseph M. Conte succinctly puts it in *Unending Design*, "On behalf of a resistant postmodernism, poststructuralist, feminist, and psychoanalytic critics celebrate the death of the subject, the revaluation of the supreme fictions of modernism, and a rising pluralism and heterogeneity. The reactionary position, often taken up by cultural neoconservatives (perhaps following the lead of Toynbee), laments the dissolution of a distinct high culture and the hierarchical social structures that support it."[2] We should note that this important debate about the "revaluation" of our "supreme fictions" has rapidly extended beyond the domain of English departments into a variety of other fields, including the study of law. The recent development of this debate in the latter field goes far beyond the isolated instance of one or two individuals (for example, Stanley Fish, formerly at Duke University, or the involvement of Jacques Derrida at the Cardozo School of Law), so that it is possible to find a number of publications nationwide that now focus on the contextual and even "literary" status of legal interpretation itself.[3]

However, when considering the relation of literature to law or the specific relation of poetry to politics, we would do well to remember that in certain fundamental ways attention to and concern with this relationship is really nothing new.[4] Indeed, as Stevens—notably, both poet and lawyer—might say, the contemporary obsession with politics and poetics is simply "like a new account of everything old" (CP, 529). In fact, it is quite possible to turn to our most traditionally canonized writers (for example, Dante, Shakespeare, Dryden, Milton, Coleridge, Emerson, and Whitman) to discover self-consciously articulated evaluations of the confluence and continuum of poetry and politics. For instance, in the 1821 "A Defence of Poetry" (easily one of the best-known and most overt statements about the political utility, purpose, and nature of poetry), Shelley quite seriously calls poets the "unacknowledged legislators of the world."[5] He in no way means this assertion in any narrowly confined aesthetic or structural sense. Countering Thomas Love Peacock's "challenge" for poets "to resign the civic crown to reasoners and mechanists," Shelley insists that poets "are not only the authors of language and of music, of the dance and architecture, and statuary, and painting; they are *the institutors of laws, and the founders of civil society.*"[6] It is with a somewhat humorous gesture that Shelley goes on to say that Plato (that philosopher who so thoroughly distrusted poetry) "was essentially a poet."[7] That particular assertion should also remind us that Plato's desire to exclude poets from his political/philosophical republic stemmed precisely from his fear of the power of poetry (which he regarded as being deceptive) in realized political life. It might not be going too far to say that despite the prevalence and impact of New Criticism in the middle part of the twentieth century, for most of literary history *the poetic has always been political.* Perhaps this fact is precisely what Stevens means when he cryptically asserts that "[p]oetry is not personal" (OP, 186) rather than espousing an Eliot-like presumption of authorial "neutrality" or individual "sacrifice" of identity, as has been so frequently assumed.

It is crucial to remember for Stevens's own use of the *lyric* that at least in the history of American literature, the supposed purity and "autonomy" of aesthetics in general and of poetry in particular was, in fact, a notion that flourished in a causal and reciprocal relation to New Criticism, a relation ironically motivated by political concerns. The most famous argument favoring aesthetic autonomy, for example, was itself a highly political argument constructed largely to allow Ezra Pound (that most political of poets) to receive in 1949 the Bollingen Prize for the poetry written while he was interred for the anti-American, pro-Fascist broadcasts he made in Italy during World War II. Furthermore, granting Pound the prize at the beginning of the cold war had the secondary political motivation of demonstrating how liberal and noncensoring the American government was in contrast to other world nations at the time. Seen in this light, the entire notion of aesthetic autonomy, at least as it has been articulated in the twentieth century, is fraught with, if not contaminated by, political motivations, contexts, and consequences. That the same argument favoring aesthetic accomplishment over political concerns would then be used the following year—as a defense against the then-widespread sentiment that Stevens's poetry was too far removed from the social realities of his time, with the consequence that Wallace Stevens would be awarded the Bollingen Prize in 1950—makes the actual political service of this supposedly "pure" aesthetic autonomy all the more striking and ironic.[8]

Yet, even if the relationship between poetry and politics is finally nothing new in either literary or cultural history, what may well be new is the growing awareness of the constitutive nature of language (whether poetic or not) that allows it to determine, in reality, political structures charged with the power alternately to privilege or to marginalize. This particular awareness has, consequently, not only led to a number of developments in ethnic and feminist theories but has also encouraged the restoration of previously un-canonized works (often written either by women or by members of ethnic minorities) that have, in turn, encouraged a recasting of our ideas about modernism, postmodernism, and even "canonization" itself.[9] It is perhaps not without some irony that some of these developments have subsequently encouraged the resuscitation of various poems by Stevens himself previously excluded from the "canonized Stevens" found in anthologies over the last few decades.[10]

This secondary consequence returns us to the faulty or at least overly restrictive traditional distinction between poets of the "inner" and "outer" worlds in which invariably Stevens has been (and frequently continues to be) aligned with the former. For example, even in the relatively recent *Lyric Contingencies*, in which the author correctly argues that Stevens's poetry de-rives from a "social sense" unavailable to Emily Dickinson, Margaret Dickie still pits Stevens against Williams and Pound along this familiar critical line: "While Williams and Ezra Pound moved from the improvisations of their earliest work toward the sustained treatment and public subject of their later long poems, Stevens remained devoted to the end to the improvisations that the lyric poem permitted and offered him."[11] I would like to argue that, while it may be true that Stevens is not as obviously concerned with the marginalizing power of language as some of us might wish and so in that sense does not seem particularly oriented toward the outer or political world, he is acutely aware—in ways that equal or surpass that of Williams or Pound, or H.D. or Mina Loy, for that matter—of the constitutive power of lan-guage in shaping the structures and experiences of our actual world. Perhaps more importantly, he is equally aware of and concerned about its corollary power for destruction. As Stevens says in the 1945 poem "Description without Place," "It is a world of words to the end of it" (CP, 345), a statement that is, intentionally, simultaneously charged with the potential for realized beauty and with the possibility of apocalyptic destruction. That is to say, both as a lawyer and as a poet (even if among his coworkers he tried to keep his vocations separate), Stevens well understood that words have power, that poetry is political, and that pushed to the extreme the "theory / Of poetry" may actually be the "theory of life" (CP, 486). Yet the critical perception of Stevens as a poet devoted to the "inner world," largely unresponsive to the actual world, remains the most prevalent perception of his work among the majority of readers and scholars of twentieth-century poetry. As Fred Mora- marco notes in the spring 2001 issue of the *Wallace Stevens Journal,* "Despite recent attempts to politicize some of his poetry, . . . for many readers, myself included, Stevens remains a doggedly apolitical poet who enchants us not with the moral force of his political views, but with the imaginative power of his ability to recreate reality through a startlingly original distortion of it."[12] Moramarco's comments echo the early deprecation of Stevens as a "dandy," a dismissal of Stevens as having no social or political concerns for his times that has remained the pervasive palimpsest inhabiting Stevens's reputation for the last forty years.[13]

One reason for this lingering misconception of Stevens's poetics among the larger critical audience of twentieth-century poetry is that, as was noted sev- eral years ago in the *Times Literary Supplement,* Stevens's critics traditionally had tended to neglect the kind of historical and contextual criticism given to other authors.[14] Only over the last ten to twelve years, as in parts of Eleanor Cook's *Poetry, Word-Play, and Word-War in Wallace Stevens,* the special issue of the *Wallace Stevens Journal* on Stevens and politics, James Longenbach's *Wallace Stevens: The Plain Sense of Things,* Alan Filreis's *Wallace Stevens and the Actual World,* and the recent publication of Angus Cleghorn's *Wallace Stevens' Poetics: The Neglected Rhetoric,* have the political dimensions of Stevens's poetics been addressed with a serious and continuing critical inter- est. (It is, of course, precisely the "politics" of "criticism" itself and what kind of criticism is revered at a particular moment that caused early work in this area, such as Joseph N. Riddel's " 'Poets' Politics'—Wallace Stevens' *Owl's Clover"* and his "Wallace Stevens' *Ideas of Order:* The Rhetoric of Politics and the Rhetoric of Poetry," to remain relatively ignored.)

Nevertheless, in contrast to the recent critical studies mentioned above, my study here is focused almost entirely on Stevens's changing strategies of poetic/political "resistance" (in the most active sense) during the years immediately surrounding World War II. I have chosen this particular focus because I find that it was during these years that Stevens's poetic involvement with the political climate of his time transformed what was already a remarkable poet into the great poet of his later years in discrete, identifiable, and important stages that either have not been recognized before or have been misrepresented by not attending to the actual chronological writing of the most seminal poems of this period. Although my discussion will eventually embrace both his early and late poetries (especially in relation to gender and race or to sexism and racism), I have chosen to focus most of this book on the poems that would eventually constitute *Parts of a World* and *Transport to Summer*, for those two volumes prove pivotal in Stevens's career, specifically demonstrating the fundamental changes that occurred in Stevens's aesthetics from one responsive to the poetics of his time to one politically responsive to the actual world. Although it may be true, as Dickie has argued, that "Stevens's interest in the community and his fellow readers" began in the 1930s with his interest in "Communism and in a potential audience for poetry on the left,"[15] that "political" interest seems far more "theoretical" than it would become with the acute "pressure" of World War II. Furthermore, in his response to the Second World War, we also find the beginnings of Stevens's change from a rather posturing "masculine" or "virile" poet, quite full of the "rage to order," to a poet increasingly open to what we might metaphorically call the "feminine" or "other," including racial "others"—an important change I regard as critical even now. The work that follows traces in detail how what Stevens would call the "violence within" came to wrestle with a growing "violence without" that culminated in a genuine "revolutionary poetics" that remains important to us today.

I should clarify that this study does not repeat the archival and contextual research already done so well by James Longenbach and Alan Filreis, whose detailed accounts of historical events, letters, newspaper articles, and poetic battles of this same period demonstrate definitively the importance of Stevens's poetic responses in a time of war. Nor does it repeat the similar kinds of archival and historical work that inform various other critics' insights into Stevens such as that of Milton Bates and George Lensing, on the one hand, and biographer Joan Richardson, on the other. For a genuinely rounded sense of Wallace Stevens in his times, the work of all these authors needs to be integrated by readers and critics alike. Although it is necessary in the following argument to delineate something of the historical and artistic conflicts that surrounded Stevens's development in these poems of his middle years, I am limiting my own contextual evidence to a few selected journals, papers, letters, and well-known facts precisely because the extensive work just mentioned has already been done so thoroughly. Despite this narrow focus, I do wish to place Stevens and his development during the war years within a fundamentally wider context, with an eye to seeing how Stevens's "revolutionary poetics" and its critical stages fit a larger picture of the intersection of poetics and politics in the twentieth century.

Finally, although it may well be true, as Elizabeth Bishop writes, that "none of the books has ever got it right," that fact does not release us, as critics, from the moral responsibility implicit in interpretation itself.[16] It is my hope, therefore, that ultimately this book may be of interest not only to Stevens's readers but to anyone genuinely interested in the transformative power of words. If we consider the enormity of our political crisis in the Persian Gulf in the early 1990s and remember the power of language in phrases such as "decision day," "high noon," "surgical strikes," "Patriot missiles," and "friendly fire" to shape reality before our eyes, and if we consider the tragedy of September 2001 and the ability of phrases such as "holy war," "infinite justice," and "enduring freedom" to determine the future shape of our world, then attending to the power of words with which we choose to describe our world seems paramount. As I have argued elsewhere, it is not the will to power but our irrepressible will to interpret that remains our most compelling challenge as critics—and as citizens of this world—today.

The following chapter begins with Stevens's initial interpretation of the poetics of his climate and his subsequent negotiation with the political climate of his times. The former may well begin with a somewhat reductive reading of William Carlos Williams, but it is also marked by a nearly impassioned and obstinate belief in the power of poetry to *mean*. As he put it in a letter one year after the end of World War II, "I have the greatest respect for him [William Carlos Williams], although there is the constant difficulty that he is more interested in the way of saying things than in what he has to say. The fact remains that we are always fundamentally interested in what a writer has to say. When we are sure of that, we pay attention to the way in which he says it, not often before" (L, 544). I hear something of the lawyer as well as of the poet in that judgment—and someone fully aware that much, if not all, that happens in the world is either deemed (maybe redeemed) or doomed through the power of words.

CHAPTER ONE

POEMS AGAINST HIS CLIMATE

Wallace Stevens's response to the climate that surrounded his middle years became, at its best, a technique for subverting the social, even political, descriptions of his world through an act of sustained though also changing poetic "resistance."[1] It was an evolving technique initially prompted, however ironically, by his artistic resistance to contemporary "objective" or "descriptive" poetry, especially that of William Carlos Williams. This response, and the ensuing poetic strategies he developed as well, inevitably pushed Stevens during the last half of his middle period more deeply into poetic theory, including the "theory of description" (CP, 345). It is not surprising that the great poems of these years (roughly 1938–45), as well as much of the prose of this period, are consistently preoccupied with poetic theory, as "The Poems of Our Climate," "Poetry Is a Destructive Force," "Notes toward a Supreme Fiction," "The Pure Good of Theory," and the earlier essays of *The Necessary Angel* all testify.

Nevertheless, just what Stevens's "theory" is has continued to be a major point of controversy among Stevens's critics, a controversy fueled by conflicting ideas expressed not only in different poems of Stevens's canon but within single poems as well.[2] For example, in "Description without Place," the evocation of the

Book of a concept only possible
In description, canon central in itself,
The thesis of the plentifullest John
(CP, 345)

celebrates what could be accurately called a "logocentric theory" of poetry,[3] that is, that words are ultimately grounded in *being*. Yet only a few lines earlier in the poem Stevens counters the possibility that language could be "central in itself" by defining description as

a desire,
. . . .
A little different from reality:
The difference that we make in what we see

And our memorials of that difference.

This "alternative theory," which anticipates poststructuralist theories of signification, reminds us that the word is never equivalent to *being* but consistently evades the "thing itself."[4]

That these two conflicting theories should appear side by side in one poem, particularly one so obviously devoted to an exploration of poetic "description," is symptomatic of Stevens's interest in both the creative capacity and the inherent liability of the linguistic medium with which he worked. Yet, however much they preoccupied both his imagination and his poetry, it is useful to remember that what critics abstract as competing theories of poetry within his verse had a greater urgency, even immediacy, for the poet himself than our criticism sometimes suggests. Although a growing number of critics have begun to show that Stevens's poetry was deeply responsive to his own contemporary climate, it seems to me that at least until the advent of World War II, the majority of Stevens's responses to his actual times remained aesthetically and cognitively at a far remove from what he would come to call the "pressure of reality." In fact, despite the title of one of his better-known poems, during his middle years Stevens's overwhelming reaction was not finally "of" but pointedly "against" the climate of his time as his poetry became increasingly engaged with the actual or political world. Put differently, during his middle period, Stevens's poetics changed from one committed to the aesthetic consolations of poetry as an enduring artifact to one countering and perhaps correcting the increasingly violent rhetoric of his actual times.

The poem entitled "The Poems of Our Climate," written in 1938, offers a useful point of departure for exploring this response. The context for this poem is quite complicated, both aesthetically and historically. As Joseph N. Riddel argued years ago, the opening lines of "The Poems of Our Climate" recall the "dix-huitième quality of Imagist exercises," although he also suggests that its main purpose is to place the imagination in a modern climate—one of "chaos and change"—as opposed to a lost, earlier climate of "orderly and fixed laws, a still life."[5] But, as Harold Bloom later pointed out, its "cold porcelain" is also the modern American substitution for Keats's "cold pastoral," an observation that allows him to conclude that the "opening irony, or alternation of imagistic presence and absence" of this "Keatsian mediation" is "perhaps Stevens's most ineluctable swerve away from poetic origins."[6] (Actually, a more overt "swerve away" from this particular "poetic origin" is to be found in a poem written one year later in which Stevens explicitly writes, "It is cold to be forever young" ["Variations on a Summer Day," CP, 233].) Although imagism and Keats and even the more generalized "chaos and change" that began to accompany the late 1930s are undoubtedly part of the larger climate that informs this poem, the self-reflective irony of the title suggests that "The Poems of Our Climate" is primarily an ironic critique of the particular *poetic* climate at the time, one dominated to a large degree in 1938 by the "objective" poetry of his well-known contemporary, William Carlos Williams, far removed from what would subsequently become Stevens's critique of the *political* climate of his time.[7]

Even this particular context of Stevens's poem is quite complicated: Stevens's and Williams's friendship, though nearly lifelong, was alternately bullying, playful, respectful, and somewhat "uneasy."[8] For example, although he once criticized Williams for being "more interested in the way of saying things than in what he has to say" (L, 544), Stevens also said, quite simply, "I love his stuff" (L, 286). But, however positive or competitive their relationship may have been, there was on Stevens's part a real misunderstanding of Williams's poetic enterprise. Stevens's conclusion, for example, that Williams "rejects the idea that meaning has the slightest value" and that he "describes a poem as a structure of little blocks" (L, 803) may be an unfair assessment, but it is one that nonetheless informed Stevens's various critiques and reviews of Williams's poetry that, in turn, broadened the misunderstanding between the poets.

Of these various critiques, the preface Stevens wrote for Williams's 1934 *Collected Poems* is of particular interest here, for it tells us quite specifically how Stevens read, or even "misread," his contemporary during this period.[9] After the opening remark that the "slightly tobaccoy odor of autumn is perceptible in these pages. Williams is past fifty," Stevens describes Williams as a "romantic poet," albeit a unique kind of romantic poet, who has a "passion for the anti-poetic." He then expresses his admiration for Williams's "sentimentality," which, he says, "cures" Williams's otherwise excessively "anti-poetic" poetry: "Something of the sentimental is necessary to fecundate the anti-poetic. Williams, by nature, is more of a realist than is commonly true in the case of a poet." Toward the end of the preface, Stevens notably praises Williams for the "ambiguity produced by bareness" and the "addition to imagism" achieved in "Young Sycamore": "The implied image, as in YOUNG SYCAMORE, the serpent that leaps up in one's imagination at his prompting, is an addition to imagism, a phase of realism which Williams has always found congenial." He then says, "In respect to manner he is a virtuoso. He writes of flowers exquisitely" (WCP, 1–4). Although Kurt Heinzelman has argued that this preface is "honorific," such praise as is given appears clearly backhanded, and it certainly "nettled" Williams.[10]

More important, the preface cues us to the ways in which "The Poems of Our Climate," written four years later, uses poems in that collection as a background, even a "con-text," for its own artistic production (within which Stevens elaborates a very different "theory of description"). For example, in addition to describing "exquisite flowers," the opening lines of the poem are noticeably "bare" and "sentimental," imitating Williams's particular form of imagism far more than "dix-huitième exercises":

Clear water in a brilliant bowl,
Pink and white carnations. The light
In the room more like a snowy air,
Reflecting snow. A newly-fallen snow
At the end of winter when afternoons return.
Pink and white carnations.
(CP, 193)

There are a number of precursors to this passage in Williams's 1934 *Collected Poems*. Williams's "The Lily," for example, begins with a description of flowers and air in much the same way that "The Poems of Our Climate" does:

The Branching head of
tiger-lilies through the window
in the air.
(WCP, 37)

Again like Stevens's poem, "Birds and Flowers" focuses on flowers, enhancing
their color with white:

the white
shellwhite
glassy, linenwhite, crystalwhite
crocuses with orange centers.
(WCP, 53)

However, "Nantucket," possibly the best-known poem in that collection, offers the most striking "pre-text" for Stevens's poem:

Flowers through the window
lavender and yellow

changed by white curtains—
Smell of cleanliness—

Sunshine of late afternoon—
On the glass tray

a glass pitcher, the tumbler
turned down, by which

a key is lying—And the
immaculate white bed.
(WCP, 42)

The exquisite flowers, glass pitcher, and "immaculate white" are the most
immediate precursors to Stevens's "pink carnations," "brilliant bowl," and
"snowy air," constituting a "source" that stands in an intensely ironic relation
to Stevens's text.

It is important to clarify that although "Nantucket" sustains the illusion
of accurate, objective description throughout the poem, in its strategy it

moves from "pure" description (if that is possible) to something quite close to phenomenological transformation as the interior is revised by the larger context of the external world. As such, the poem is precisely what David Walker calls a "transparent lyric," in which the "dramatic center" of the poem has been shifted from a "lyric speaker to the reading experience itself."[11] Yet Stevens's preface to the 1934 *Collected Poems*, in which this poem was included, in no way acknowledges that facet of Williams's poetry, and "The Poems of Our Climate," as allusion to Williams, certainly does not.

However, as a notable critic has argued in a different context, "The etiology of the allusion, like the etiology of the word, originates in ignorance, in the inevitable slippage of understanding that divides us from our past."[12] Such slippage, it seems to me, is also inevitable (and perhaps intentional) in contemporary allusions. From this perspective, "The Poems of Our Climate" may be said to demonstrate Stevens's "ignorance" of Williams's poetry or, more specifically, of Williams's poetic strategy. However much we may find that Williams ultimately succeeds in evoking the "act of the mind" (CP, 240) that Stevens desires of modern poetry, such "objective" poetry remains for Stevens far too "anti-poetic." Against what he describes in "Rubbings of Reality" as Williams's desire to present an "exact definition" of his subject (OP, 245), Stevens attempts to demonstrate that the subject is "not seen / As the observer wills" (CP, 197)—and most certainly not if it is willed to be seen "objectively."

As he will continue to do so, with increasing sophistication throughout the poems of these middle years, Stevens counters the notion of objective, descriptive poetry in "The Poems of Our Climate" by subverting the notion of description itself—in this case by exploiting the latent, if not inherent, irony of textual allusion in order to debase both Williams's subjects and his style of writing. Thus, immediately after the opening lines (cited above), he clarifies his somewhat contemptuous attitude toward such poetry, saying, "[O]ne desires / So much more than that" (a statement reiterated again in the second stanza: "Still one would want more, one would need more, / More than a world of white and snowy scents"). This self-reflective intrusion clearly describes the critical distance between itself and its pre-text, intentionally divorcing the poem from the poetry inscribed in its own first lines.

The crucial rupturing of text and pre-text occurs, however, before that intrusion and can be described through the difference between Stevens's poetic strategy and that of Williams. In contrast to the "objective" descriptions sustained throughout "Nantucket," "The Poems of Our Climate" immediately violates the possibility of objective description, primarily through the similes of its second sentence:

> The light
> In the room more like a snowy air,
> Reflecting snow.

These similes ensure that the descriptions are not merely objective. Quite subtly but irrevocably, the words "like" and "reflecting" disrupt the illusion of verisimilitude in language itself, debasing, in consequence, the very kind of poetry they pretend to imitate. The opening passage is not, finally, a "Williams's exercise" but a deliberate act of "sub-version." Such subversions continue throughout the poem. The "vital I" of the second stanza (recalling Williams's "eye") is "evilly compounded" here. Even if it were possible to attain some "complete simplicity," a "world of white, / A World of clear water, brilliant-edged," says Stevens,

> There would still remain the never-resting mind,
> So that one would want to escape, come back
> To what had been so long composed.

The irony here is devastating. Against the presumption of stasis in artistic "composition"—elaborated in Williams's "A Sort of a Song" as "Compose. (No ideas / but in things)"—Stevens's poem reminds us that what has really been "composed" is this "compounded" world and an "evilly compounded" (and thus "vital") "I" that continually confronts the radical drift between the world and the words through which we describe the world. The "perfect" world of Williams's sharp-edged delineations is not, at least according to Stevens, possible, either in life or in poetry, and this constitutes part of a "theory" that he reiterates from "Sunday Morning" to "Notes toward a Supreme Fiction." Pushed to its extreme, then, "The Poems of Our Climate" discloses "description" as "de-scription."

As sophisticated as this strategy may seem to contemporary critics, it must be stressed that in 1938 Stevens did not intend to "deconstruct" poetry, either Williams's or his own. Despite his acute awareness that language may be a "Destructive Force" (CP, 192), Stevens still insists upon the creative capacity of the medium in which he works. Thus, after disrupting the "still life" of Williams's "objective" poetry, Stevens concludes "The Poems of

Our Climate" by validating language as the only (however ironic) source of meaning:

> The imperfect is our paradise.
> Note that, in this bitterness, delight,
> Since the imperfect is so hot in us,
> Lies in flawed words and stubborn sounds.
> (CP, 194)

On the one hand, Stevens's affirmation of the "imperfect" is made at the expense of Williams's "perfectionisms."[13] On the other, this affirmative play is a serious confirmation of the very "reflective" nature of both language and the "never-resting mind." As many modern critics have shown, and as Stevens seems to have fully realized, both language and the mind depend upon "original" rupture.[14] The poem, then, succeeds as a tour de force in which the "original" parody of Williams's descriptive poetry ironically comes to describe the elusive, even allusive, relation of world, mind, and word. Thus, although it may be a poem more "against" than "of" its climate, it is one that transcends its climate through the not-so-casual litter of its words.

The intertextual play of "The Poems of Our Climate" is obviously complicated by Stevens's ongoing, personal relationship with Williams as well as by its interaction with other poems written at approximately the same time.[15] Significantly, in both its original publication as part of "Canonica" and later as part of *Parts of a World*, Stevens chose to precede "The Poems of Our Climate" with "Poetry Is a Destructive Force" and to follow it with "Prelude to Objects," the title of which is an obvious gesture toward Williams.[16] In the latter poem Stevens once again undermines "objective" poetry even as he affirms the creative power of poetic "conceits." For example, after seeming to "grant" the hypothesis of accurate reflection ("Granted each picture is a glass"), Stevens fractures the possibility of accurate reflection with the assertion that "the walls are mirrors multiplied." Stevens then "de-scribes" both the power of conception and the lewdness of deception inherent in poetic "conceits" by telling the "Poet" to

> Fix quiet. Take the place
> Of parents, lewdest of ancestors.
> We are conceived in your conceits.
> (CP, 195)

Stevens used this "Canonica" of 1938, in its entirety, as the first twelve poems of *Parts of a World*, first published in 1942. It is a group of poems that clearly, if somewhat playfully at times, is intended to summarize Stevens's maturing sense of aesthetics. Williams, again, is not the only "context" for this "Canonica." The first poem of the group, "Parochial Theme," challenges the most traditional of poetry and themes. In addition, as Glen MacLeod has convincingly argued, "Canonica" in particular bears a relation to surrealism and Dutch painting, as well as serving as a specific rejection of the kind of "strict rationalism" associated with the "geometric-abstract tradition" in the visual arts. [17] However, the majority of the poems, such as "Study of Two Pears," "The Glass of Water," "Add This to Rhetoric" (perhaps a specific "revision" of Williams's "To a Solitary Disciple"), and "Dry Loaf," are rather obviously pitted against "objective" poetry. In all of these poems Stevens exposes descriptive "delineations" (OP, 245) of reality, which Stevens says Williams tries to create, as mere "rubbings of a glass in which we peer" (an ironic phrase taken from "Notes toward a Supreme Fiction" [CP, 398], anticipating Stevens's critique of Williams in "Rubbings of Reality" [OP, 244–45]).

As intricately related to Williams's poetry as these poems are, it is appropriately the last of the "Canonica," "The Latest Freed Man," that most clearly anticipates the "canon" developed in the later poems of this middle period:

> Tired of the old descriptions of the world,
> The latest freed man rose at six and sat
> On the edge of his bed. He said,
>   "I suppose there is
> A doctrine to this landscape. Yet, having just
> Escaped from the truth, the morning is color and mist,
> Which is enough. . . . "
> . . . .
> It was how the sun came shining into his room:
> To be without a description of to be,
> For a moment on rising, at the edge of the bed, to be,
> To have the ant of the self changed to an ox
> With its organic boomings, to be changed
> From a doctor into an ox.
> (CP, 204–5)

Here Stevens suggests both that the "old descriptions" can be an imprison-
ing "doctrine" that denies *being* and that description is not only inevitable
but also inescapable. With a playful gesture toward the poet he elsewhere
calls "old Dr. Williams" (L, 286), "The Latest Freed Man" describes the
possible freedom from "doctrinal" descriptions through subversive poetic
descriptions.

Stevens, it would appear then, is almost obsessed during this period with
demonstrating that the word has the power to create, that "[i]n the way
you speak / You arrange, the thing is posed" (CP, 198), and that for this very
reason it is all the more crucial that language not be taken naively for the
"thing itself," that the most exquisite images be recognized as an "evading
metaphor" (CP, 199). The increased urgency for this recognition, at least on
the part of Stevens, is implied by the degree to which he reiterated this point
in the many poems of this period, such as "Illustrations of the Poetic as a
Sense," "The Sense of the Sleight-of-Hand Man," and "A Dish of Peaches in
Russia" (a poem that rather ferociously counters Williams's "This Is Just to
Say" and its well-known plums). But this urgent recognition is made quite
explicit in one of the later poems of this period, "Description without Place"
(1945), a poem that proves pivotal to Stevens's developing poetics not only
in relation to this "aesthetic" stage but to other stages in his evolving poetics
to be discussed in the following chapters:

> Things are as they seemed to Calvin or to Anne
> Of England, to Pablo Neruda in Ceylon,
>
> To Nietzsche in Basel, to Lenin by a lake.
> . . . .
> The eye of Lenin kept the far-off shapes.
> His mind raised up, down-drowned, the chariots.
> And reaches, beaches, tomorrow's regions became
> One thinking of apocalyptic legions.
> (CP, 341–43)

The possible "apocalyptic" extension of the "eye," that is, the potential consequence of our interpretations of reality made precisely through descriptions
of reality, leads Stevens to conclude in another poem written in the same year
that "the nicer knowledge of / Belief" is that "what it believes in is not true"
(CP, 332). This, as the title tells us, is "The Pure Good of Theory."

Stevens rehearses similar themes in many of the poems written during this period. In "Certain Phenomena of Sound" (1942), to choose just one example, the "vital I" is potentially reduced to a linguistic sign inscribed in the word *Semiramide:*

> There is no life except in the word of it.
> I write *Semiramide* and in the script
> I am and have a being and play a part.
> You are that white Eulalia of the name.
> (CP, 287)

Yet as the poem demonstrates, the "I" is present, ironically but necessarily, in its description—in this case, through *intratextual* allusions (such as the "I am" that also appears "in the script"). As Stevens explains, with a certain clarity and urgency, "the power of literature is that in describing the world it creates what it describes. Those things that are not described do not exist, so that in putting together a review like ORIGENES you are really putting together a world. You are describing a world and by describing it you are creating it" (L, 495). In this letter, written in 1945, there is an implied responsibility, perhaps even an implicit moral imperative, in choosing our descriptions that is not found in "The Poems of Our Climate." That imperative is, strictly speaking, phenomenological, for in 1939 the world went to war again.

The poems written between the "Canonica" (1938) and the "canon central in itself" of "Description without Place" (1945) mark the rapid maturing of a poet into one of the greatest poets of the twentieth century. In part, this development may be accounted for by Stevens's working through his own "theory of poetry," which meant, among other things, that it "must not be fixed" (NA, 34). For Stevens, the subject of poetry is the "act of the mind," with its implicit movement and ambiguity, rather than " 'a collection of solid, static objects extended in space'" (NA, 25), with its implicit stasis and flat objectivity. As he says with great force in "Extracts from Addresses to the Academy of Fine Ideas" (1940), the "mind is the end and must be satisfied" (CP, 257), and seemingly flat descriptions, like those in "Nantucket," would never do.

Yet despite his persistent inquiries into the nature and theory of poetry, and despite his rather personal response to Williams, Stevens's nearly explosive poetic growth during these few years must finally be accounted for by the most significant element in his climate after 1939, the Second World War. In "Forces, the Will & the Weather" (possibly with a pun on Williams and his essay "Against the Weather" of the same year),[18] Stevens suggests, with humor in this case, one of the potential catastrophes of the war:

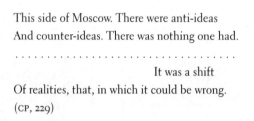

> There was not an idea
>
> This side of Moscow. There were anti-ideas
> And counter-ideas. There was nothing one had.
> . . . .
>   It was a shift
> Of realities, that, in which it could be wrong.
> (CP, 229)

The "latest freed man" of the "Canonica" is no longer free in this poem, having become imprisoned by the times and its overpowering ideas. The "shift / Of realities," Stevens warns, with both aesthetic and ethical consequences, "could be wrong."

Part of this shift included the new kind of poetry that began to enter the climate, that is, antiwar poems such as those of Karl Shapiro and Randall Jarrell that, following the new tradition of war poetry established in the Great War, were meant to be "objective" (albeit in a way entirely different from that of Williams's poetry) and specifically antiheroic.[19] Thus, despite the ongoing criticism of Williams's kind of "objectivist" poetry that may have influenced "Forces, the Will & the Weather," the most critical "shift / Of realities" appears, at least for Stevens, to have been created precisely by the more generalized and violent "descriptions" of his time rather than by any particular poetics. As he had eloquently, though painfully, explained in the 1936 essay "The Irrational Element in Poetry," even before the Second World War had begun

> [t]he pressure of the contemporaneous from the time of the beginning of the World War to the present time has been constant and extreme. No one can have lived apart in a happy oblivion. For a long time before the war nothing was more common. In those days the sea was full of yachts and the yachts were full of millionaires. It was a time when only maniacs had disturbing things to say. . . . People said that if the war continued it would end civilization, just as they say now that another such war will end civilization. It is one thing to talk about the end of civilization and another to feel that the thing is not merely possible but measurably probable. (OP, 229)

There may be a possible reference here to Williams's 1935 poem, "The Yachts," a reference that, given the "horror of the race" described in that poem, is once again highly ambiguous. Nevertheless, Stevens's reaction to modern war is quite clear, as it is in many of his poems written during the actual war years.

After the "Canonica" of 1938, most of the poems of Stevens's middle period are explicitly concerned with this pressure and with finding what will "suffice" to resist its suffocating power, as is the essay "The Noble Rider and the Sound of Words," first read at Princeton in 1941. The third section of that essay is devoted to explaining how "an extraordinary pressure of news—let us say, *news incomparably more pretentious than any description of it*"—is threatening the "consciousness to the exclusion of any power of contemplation" (NA, 20, my emphasis). He goes on to explain, more suggestively, that "[l]ittle of what we have believed has been true. Only the prophecies are true" (NA, 21).[20] It is for these reasons—both the pressure that necessitates resistance and the implied responsibility of what we choose to prophesy—that Stevens insists that the measure of the poet is, "in spite of all the passions of all the lovers of the truth," a "measure of his power to abstract himself, and to withdraw with him into his abstraction the reality on which the lovers of truth insist" (NA, 23), that is, quite specifically during this period, the "violence from within that protects us from a violence without" (NA, 36).

Similarly, "Extracts from Addresses to the Academy of Fine Ideas," written in 1940, also insists on both the liability of language as well as its necessity. It concludes with an especially harsh section that asks, specifically in relation to the war, whether we "live in evil and afterward / Lie harshly buried there." Yet the same section of the poem begins by saying that although "[w]e live in a camp," "[s]tanzas of final peace / Lie in the heart's residuum" (CP, 258), stanzas presumably of the "new" world in which "all men are priests":

They preach and they are preaching in a land
To be described. They are preaching in a time
To be described.
(CP, 254)

This new world, however, as Stevens well knows, has not yet been described; the final lines of the poem say, "Behold the men in helmets borne on steel, / Discolored, how they are going to defeat" (CP, 259). Yet the possibility of a land and a time yet "[t]o be described" (or "prophesized," to use the vocabulary

of "The Noble Rider and the Sound of Words") is the ironically nostalgic
center of the poem:

> He . . . wanted to think his way to life,
> To be happy because people were thinking to be.
> They had to think it to be. He wanted that,
> To face the weather and be unable to tell
> How much of it was light and how much thought,
> In these Elysia, these origins.
> (CP, 257)

This "he" who "think[s] his way to life" is placed in direct opposition in this
poem to "Ercole," whose way of thinking is the "way to death" (CP, 256).

Stevens's resistance to that "violence without" is readily seen in a poem
entitled, appropriately enough, "Examination of the Hero in a Time of War"
(1942), the poem with which he chose to conclude *Parts of a World* (and
to which I will return in chapter 2). In contrast to "realistic," antiheroic
war poems, this one is intentionally abstract and, to some degree, idealistic:
"Unless we believe in the hero," Stevens asks, "what is there / To believe?"
(CP, 275). Yet as he clarifies later in the poem, the hero he has "in mind"
cannot be reduced to a particular image:

> It is not an image. It is a feeling.
> There is no image of the hero.
> There is a feeling as definition.
> . . . .
> The hero is a feeling, a man seen
> As if the eye was an emotion,
> As if in seeing we saw our feeling
> In the object seen and saved that mystic
> Against the sight, the penetrating,
> Pure eye.
> (CP, 278–79)

In contrast to any attempt to arrive at a precise description of this "hero,"
Stevens insists upon trying to capture the "feeling, / In the object," the
emotion that ironically "describes" and "saves" the human from the "pene-
trating, / Pure eye," perhaps even an "objective" eye. At the very least, this

feeling is pitted elsewhere in the poem against the *"dry descriptions"* of images and allegory upon which, Stevens says, we cannot live (my emphasis).

Although the "con-text" for this poem of his middle years is no longer strictly Williams, we see in "Examination of the Hero in a Time of War" a certain resistance to his climate—again, in the interest of mental freedom—that was learned, at least in part, from his resistance to the earlier "objective" poetry. This rather odd conjunction of Stevens's preoccupation with the limitations of objective poetry and with the pressure of the Second World War suggested by "Examination" does not mean, of course, that Stevens felt that the forces behind the poems of his climate equaled the forces behind the war. Rather, this conjunction suggests the degree to which Stevens recognized that words taken naively as fact are dangerous—even as he insists that without words people are not only not heroes but less than human. Believing in the "hero" becomes metonymically equivalent to believing in poetry and in its ability to "truly bear" (CP, 281) and bare our truer selves. "Examination of the Hero in a Time of War" thus provides a specific marker for the number or "parts" of a world to which Stevens responds in a book that begins with "Canonica" (and his aesthetic resistance to Williams), only to end with poetic resistance to war. However, looking forward to the following chapters, I should also clarify here that this poem proves important in demonstrating yet another stage of Stevens's evolving poetics—essentially a stage in which Stevens went through a difficult change from the felt need for aesthetic disagreement, through political "resistance," to a more torturous necessity to "witness" to the horrors of his time. This critical change explains why much of his poetic production during this period can be seen as a subversion of and resistance to the political descriptions of his world that had increasingly come to dominate it in escalating violence. "Resistance," he had already clarified in "The Irrational Element in Poetry," "is the opposite of escape" (OP, 230). Not "revolving in crystal" at all.[21] The following chapters take up Stevens's growing insistence that both poetically and politically, "resistance" (which, etymologically, means "stand") is the necessary response to a violent (and increasingly violent) reality.

CHAPTER TWO

A CRITICAL MISPRISION

Between the "Canonica" of 1938 and "Description without Place" of 1945, Stevens's poetic responses to World War II changed markedly, rapidly evolving through a series of critical stages we have not yet fully begun to appreciate. Following his earlier resistance to "objectivism," Stevens's first reaction to war is marked not only by the need to "think about war," as he writes in "Of Modern Poetry" (1940), but also by the need to resist the overwhelming violence of war with the strength of the imagination, including the imaginative strength to construct formal and aesthetically enduring poetic structures. Subsequently, Stevens's response to the horrors of World War II would be to confront the possible inadequacy of this first strategy and to explore the need for poetry to register the actual *mal* of war. A subsequent and third response to the violence of his times would come to look forward to a new normalcy that would be needed after the end of the war and that would require poets' imaginative and constructive descriptions. However, as Stevens rapidly discovered, such a new normalcy could not stand on the old orders or "masculine myths" that he finally came to realize had proven false but would require an altogether new language and vision. All these stages—and the poetic strategies Stevens developed to accommodate and articulate his changing responses to the "actual world"—thus eventually merged in a form of poetry open to feminist and other ethical concerns. The great poems of his later years are, in fact, the ultimate expression of Stevens's changed and even "revolutionary poetics," a poetics that remains important to us as readers and writers in our own troubled world today.

Between the onset and the conclusion of World War II, in poem after poem, Stevens addresses the need for poetry to respond to that menacing reality, however difficult doing so might be. For example, in his seminal poem "Of Modern Poetry," Stevens says quite specifically that modern poetry "has to face the men of the time and to meet / The women of the time. It has to think about war / And it has to find what will suffice," even as modern poetry must also describe its difference from "what / Was in the script" (CP, 239–40). In "Man and Bottle," also written in 1940, he addresses the difficulty even more directly:

> [The mind] has to content the reason concerning war,
> It has to persuade that war is part of itself,
> A manner of thinking, a mode
> Of destroying, as the mind destroys,
>
> An aversion, as the world is averted
> From an old delusion, an old affair with the sun,
> An impossible aberration with the moon,
> A grossness of peace.
> (CP, 239)

This poem is directed, in part, against nineteenth-century aesthetics, the "romantic tenements / Of rose and ice" (CP, 239), as he calls it in the same poem. But however much Stevens may have been criticized for a lack of social awareness, the poem is also specifically constructed as a resistance to the war, as are most of his major poems from this period.[1] Its inherent freedom lies in the subversive trope in which war is subsumed as an analogy for the "mind" and its "mode / Of destroying"—a "mode" that, within the poem, succeeds precisely in "de-scribing" the ominous pressure of 1940. As the lines above imply, this act is a deliberate "a-version."

However, "a-version" certainly has the potential of being judged negatively as escapism, as Marjorie Perloff and others have done—a fact that Stevens anticipated in "The Noble Rider and the Sound of Words." In fact, with only a few exceptions, for over fifty years—from Stanley Burnshaw's review in *New Masses* (1935) to Perloff's "Revolving in Crystal" (1985)—there has been a largely unbroken tradition of regarding Stevens's poetry as socially irrelevant, socially unconcerned, and even socially irresponsible.[2] Even if we are not willing to go as far as Perloff in criticizing Stevens for trying to create a certain aesthetic order—even truth and beauty—in the actual arrangement of "Notes toward a Supreme Fiction" ("one poem per page, ten poems per section, seven tercets per poem, the three group titles on separate pages"), while Americans were losing heavily in the Battle of Bataan or gaining victory in the Battle of Midway, while the whole world was at war once again,[3] there has remained a relatively large consensus that Stevens was finally an aesthete—removed, often ironic, and (worse) rich. It is easy, even tempting, to concur with this critical consensus, given the ample supporting evidence (even ammunition) for this position in both his poetry and prose. As the Second World War began and then intensified, Stevens was writing poems with titles such as "Of Bright & Blue Birds & the Gala Sun" (1940), "Desire & the Object" (1942), "Holiday in Reality" (1944), and "God Is Good. It Is a Beautiful Night" (1942). Notably, the last one mentioned was written as the entire male population of the Czech village of Lidice was being exterminated, the women shipped to camps, and the children dispersed, nameless. It has been easy for critics to conclude that Stevens was serious, even maniacally so, in his insistence that "[e]thics are no more a part of poetry than they are of painting" (OP, 190), that "[p]oetry is not personal" (OP, 186) and certainly not political. From this perspective, if Stevens really meant that "[p]oetry increases the feeling for reality" (OP, 188), the kind of "reality" he meant must be utterly removed, encased, from the reality then felt by the world. "Revolving in Crystal," as it were.[4]

In addition to such poems and excerpts from his *Adagia*, it is possible to find ample evidence of Stevens's apparent social irresponsibility in both public essays and private letters. For example, in "The Noble Rider and the Sound of Words," which was written during the middle of World War II, Stevens claims that he does "not think that a poet owes any more as a social obligation than he owes as a moral obligation," adding that "if there is anything concerning poetry about which people agree it is that the role of the poet is not to be found in morals" (NA, 27–28). Furthermore, it seems, at least on the surface, that Stevens was being more than insensitive to the political realities and cruelties of his times when he wrote to Oscar Williams on 4 December 1944 that a "prose commentary on War and Poetry is out of the question. I wonder if the war has not ceased to affect us except as a part of necessity, as something that must be carried on and finished, with no end to the sacrifice involved. But I think that even the men in the Army etc. feel that it is no longer anything except an overwhelming grind" (L, 479). It might well be argued that the actual members of the army would not have agreed that the war had "ceased to affect" them. And, since Stevens goes on to add that the "big thing in the world today, the thing that really involves the future, is not the war, but the leftist movement," which he then equates to the "labor movement" (L, 479), one could conclude that the only thing that affected Stevens in any political sense was his pocketbook.[5] Moreover, it could seem, precisely, that Stevens preferred luxurious indulgences to any specific consideration of a "reality" he so frequently named, but *only* as a name, when he writes on 6 September 1945, just four days after World War II had officially ended, that "[s]itting there [in his garden at home], with a little of Kraft's Limburger Spread and a glass or two of a really decent wine, with not a voice in the universe and with those big, fat pigeons moving round, keeping an eye on me and doing queer things to keep me awake, all of these things make The New Republic and its contents (most of the time) of no account" (L, 512).

I wish to add, looking forward to the next chapter, that most of the contents of the *New Republic* in 1945 were specifically focused on the war and not on literary reviews, such as Jean Wahl's review of John Crowe Ransom that prompted this particular letter.[6] In fact, it is difficult to imagine a statement more exactly at odds with what Stevens actually felt during World War II, so it suffices to reverse the terms—that is to say, the parenthetical "repression" announces precisely that "most of the time" the contents of the *New Republic* were very much of "account" in Stevens's imagination. This reading of the letter is indicated, even demarked, by the paragraph immediately preceding the one just cited. There, in response to whether or not he had seen the review, Stevens answers no, with the following explanation: "I am going through a period in which I am inexpressibly sick of all sorts of fault-finding, and if Wahl has been finding fault with Ransom, I don't want to know anything about it. I suppose this state of mind comes from reading what the British say about the Americans and what the Americans say about the Japs, and so on" (L, 511). In the following argument, I will come back to this journal and to a number of articles published in it during World War II as a limited but very specific context for extending our understanding of Stevens's wartime poems, including the insights offered by a few critics such as Alan Filreis, James Longenbach, and Eleanor Cook.

But for now it is understandable why traditionally many critics might have concluded that Stevens intentionally played the part of the ostrich, sticking his head in the sand, willfully and persistently. As late as 1954 he writes, "I cannot say that there is any way to adapt myself to the idea that I am living in the Atomic Age and I think it a lot of nonsense to try to adapt oneself to such a thing" (L, 839). We are forced to consider, if not to conclude, that when Stevens explains in a 1940 letter that he makes "no reference in this letter to the war," that "[i]t goes without saying that our minds are full of it" (L, 356), he is uttering a nearly insidious "fiction," as it were—that he is virtually oblivious to the war, enclosed in some "revolving crystalline" (NA, 88) sustained by imaginative musings and economic security.

Yet if we want to be fair to the actual climate surrounding Stevens's aesthetic pronouncements during this time, we should note that many writers during this period espoused the same kind of aesthetic distancing noted in "The Noble Rider and the Sound of Words." Allen Tate, for example, sounds as forceful as Stevens when he says, "The success or failure of a political idea is none of my business; my business is to render in words the experience of people, whatever movement of ideas they may be caught up in. An artist who gets into a political movement because he thinks it is the coming thing, is a weakling" (PR, 29). Similarly, in response to the actual question "What do you think the responsibilities of writers in general are when and if war [the Second World War] comes?" James T. Farrell replies, "It is difficult for me to answer your last question because the real estate business has never been my *métier*. Personally, I have no economic interests in Chile, Paraguay, Uruguay, Bolivia, Brazil . . . Iceland, Finland, Greenland . . . not to mention the Suez Canal, Ethiopia, or the Island of Yap" (PR, 33). Katherine Anne Porter answers that the writer's "prime responsibility 'when and if war comes' is not to go mad," although she goes on to clarify that she means not being deceived by propagandistic rhetoric, which would argue that the "present violence" will end in "something new and blissful" (PR, 39). As Wallace Stevens would put it succinctly one year later (with reference, I think, to the propaganda of World War II as well as to that of the war before—"the war to end all wars"), "The good is evil's last invention" (CP, 253). Similarly, although with more ambivalence, Lionel Trilling argues that "however legitimate and laudable" is the "intention" of "literature of social protest" in "arousing pity and anger, in actual fact, because of its artistic failures, it constitutes a form of 'escapism' " (PR, 109). And Louise Bogan complains most bitterly about the pressure on the artist to be socially "responsible": "[T]he American 'cultural' background is thick with ideas of 'success' and 'morality.' So a piece of writing which is worth nothing, and means nothing (*but itself*) is, to readers at large, silly and somewhat immoral. 'Serious writing' has come to mean, to the public, the pompous or thinly documentary. The truly serious piece of work, where a situation is explored at all levels, *disinterestedly, for its own sake,* is outlawed" (PR, 106, my emphasis).

The context of all these remarks is "The Situation in American Writing," published in two parts in the *Partisan Review* in the summer of 1939 before the onset of the Second World War and, ironically, in the early fall of the same year after its eruption.[7] In other words, all of the responses had been written before another world war became a reality. Interestingly, the possibility of aesthetic distancing that the journal was supporting is ironically challenged in the second of these two issues, which concludes, in big block letters, with "WAR IS THE ISSUE!" as the exclamatory title of the final editorial, which both announces the war and, with the pun on "Issue," provocatively intimates a profound relationship between politics and words, or literal action and literature.[8] In this same series, Wallace Stevens replies, with what seems to me a nearly perfect Stevensian enigma, "The role of the writer in war remains the fundamental role of the writer intensified and concentrated" (PR, 40). Only earlier, in response to a very different question ("Do you think of yourself as writing for a definite audience?"), is there any clue to what this "role" may be. There he answers, "I do not visualize any audience. To me poetry is one of the sanctions of life and I write it because it helps me to accept and validate my experience" (PR, 39). The reading of Stevens's response to his climate that would insist he was clearly apolitical, if not irresponsible, to his times would attend to his admission that he does not envision any audience. An alternative reading, with which I finally concur, would focus on this embryonic formulation of poetry as a sanction—possibly even a redemption—in the violence and poverty of life, a formulation that would expand, with great rapidity once a second world war began, from a private to a public sanction deeply concerned with the polis, even the cosmos-polis.

However, before turning to that interpretation, I offer one other fairly damning statement from Stevens. Just prior to his assertion that the writer's role was "intensified and concentrated" in war, Stevens wrote the following in response to the same question: "I don't think that the United States should enter into the next world war, if there is to be another, unless it does so with the idea of dominating the world that comes out of it, or unless it is required to enter it in self-defense. The question respecting the responsibility of writers in war is a very theoretical question respecting an extremely practical state of affairs. A *war is a military state of affairs, not a literary one*" (PR, 40, my emphasis). Given the turn of historical events (our entering the war in actual self-defense after Pearl Harbor and our later use of two atomic bombs), Stevens's either/or formulation here proves ironically constitutive of the kind of thinking that encourages military violence. However, at the end of this unsympathetic reading of Stevens, it is critical to say that my overriding thesis in this study is that during World War II Stevens came to conclude that war is a literary state of affairs rather than a separate state of affairs, that "War *Is* the Issue"—the issue of our words.

Given the evidence just marshaled, it may seem almost perverse to insist that there is another interpretation of Stevens's response to (or negotiation through) his climate, one that is, ultimately, far more accurate to him both as a person and a poet. Yet as we are beginning to see, the myth of a Stevens removed from history can be sustained only through utter repression of his overwhelming response to global warfare, particularly World War II. [9] As early as 20 September 1939, three weeks after Hitler had begun his invasion of Poland and was bombing Warsaw, Stevens writes, "As the news of the development of the war comes in, I feel a horror of it: a horror of the fact that such a thing could occur" and goes on to call it an "unbelievable catastrophe" (L, 342–43).[10] His "horror" is not, I think, due to merely personal reasons but to deeply felt ethical reasons that would be instantiated in his poetry over the subsequent years. In fact, we must immediately revise our possible misreading of "The Noble Rider and the Sound of Words" as an essay espousing aesthetic *irresponsibility*. In that essay, Stevens is careful to explain that when he defines poetry, the imagination, and the mind as a "violence from within that protects us from a violence without" (NA, 36), he means by the "pressure of reality" a "pressure of an external event or events on the consciousness to the exclusion of any power of contemplation" (NA, 20). After saying that "the definition ought to be exact," he goes on to describe "a whole generation" and "a world at war," news of "Europe, Asia and Africa all at one time" (NA, 20–21). As the contents of contemporaneous issues of the *New Republic* well testify, the news was indeed of Europe, Asia, Africa all at one time, not only in the journals and the newspapers but also on the radio. In fact, during the month Stevens was composing this essay (February 1941), one disturbing article entitled "What Can We Defend?" makes the alarming point that "over half a world" is of immediate and pressing consequence to the United States, constituting "danger zones" to future American security.[11] It is resistance to what the editors call the "coming of *total war*" (my emphasis) in that article that Stevens sets himself—and the creative act of the imagination—in both "The Noble Rider and the Sound of Words" and the best poems of this period.

We should remember that "resistance," both in poetry and in the political reality of World War II, is neither dismissive nor escapist but an active stand taken against a reality or presence we might describe as being "too strong."[12] One telling example is the evolution of the word "theater," one that had formerly been restricted to the arts but that became disturbingly descriptive of war. Despite its initial aesthetic meaning, during World War I the word "theater" (or "theatre") had come to include the meaning in the phrase "theatre of war" (first coined by Winston Churchill in 1914, according to the *Supplement* to the *Oxford English Dictionary*).[13] By World War II, knowledge of this new connotation of "theater" was simply presumed when speaking of the "Pacific theater" and other geographic "theaters" of war. Thus, in spite of Stevens's calling for an internal violence in "The Noble Rider and the Sound of Words" that could protect us against the external and overwhelming violence of World War II, Stevens also insists in his "Two Theoretic Poems" of 1940 ("Man and Bottle" and "Of Modern Poetry") that because the "theatre was changed / To something else" (CP, 239) in this modern world, a new poetry "has to content the reason concerning war" (CP, 239), and "[i]t has to think about war / And it has to find what will suffice" (CP, 240).[14]

Given how far removed from actual war Stevens was, both by age and occupation, what is most striking about Stevens's poetry during this period is the degree to which it does actually begin to "think about war." In ways that most critics have either overlooked or dismissed entirely, the violent and changed "theater" begins to enter into Stevens's verse, sometimes in extremely subtle ways and sometimes with disturbingly apocalyptic images. For example, "Girl in a Nightgown" (the poem that precedes "Connoisseur of Chaos" in *Parts of a World*) expresses a pervasive cultural angst that seems far more attuned to the possibility of apocalyptic violence than to the earlier modernist malaise. In contrast to his earlier female character in "Sunday Morning" who dreams of something that will compensate for the loss of religious faith, the girl in the nightgown rather startlingly has no dreams—and no illusions of compensation:

Once it was, the repose of night,
Was a place, strong place, in which to sleep.

It is shaken now. It will burst into flames,
Either now or tomorrow or the day after that.
(CP, 214)

The apocalyptic vision here is not a lament against change, temporality, or imperfection, although, as in "The Poems of Our Climate," this poem specifically rejects any cold pastoral in favor of a very earthly and temporally laden "play": "The night should be warm and fluters' fortune / Should play in the trees when morning comes." But as the subjunctive "Should" reminds us, such an appealing morning is no longer possible in the grim "weather" the poem describes. Instead,

Like a tottering, a falling and an end,
Again and again, always there,
Massive drums and leaden trumpets,
Perceived by feeling instead of sense,
A revolution of things colliding.
Phrases! But of fear and of fate.
(CP, 214)

As Stevens suggests in the last line, fear and possibly hatred arise through words ("Phrases," or the rhetoric of war), so that the coming of war is, indeed, *cata-strophic* in the most elemental sense, with the consequence that the "truth and beauty" proffered by the supposedly revolutionary poets of the romantic period is no longer viable—if it ever was.

Yet for our purposes here, perhaps the most remarkable poem of those that would comprise *Parts of a World* is the small poem of 1939 entitled "A Dish of Peaches in Russia" (cited in full below), one that is rarely mentioned in Stevens criticism. It demonstrates in praxis the transformation Stevens makes from his earlier aesthetic resistance to objectivism to his increasingly political resistance to the violence of his times:[15]

With my whole body I taste these peaches,
I touch them and smell them. Who speaks?

I absorb them as the Angevine
Absorbs Anjou. I see them as a lover sees,

As a young lover sees the first buds of spring
And as the black Spaniard plays his guitar.

Who speaks? But it must be that I,
That animal, that Russian, that exile, for whom

The bells of the chapel pullulate sounds at
Heart. The peaches are large and round,

Ah! and red; and they have peach fuzz, ah!
They are full of juice and the skin is soft.

They are full of the colors of my village
And of fair weather, summer, dew, peace.

The room is quiet where they are.
The windows are open. The sunlight fills

The curtains. Even the drifting of the curtains,
Slight as it is, disturbs me. I did not know

That such ferocities could tear
One self from another, as these peaches do.
(CP, 224)

As suggested in the preceding chapter, this poem could easily be read as a subversion of Williams's well-known poem "This Is Just to Say," in which Williams not only confesses to having stolen and eaten the plums from the icebox but revels (while apologizing) in how "cold" and "sweet" they were. Stevens, it would appear, decides to outdo Williams, for his peaches—"large," "round," "red," fuzzy, soft, and notably "full of juice"—are so obviously even more sensual and seductive than Williams's plums. From this perspective, "A Dish of Peaches in Russia" engages in something like a poetic duel in which the peaches, fortified with a nearly overwhelming number of attributes and "complications," again subvert, even conquer Williams's relative "simplicity." In fact, with the exception of the evoked but withheld reality of what it would really mean in 1939 to be a Russian or for an "Angevine" to absorb "Anjou," the first twelve lines of this poem could be interpreted as a virtual appendix to the poems in "Canonica." It is not surprising, then, that this poem initially appeared in *Poetry* as one of a number of poems collectively entitled "Illustrations of the Poetic as a Sense."[16] For Stevens, the poetic is never merely objective.

However, this seemingly innocuous poem proves to be a major poem of discovery for both poet and critic. Read carefully, particularly, I might add, with the kind of rereading Michael Riffaterre advocates when a text contains a literary involucrum,[17] the last lines of this poem take on an entirely different dimension, becoming ominous in a way that is only understandable in relation to the "violence" of reality or the "actual world," however much the *nominal subject* of the poem and the textual interplay with Williams's poem might erroneously be interpreted as avoiding that reality. That is to say, while initially published in a group of poems very similar to "Canonica," "A Dish of Peaches in Russia" turns political if not prophetic, evoking a sense of the actual change in the political climate that occurred, in reality, that summer.

This rereading is forced upon us by a noticeable thematic aberration. Given what we have seen of Stevens's poetic and philosophical sensibility in the preceding chapter, we should expect Stevens—or the Russian persona—to prefer change, mutability, and "imperfections" over stasis, as Stevens consistently does in his poetry, from "Sunday Morning" to "The Poems of Our Climate." With his earlier rejection of the "still curtains" and "immaculate white" of Williams's "Nantucket" in mind, we should expect a celebration not only of the juiciness and sensuality of the peaches but of the temporal change and mutability implicit in "the drifting of the curtains." But the speaker—and, importantly, we never really know who speaks—makes a striking and unexpected statement. As "[s]light as it is," the speaker says, "[e]ven the drifting of the curtains . . . disturbs me." This "disturbance" works on the order of an involucrum, a literary disruption that forces us to reread the poem with the particular purpose of discovering why something as pleasant as drifting curtains would prove so distressing. As Dolores Frese explains, "More than a decade ago, Michael Riffaterre correctly insisted that the *literary* phenomenology of any genuinely poetic text—a phenomenology lodged in those features that distinguish it from oral performance, however inspired or accomplished—will always be found precisely in those textual disruptions or 'ungrammaticalities' that initially scandalize attentive readers who are attempting to make their way smoothly and sequentially through a written work."[18] And the "scandal" here is not just the lascivious nature of the peaches or Stevens's intertextual play with "This Is Just to Say" or even the literal "disruption" of drifting curtains but rather the unexpected desire of the speaker to repress what is ironically reified in virtually every other previous poem by Stevens, and that is precisely the "scandalous" nature of change, mutability, imperfection.

The only explanation for this unexpected reaction or repression is to be found in the violence of reality prescinded from the discussion above—a genuinely "disturbing" reality, one quite at odds with the sensual ease supposedly experienced by the speaker. Although we are told that the speaker absorbs the peaches "as the Angevine / Absorbs Anjou" and that the peaches "are full of the colors of [his] village / And of fair weather, summer, dew, peace," in the year this poem was written, the last cited word here proves to be intensely ironic. By 1939 there had already been that "shift / Of realities" that "could be wrong," that is, the world was at war again. The speaker of "A Dish of Peaches in Russia" is already nostalgically recalling a time when fair weather and peace were the reality and is (unsuccessfully, I might add) trying to repress from his own consciousness the subsequent change in reality of what Stevens would come to call the "violence without." Only this "outer" or actual world accounts for the speaker's unexpected rejection of change and for his desire to keep a certain stasis in place that would necessarily be equivalent to that "cold pastoral" Stevens as poet almost always rejects. Thus, the unstated cause for what "disturbs" the speaker functions in the poem as a kind of "white text," allowing us to de-cipher, as it were, the actual informing reality of the poem as being quite the opposite of the speaker's nostalgic rhetoric. In fact, the actual political climate in 1939 was something far closer to "bad weather, winter, snow, war" than to the speaker's desired hedonistic haven of "fair weather, summer, dew, peace."

The political reality contextualizing this poem thus accounts for the unexpected intensity of the last lines. The peaches bear such "ferocities" not because they tear Stevens from Williams (though they do, in the context of "This Is Just to Say") or because they tear a part of Stevens from himself (though they may) but because they tear through the speaker's repression of reality, reminding him with their sensuality of the physical violence very likely to occur. Stevens's desire to engage with as well as to resist this disturbing reality is made clear in a letter of the same year: "Poetry is a thing that engages, or should engage, . . . men of serious intelligence," he writes, adding, "every poet of any interest considers himself a person concerned with something essential and vital" (L, 414). And, we might add, such a statement applies to other forms of "serious" writing as well, with interesting convergences to Stevens's own poetry. Although Ernest Hemingway had been reporting on the civil war in Spain since 1937, predicting a second world war he specifically warned us against entering (even as early as 1935), he did not begin *For Whom the Bell Tolls* until 1939, and the novel was not published until 1940. And yet, from the lover, to the black Spaniard, to the exiled Russian, certain fundamental characters and images as well as the larger thematic of Stevens's poem (which shows how the violence of war interrupts normal life, including food and love) prove uncannily similar to those of Hemingway's novel. Thus "A Dish of Peaches in Russia" marks a particular turning point in Stevens's career in which a certain aesthetic resistance intersects with his growing sense of political resistance, creating in that intersection a new artistic strength that would increasingly inform Stevens's work over the next several years.

Even if, as Alan Filreis has recently asserted, Stevens's initial reaction to the prospect of American involvement followed the popular tendency toward supporting isolationism,[19] the number of poems Stevens wrote after World War II began that specifically refer to war indicates the degree to which it occupied both his poetry and his thought. In addition to "Man and Bottle" and "Of Modern Poetry," by early 1940 Stevens had already published "Martial Cadenza," a poem that calls for "ever-living" time rather than the impoverished "world without time," "full / Of the silence before the armies" (CP, 237–38). In the same year Stevens also published "Yellow Afternoon," an extremely moving poem in which "life of the fatal unity of war" (CP, 236) is the cause for personal despair.[20] It might still be possible to argue that all these instances are merely theoretical speculations on the question asked in the *Partisan Review* (what is the writer's responsibility in a time of war?), that in these poems he is deliberately "musing the obscure" (CP, 88) by avoiding, effectively, his actual times. But within the context of the larger "isolationalist" feelings in the country,[21] Stevens appears actually engaged in thinking through the consequences of another violence on a global scale, even if in understandably abstract terms.

However, I find it crucial to understanding Stevens's response to his climate, including the composition of "Notes toward a Supreme Fiction," to note that after Pearl Harbor (in other words, after the war had become a reality for Americans rather than an abstraction) Stevens's responses became much more specific, with largely unrecognized loci in the events and atmosphere of the time, uttered with a voice that speaks prophetically at times, publicly, and certainly politically. I should clarify, with emphasis on the plurality, that *world events* increasingly informed Stevens's verse throughout the war. It is obviously not the case that *one* Jewish person was killed, or that *one* country fell to the Axis powers, or that even *one* continent (with something like an identifiable front line) defined the realm of violence. It is understandable, then, that Stevens's responses to the events of his time necessarily take on something of the abstraction that the sheer magnitude of the horrors in World War II inevitably meant, especially for those Americans who remained on American soil, making it sometimes difficult to offer particularized contexts for some of Stevens's work. The possibility of historical slippage in this regard presents a crucial difficulty, one that has simultaneously allowed one critic to argue (incorrectly, I believe) that "The Auroras of Autumn" refers to the atomic bomb and another to promote, from a totally different perspective, a pairing of Stevens's letters with a "checklist" of calamitous world events while he arranged "Notes toward a Supreme Fiction." [22] Certainly, given a poet who would continually struggle with the difficult line between art and reality, it is almost inevitable that we would be tempted to conclude that Stevens was either more referential or less responsive to his times than perhaps he really was. As Charles Mauron writes in *Aesthetics and Psychology*, and in words that apply well to Wallace Stevens (and that Stevens himself underscored in his own copy of Mauron's book): "The whole question is where to draw the line between life and art." [23]

Despite this warning, I think it is possible to see that Stevens did write in response—and in resistance—to the events of this time, including the bombing of Pearl Harbor, the destruction of European cities (by Americans as well as by the Axis powers), the fear of being at war on American soil under the escalating horrors of Hitler's slaughter, and the atomic bomb itself. [24] In the fall of 1941 Stevens had already produced many of the more "theoretical" war poems mentioned above, some of them (like "Of Modern Poetry") frequently recognized as seminal though not necessarily as political poems and others (such as "Extracts from Addresses to the Academy of Fine Ideas") in which he anticipates what may well be his finest antiwar poem, "Description without Place." In "Extracts from Addresses to the Academy of Fine Ideas," Stevens writes within the context of "men in helmets borne on steel" (CP, 259) that the priests of a new world

> are preaching in a land
> To be described. They are preaching in a time
> To be described.
> (CP, 254)

In "Description without Place," Stevens exposes the "death of a soldier" as "seemings" of an "arrogant" young poet (CP, 341, 340), calling attention to the long and unfortunate promotion of war by poets themselves.

Yet in December 1941, as we all know, Japan chose to bomb Pearl Harbor. What is of particular interest in establishing the context of Stevens's first poem published after that tragedy ("Montrachet-le-Jardin," which appeared three months later) is the reminder that even before Pearl Harbor it was the Japanese (the "Asians," as Stevens may have termed them in his poetry, following the contemporary phraseology that would refer to "Greater East Asia" or "What Next in Asia?") and not the Germans in general nor Hitler in particular who posed the most immediate threat to America.[25] During the summer and fall of 1941 the government was preoccupied with "appeasement." Yet, in the *New Republic* at least, the rhetoric began to get more violent. The fall issues in particular contained articles or editorials that repeatedly urged America to "Call Japan's Bluff!" or to "Stay Tough with Japan" or to "Hold the Pacific!"[26] The belated attempts to create some sort of "appeasement" or compromise between the United States and Japan certainly failed. Yet even before the actual bombing of Pearl Harbor, the American people and American press began to regard the Japanese as something akin to monsters. There was the (fictional) theory published at this very time that the Japanese "gestated for only six months in the womb," in addition to what Paul Fussell has described as the general American view of the Japanese as inferior, subhuman, even insectlike creatures.[27] It was also during 1941 that Stevens wrote "The News and the Weather," a poem that moves, at least in section 1, well beyond the prophetic worry of the 1939 "Forces, the Will & the Weather" (that is, that the new climate "could be wrong") to an outright sarcastic derision of contemporary American rhetoric, including specifically racist rhetoric:[28]

> The blue sun in his red cockade
> Walked the United States today,
>
> Taller than any eye could see,
> Older than any man could be.
>
> He caught the flags and the picket-lines
> Of people, round the auto-works:
>
> His manner slickened them. He milled
> In the rowdy serpentines. He drilled.
> (CP, 264)

It may be to Stevens's credit here that there is an elliptically stated alignment in this section between mass production and mass responsiveness to the swaggering manner of militaristic rhetoric and pomposity.

After the attack on Pearl Harbor, American reaction and rhetoric became even more intense. In the very first issue of the *New Republic* to go to press after the bombing, William Harlan Hale writes in "After Pearl Harbor" that whereas Hitler's aim has always been "total," that is, the *"annihilation of the enemy,"* Japan can only seek "to drive us out of the Western Pacific," and that whereas Japan's objectives are therefore "limited," "[o]ur objective, on the other hand, is total: it is to destroy Japan as a military power. We are committing our forces for an entire victory over the aggressor." The defeat of Japan's fleet, Hale adds, "is the end of Japan."[29] He does not seem to mean this in any figurative way. His explicit comparison of what the American aim should be toward the Japanese to Hitler's "aim" must inevitably seem, after Hiroshima or at the very least after the *second* bomb, profoundly disturbing. In this context, Stevens's "The News and the Weather" signals a prophetic and genuinely profound disgust with the kind of propagandistic rhetoric abounding in the journals and, presumably, on the radios as well.

Stevens's first published poem after Pearl Harbor—"Montrachet-le-Jardin," which, notably, appeared in the *Partisan Review* once again—evokes the "hero's being, the deliverer / Delivering the prisoner *by his words*" (CP, 261, my emphasis) in lines that anticipate the well-known coda to his major poem published the next year, "Notes toward a Supreme Fiction," and that certainly suggest the possibility of a social obligation carried out poetically. Yet within this particular historical context, perhaps the most telling lines of "Montrachet-le-Jardin" (which Stevens placed immediately *before* "The News and the Weather" in *Parts of a World*, as if to contextualize, even to counter, the growing rhetoric of the United States of 1939) are these:

Consider how the speechless, invisible gods
Ruled us before, from over Asia, by
Our merest apprehension of their will.
(CP, 262)

Yet Stevens does not indulge in either racial or ethnic condemnation. Whether prompted by his earlier readings in Buddhism or not,[30] what is most remarkable about this poem, given its actual historical context, is that the next crucial stanzas of the poem appeal to the possible common good in humanity:

There must be mercy in Asia and divine
Shadows of scholars bent upon their books,
Divine orations from lean sacristans

Of the good, speaking of good in the voice of men.
All men can speak of it in the voice of gods.
But to speak simply of good is like to love.
(CP, 262)

For a man and a poet who has so often been characterized as being essentially a WASP, and for a man who had written, as we have seen, that we should not enter this war unless we intended total domination of Japan, these lines written at that time resonate with a particular generosity, something more than tolerance, with a tone approaching prayer—and it is a tone no longer seeking personal validation of experience. "There must be mercy" has the same fictional quality, and specific ethical and political appeal, as "It Must Be Abstract," "It Must Change," and "It Must Give Pleasure," all of which evoke what Drucilla Cornell has called in a different context the ethical world of the "not yet" as a possibility we have the power to create.[31] As the coda to "Notes toward a Supreme Fiction" makes clear, the context of all these imperatives *is* the world at war, where the real war of the soldier and the war of the poet "are one" (CP, 407). However much we may criticize Stevens for his conservatism and sometimes undeniable racism in other instances (though the latter charge against Stevens is the subject of the last chapter), "There must be mercy in Asia" at that particular moment in time is ultimately an intensely political—and ethical—statement, one that I much prefer to those that ended in the internment of American Japanese,[32] and a statement of spiritual generosity to which we should continue to attend even now.

Another poem of 1942, "Examination of the Hero in a Time of War" (the poem with which Stevens concluded *Parts of a World*), has as its context the bombing of European cities, which, beginning with the total destruction of Warsaw, had spread either as a reality or as a threat from Stalingrad to London but which was also being engaged in by Americans, who were then bombing, quite heavily, the Axis European cities. (A subsequent issue of the *New Republic* would ask whether this strategy were necessary and if it would not alienate our own allies.)[33] Although the poem is quite long, three particular passages prove quite salient here. The first is the beginning of section 2:

The Got whome [*sic*] we serve is able to deliver
Us. Good chemistry, good common man, what
Of that angelic sword? Creature of
Ten times ten times dynamite, convulsive
Angel, convulsive shatterer, gun,
Click, click, the Got whom we serve is able
Still, still to deliver us.
(CP, 273)

Given what we know to have been the reality in Europe in 1942, given what
Stevens knew to be the reality in that year, the devastating irony of this prayer
proves extraordinarily painful even as it once again evokes tolerance for all
supposed "sides" of the war. As he had already said in 1941, specifically in
"The Noble Rider and the Sound of Words," he is "thinking of life in a state
of violence, not physically, as yet for Americans, but physically violent for
millions of our friends and *for still more millions of our enemies and spiritually
violent . . . for everyone alive*" (NA, 26–27, my emphasis).

In the seventh section of this poem, Stevens suggests that one consequence
of modern technological warfare is to create (ironically) a situation in which
there is no "safe rear" and, consequently, to level the difference between the
armed forces and civilians:

Gazette Guerrière. A man might happen
To prefer *L'Observateur de la Paix,* since
The hero of the *Gazette* and the hero
Of *L'Observateur,* the classic hero
And the bourgeois, are different, much.
The classic changed. There have been many.
And there are many bourgeois heroes.
(CP, 276)

These lines also imply that this situation—and its possible cure—is a function
of what we will choose to read, how we will describe the world. And yet,
despite the appeal to the "many bourgeois heroes," Stevens still very much
wants to believe in the "hero" as a "feeling" (CP, 278) in this poem: "Unless
we believe in the hero," he asks, "what is there / To believe?" (CP, 275).
In contrast to the perspective, the "belief," if you will, that prompted W. H.
Auden's remarks in "The Poet and the City" that the "[c]haracteristic style of

'Modern' poetry . . . is the speech of one person addressing one person," since any attempt to speak for society "sounds phony," and in contrast to Auden's statements that the characteristic modern hero "is neither the 'Great Man' nor the romantic rebel . . . but the man or woman" who "manages to acquire and preserve a face of his own,"[34] Stevens insists upon the possibility of a "hero" (not the "Got whome we serve") who can "save us":

> It is not an image. It is a feeling.
> There is no image of the hero.
> . . . .
> The hero is a feeling, a man seen
> As if the eye was an emotion,
> As if in seeing we saw our feeling
> In the object seen and saved that mystic
> Against the sight, the penetrating,
> Pure eye. Instead of allegory,
> We have and are the man, capable
> Of his brave quickenings, the human
> Accelerations that seem inhuman.
> (CP, 278–79)

The genuine *need* for such a belief, even though proffered as a possible fiction within the poem, has as its specific context not the "objectivist" poetry noted in the previous chapter but the acute possibility of being, at any moment, a victim of violence, in any city, in any home, as well as the more generalized horrors of the war.[35] As Stevens explains in "The Noble Rider and the Sound of Words," the poet's "role is to help people to live their lives" (NA, 30).

In that essay (first written in 1941 and subsequently published during the chaos of 1942), Stevens admits that the "poetic process" he is describing could be analyzed as an "escapist process," but he also insists that we cannot "suppose" that he is using the word "escapist" in a "pejorative sense" (NA, 30–31). Citing a remark from Dr. Joad as his point of contrast, Stevens's explanation of this "poetic process" is placed in contrast to the growing sense of the "[u]nreal city," a place of poverty and disillusionment not just in literature but *in reality*. If, Stevens says, "without elaborating this complete poverty, if suddenly we hear a different and *familiar* description of the place" ("This City now doth, like a garment, wear / The beauty of the morning, silent bare"), "if we have this experience, we know how poets help people to live their lives" (NA, 31, my emphasis). The "familiar" poetically, not the strange or "unreal" poverty and violence of the actual times, is a place where we can live, and, Stevens adds, "This illustration must serve for all the rest" (NA, 31). In the next chapter I take this admonition seriously and explore how Stevens's most famous poem of 1942, "Notes toward a Supreme Fiction," could be seen as a "familiar," a "real city," as it were, though certainly not in any objective sense, "where we can live."

CHAPTER THREE

FORMAL RESISTANCE

The previously described historical context accounts for Stevens's simultane-
ous aesthetic resistance to his times and for the inherent aesthetic consolation
he intended to offer in his most famous of wartime poems, "Notes toward a
Supreme Fiction." This is not to say that the poem readily announces such an
idealistic agenda. At least until its final canto (and then, subsequently, with
the prologue Stevens added to this highly formal composition), the poem
remains acutely skeptical of any ultimate consolation on this earth. However,
the strange idealism fueling the poem was Stevens's specific attempt to find
in the aesthetic structure—in the actual form—of the poem a place where
we could "live," a structure that would "satisfy" in the way that the actual
form of *The Divine Comedy* provided a formal sanctuary for Dante in his own
deeply troubled times.[1] In 1942, the year Stevens published this poem (as well
as "Montrachet-le-Jardin" and "Examination of the Hero in a Time of War"),
the position of the Allies in general but of U.S. troops in particular was such
that Paul Fussell has written of that year that "we never needed consolation
more."[2] However, for Stevens, that "finding of a satisfaction" was not, at
least initially, coupled with religious faith—a fact that for Stevens and for
others in what he had earlier termed the "epic of disbelief" (CP, 122) made
the necessity of formal or aesthetic consolation all the more acute. Stevens's

decision to model a modern but secular "Supreme Fiction"—or, rather, notes *toward* such a fiction—actually intensified the difficulty in achieving such a desired consolation. For whether believers or not, both Stevens and Dante before him faced not only the problem of achieving some kind of consolation in words against the backdrop of political chaos but an equally acute anxiety about linguistic mutability—about the ability of words to mean in time and, over time, to mean at all.

Obviously, Stevens's title alone, with the plural and nebulous "Notes toward" and the indefinite "a" that precedes the desired "Supreme Fiction," announces the felt impossibility of ever achieving the kind of certitude and authority that allowed Dante to be "the voice of the Middle Ages" (NA, 29), as Stevens put it in "The Noble Rider and the Sound of Words." Yet the coda, addressed finally to the "Soldier," places the poem's rather metaphysical concerns back in the historical reality of war and reminds us of the necessity for such consoling authority—a necessity Dante experienced as well with the ongoing and escalating wars between the Guelfs and Ghibellines, engendering for both poets the desire for poetry to provide a stasis against temporal mutability.

As Thomas M. Greene has deftly demonstrated in *The Light in Troy*, in *The Divine Comedy* (and in the *Paradiso* in particular) Dante was obsessed with the problem of linguistic mutability.[3] It is perhaps this somewhat surprising theoretical connection that made Dante amenable to Stevens. Fearing, as many authors before him had, that with the passage of time and linguistic drift his work would become unreadable or untranslatable, Dante the poet has Dante the pilgrim question Adam about the first language spoken in Eden. To the pilgrim's surprise, Adam replies that the "first language" had disappeared even before the building of the tower of Babel and that, furthermore,

> nullo effetto mai razionabile,
> per lo piacere uman che rinovella
> seguendo il cielo, sempre fu durabile.

> [no product of whatever reason—since human choice is renewed with the course
>   of heaven—can last forever.]
> (*Paradiso* 26, ll. 127–29)

Greene argues that despite Adam's joy, to which other lines of this canto testify, Adam's "discourse remains a classic statement of a perception that has troubled men since Plato: the scandal of the mutability, the ungrounded contingency of language."[4] Wallace Stevens obviously shared this troubling perception, though perhaps more acutely than many (and certainly more than William Carlos Williams, who, in his 1939 "Against the Weather," called for poetic revolution every ten years).[5] "The loss of a language," Stevens once wrote, with great understatement, "creates confusion or dumbness" (OP, 185). As Joan Richardson notes in her biography, Stevens "wanted anyone at any future time" to be able to read him, a desire that she says motivated Stevens's tendency toward abstraction, a tendency overtly expressed in "Notes toward a Supreme Fiction" as the imperative "It Must Be Abstract": in this desire, Stevens "wanted to outdo even Dante," whose particular "references bound him too closely, in Stevens's terms, to his historical moment."[6]

It is curious that the specific relation of Stevens's text to *The Divine Comedy* has been so unexplored, especially since the ongoing influence of Dante on Stevens is generally recognized. As Stevens's letters testify, the poet was thoroughly familiar with Dante's poem, both in the original and (presumably) in translation through the labor of his friend Walter Arensberg.[7] Not surprisingly, critics have found that many of Stevens's poems echo Dante's work, from the early "The Comedian as the Letter C" and "The Emperor of Ice-Cream" to later works such as "Esthétique du Mal," "An Ordinary Evening in New Haven," and "Not Ideas about the Thing but the Thing Itself."[8] Yet "Notes," which attempts both to reenvision and to "revise" *The Divine Comedy*, is usually discussed in relation to the Bible, Genesis in particular, or various writers such as Coleridge, Whitman, Shelley, Wordsworth, and Milton.[9] I should clarify that I am not denying the validity of such influences on Stevens's poem; rather, I am asserting that for "Notes toward a Supreme Fiction" Dante's *Divine Comedy* constitutes what Thomas Greene would call a "single privileged predecessor" to which Stevens's seminal poem is bound with "particularly intricate knots."[10]

The relative lack of discussion of the formal relation of Stevens's "Notes toward a Supreme Fiction" to Dante's *Divine Comedy* may be due to the earlier critical conviction, most forcefully voiced by Joseph Riddel, that the form of the poem is not revealing, a conviction that could easily discourage recognizing, much less exploring, Stevens's allusion to Dante in the actual structural arrangement of the poem. Having noted the "three major divisions, consisting of ten cantos each," and the "obvious trinity" of those sections, he goes on to assert that *"like other of Stevens's long poems, 'Notes' cannot be defined by external form.*"[11] Curiously, Marie Borroff insists that Stevens's poem lacks "architectonic unity."[12] Although Richardson implies that at the time of the poem's publication Allen Tate perceived a similarity between Stevens and Dante when speculating on what kind of poetry Stevens would produce if he wrote in strict terza rima,[13] only Marjorie Perloff has stressed the formal composition of the poem, albeit in a negative way. Drawing upon his letters, in which he expresses his concern with the physical arrangement of the poem, Perloff summarizes what she suggestively calls the "numerology" of his "Notes" this way: "Thirty poems divided into three equal sections, each with a title. Further, thirty (poems) times seven (stanzas) times three (lines) equals 630 lines. One poem per page equals thirty pages, plus [three] separate nearly blank pages for the subtitles: in short, a perfect geometric whole."[14] If we add to this compositional summary the fact that the "geometric perfection" of this text ends up being followed rather than being introduced by one unnumbered canto of the same metrical form and that when initially composed the first canto of the poem bore "the caption REFACIMENTO" (L, 431), then what I would call the *formal* allusion to and neat inversion of *The Divine Comedy* seems readily apparent.[15] With this highly controlled form, the architecture of "Notes" actually has even more in common with *The Divine Comedy* than does "An Ordinary Evening in New Haven," a poem that Eleanor Cook has convincingly argued alludes to Dante's work.[16] Interestingly, the title of "An Ordinary Evening in New Haven" specifically revises the "heaven-haven" (CP, 399) of the first canto of the third section of "Notes," that is, the first canto in which Stevens obviously attempts to offer a "terrestrial" counterpart to Dante's *Paradiso.*[17] In fact, I would argue that "An Ordinary Evening in New Haven" (which also has thirty-one cantos of a nearly identical arrangement but without the sectional breaks) signals Stevens's subsequent dissatisfaction with the success of "Notes" in having accomplished the goal finally announced in "Imagination as Value" (1948). There he says, with what I regard as a wistful and retrospective denigration of "Notes," that although the "great poems of heaven and hell have been written," the "great poem of the earth remains to be written" (NA, 142).

Yet when he began "Notes toward a Supreme Fiction," Stevens was quite consciously trying to compose a modern and secular *Divine Comedy,* one that could relieve the anxiety not only about linguistic mutability but also about political mutations—indeed, one that could offer a sanction in life—but without recourse to the absolute Logos to which Dante could appeal. "After one has abandoned a belief in god," he writes in his *Adagia*, "poetry is that essence which takes its place as life's redemption" (OP, 185). In fact, much of the poem can be seen as an attempt to *confirm* linguistic mutability (and to subvert the grounding in logocentric authority to which he at least felt Dante could ultimately appeal) in order to prove what he had earlier argued in "The Poems of Our Climate"—that the "imperfect," not the perfect, "is our paradise" (CP, 194). Given the historical realities of his times, this purpose was certainly ambitious if not actually courageous.

Stevens's poem wrestles with *The Divine Comedy* in a variety of ways, with echoes ranging from simple allusion (through the similarity in form and numerology), through parody (as in the third section of Stevens's poem when the maiden Bawda, one of "love's characters come face to face" [CP, 401], parodies not only Beatrice's facing Dante but also the actual "characters" of love Dante sees in the eighteenth canto of the *Paradiso*),[18] to the previously noted, shared anxiety about linguistic mutability. I regard it as no accident that Stevens writes, as a self-conscious critique within "Notes," that the poem moves from "the poet's gibberish to / The gibberish of the *vulgate* and back again" (CP, 396, my emphasis), a statement that at once deflates the exalted role of the poet and of language itself while exposing a dilemma faced by Stevens similar to that faced by Dante when abandoning the traditional Latin. For both, the need to make poetry "modern" necessitated a hyperanxiety about the nature and reliability of language (as it did for Williams as well, although prosodically, at least, in obviously very different ways), for this linguistic anxiety was deeply, inextricably entwined with political contexts and consequences.

With this fact in mind, it seems fair to say that far from signaling an irresponsible reaction to the war, the sheer creation of such consciously *composed* poetry may have been for Stevens, as it was for Dante, an act of moral courage—an active, even spiritual "resistance" (OP, 230) to the political chaos of his times.[19] At the very least, such aesthetic composure offered Stevens what he reveals to have been a necessary "support" during his own violent times: "In the absence of a belief in God, the mind turns to its own creations and examines them, not alone from the aesthetic point of view, but for what they reveal, for what they validate and invalidate, for the support that they give" (OP, 186). Yet as this quotation suggests, without the faith in the divine absolute that would endow the structure, even the numerology, of a poem with universal meaning, a modern "supreme fiction" could not, as Stevens

well knew, find its "satisfaction" (CP, 240) in the assumptions and arguments
that presumably sustained Dante. Hence, the tripartite structure, with the
urgent imperatives heading each section, emerges once again as a literary
involucrum, inviting us to read each section of Stevens's poem as much
against, as in concord with, its corresponding book in Dante's trilogy.

Put simply, a modern supreme fiction "Must Be Abstract," as opposed to
the concrete and historically bound Inferno Dante envisions.[20] To satisfy the
modern and secularized mind, that supreme fiction also "Must Change,"
an imperative that I regard as a subtle reversal of the dogmatic assumptions
underlying Dante's text and, simultaneously, a surprising confirmation of the
function of Purgatory (with the consequence that the verb "change" carries
both an intransitive and a transitive meaning). Last, but not least, a modern
supreme fiction "Must Give Pleasure," as Dante's Paradise "must" as well,
but with specifically secular rather than sacred beatitude. In other words,
for Stevens, poetry must satisfy the same *function* it did for Dante—the
construction of "belief" that is "like to love" (CP, 262), as he says in another
wartime poem—but without either the logocentric or "realistic" underpin-
nings (whether philosophically or spiritually conceived) it had for Dante.

This "critique of Paradise" (CP, 305), as Stevens would call it in another
poem, or, more accurately, this argument against the metaphysical and the-
ological assumptions underlying Dante's text is carried out in the larger patterns of each section and in particular lines within individual cantos. To give
but one example of the latter, when the captain and maiden Bawda refuse to
marry in the third section of "Notes," with this rather odd "ceremonial hymn"
("Anon / We loved but would no marriage make"), and then *do* marry "well"
because "the marriage-place / Was what they loved" (CP, 401), they repeat in a
somewhat subversive action a distinction Dante draws in the *Paradiso* (canto
5) between the *content* of vows and the *act* of vowing. I should add that the
parody of Beatrice as the earthly directed Bawda is continued in the fourth
canto of section 3 with such lines as "Bawda loved the captain as she loved the
sun," with the possible hedonistic reinterpretation of "Son" (CP, 401) as "sun"
that appears in so many of Stevens's poems from "Sunday Morning" on.

Not surprisingly, then, not only does Stevens's first section, "It Must Be
Abstract," reject the concrete formulation of the *Inferno* (which, by its con-
creteness, precludes us now from believing it), but it also rejects the form of
the Trinity associated with Dante's first book (i.e., the power of the Father)
when it tells us

> Never [to] suppose an inventing mind as source
> Of this idea nor for that mind compose
> A voluminous master folded in his fire.
> (CP, 381)

Other aspects of the Trinity normally associated with Dante's trilogy are subverted in the subsequent two sections of Stevens's poem as well. Section 2, for example, evokes in its first canto the "Wisdom of the Son," or the resurrection of the Incarnated Word, only to dismiss that possibility with a deft simile:

> The old seraph, parcel-gilded, among violets
> Inhaled the appointed odor, while the doves
> Rose up like phantoms from chronologies.
> (CP, 389)

Even the possibility of the Word's ever being made incarnate is undermined in the sixth canto of section 2 (a canto that subverts the idea of communion as well along with a glib parodic gesture to Shelley):

> Bethou him, you
> And you, bethou him and bethou. It is
> A sound like any other. It will end.
> (CP, 394)

Finally, the Love of the Holy Spirit, corresponding in Dante's text with the *Paradiso*, is replaced in the last canto of Stevens's third section by the poet's desire for the "[f]at girl, terrestrial, my summer, my night," something that Stevens further insists (in contrast to Dante's ultimate vision) must be found "in difference," in "a change not quite completed" (CP, 406).

"Notes toward a Supreme Fiction," then, is consistently engaged with Dante's text, specifically in what we might call a contra-diction of the very "logocentric" assumptions of Dante's poem, even as it tries to offer poetry as a kind of redemptive force in the "epic of disbelief" (CP, 122). For example, in the first section of "Notes," Stevens exposes the "Logos and Logic, crystal hypothesis" (CP, 387), that is, the very underpinning of all Western philosophical theology, as something that desires to be but cannot be the "[b]eau linguist" (CP, 387). Far more rigorously than Dante, who after all follows reason in the figure of Virgil through the Inferno into Purgatory,

Stevens rejects the rationale of philosophical discourse. From the ridiculed "prodigious scholar" (CP, 381) of the second canto of the first section to the concluding and flippant farewell that "[t]hey will get it straight one day at the Sorbonne . . . / Pleased that the irrational is rational" (CP, 407), "Notes toward a Supreme Fiction" scoffs at the idea of *the* supreme idea so rigorously desired throughout the history of Western metaphysics.

Stevens confronts the consequences of this textual "pre-dicament" most acutely in the third section of his poem, that section in which he most clearly attempts to offer, in contrast to Dante's beatific vision, what he elsewhere calls the "acutest speech" of "human things" (CP, 300). Yet, as may be obvious, this attempt places Stevens essentially in the position of God as creator, a consequence that may be literally inscribed within the poem. Although this suggestion must remain tentative, even controversial, it is possible that following Walter Arensberg's numerous readings of Dante's "signature" in *The Divine Comedy*,[21] Stevens intentionally inscribes his own name through the cryptology of lines that ask, specifically,

> What am I to believe? If the angel in his cloud,
> Serenely gazing at the violent abyss,
> Plucks on his strings to pluck abysmal glory,
>
> . . . .
> Am I that imagine this angel less satisfied?
> (CP, 404)

The letters composing the words "Wallace Stevens" can be found in the first and second lines, respectively, of this excerpt. What mitigates against this speculation is that whereas Arensberg managed to find "Dante Poet" in several lines of *The Divine Comedy*, the word "Poet" cannot be found in the third line above—a curious omission if Stevens were following his friend's interest in cryptology.[22] Nonetheless, Stevens notably concludes this meditation on what "to believe" with this line, "I have not but I am and as I am, I am" (CP, 405), in which he specifically shifts biblical creative power— that "I am that I am"—to the individual self.

This desire to become (rather than to converge with) the creator accounts for the apparent contradiction in the last numbered canto of "Notes" to produce a language that could fulfill the very "logocentric" conception of language Stevens has subverted throughout the poem. Having begun the poem by insisting that

The sun
Must bear no name, gold flourisher, but be
In the difficulty of what it is to be
(CP, 381)

and having thoroughly exposed through his "revision" of *The Divine Comedy* that the logocentric desire for absolute unity is a nostalgic fiction, Stevens surprisingly announces in the last numbered canto of his poem his own desire for an ultimate (linguistic) unity with a "terrestrial" (not beatific) being. He wants "to name" his own feminine muse, that "[f]at girl, terrestrial," and to name her "flatly, waste no words" (CP, 406). Of course, this he cannot do (as Dante well knows; compare *Paradiso* 1, ll. 70–72), not even with recourse to the very logocentric conception of the Word that he has attempted to "outdo" in his modern revision of *The Divine Comedy*. It is with the greatest of ironies that the mutability or temporal break that language necessitates—that which forces Dante in the end to report the moment of absolute union as memory, in the past—finds its ultimate (even unavoidable) parallel in the withheld, future mood of Stevens's attempt to speak of this earth exactly:

Until flicked by feeling, in a gildered street,
I call you by name, my green, my fluent mundo.
You will have stopped revolving except in crystal.
(CP, 407)

This final irony, for it is acutely ironic, explains why Stevens's poem remains, poignantly and necessarily, only "*Notes toward* a Supreme Fiction." Not even the earth (much less the divine) can be confirmed through what Stevens calls the "evasion[s]" (CP, 396) of our words.

Yet the rather obvious failure of "Notes toward a Supreme Fiction" to redeem successfully our anxiety about linguistic mutability (indeed, all mutability) also accounts for the unexpected recourse to Christological imagery in the poem's final, unnumbered canto. With reference to "twelve wines" and the "bread of faithful speech," Stevens (however ironically) concludes:

How simply the fictive hero becomes the real;
How gladly with proper words the soldier dies,
If he must, or lives on the bread of faithful speech.
(CP, 408)

This final appeal to the very Christology that Stevens has been trying to subvert with his modern *Comedy* makes his subsequent (and previously mentioned) remark that the "great poem *of the earth* remains to be written" almost painful (my emphasis). At the end of his poem, against all his desire to do otherwise, Stevens cannot "ground" the consolation he desires for poetry to achieve without appealing to the very metaphysics rejected throughout the rest of the poem. It is there that Stevens finally and explicitly offers poetry, perhaps even his "Notes," as a "consolation" to men at war. And yet this very internal contradiction may itself be a mark of genius. For having so successfully undermined our faith in language, having so consistently reminded us of its "fictionality," the words of the poem's last (conditional) imperative, "If he must [die]," disturbingly remind us that it is a fiction that a soldier "must die," that we "must" have war. The alternative, the poem implies in its final line, is to live, perhaps by changing our language, even the political "descriptions" that could be said to be controlling the world. As already noted in "The Noble Rider and the Sound of Words," Stevens overtly asserts that the poet's function is "to help people to live their lives" (NA, 29), a "belief" that he fully articulates in the coda to "Notes toward a Supreme Fiction" (1942):

> Soldier, there is a war between the mind
> And sky, between thought and day and night. It is
> For that the poet is always in the sun,
>
> Patches the moon together in his room
> To his Virgilian cadences, up down,
> Up down. It is a war that never ends.
>
> Yet it depends on yours. The two are one.
> (CP, 407)

This coda is therefore not, as M. L. Rosenthal and Sally M. Gall have remarked, a "mawkish" afterthought, tacked on at the end to adapt "his metaphysical groping on the subject of language to a momentarily political end."[23] While it follows the rest of the poem, so that the concern with the war is not immediately apparent in the numbered cantos, the coda explains quite clearly one of the "necessities" of a "supreme fiction" in poetry. As such, this coda is the culminating expression in Stevens's work, up to that time, of his thinking deeply about the relation between the descriptions of our world achieved in poetry and the descriptions of our world realized in politics (and specifically in war). That "relation," Stevens had already insisted in "The Irrational Element in Poetry," is one of a "possible conversion":

> The trouble is that the greater the pressure of the contemporaneous, the greater the resistance. Resistance is the opposite of escape. The poet who wishes to con-template the good in the midst of confusion is like the mystic who wishes to contemplate God in the midst of evil. . . . In poetry, to that extent, the subject is not the contemporaneous, because that is only the nominal subject, but the poetry of the contemporaneous. Resistance to the pressure of ominous and destructive circumstance consists of its conversion, so far as possible, into a different, an explicable, an amenable circumstance. (OP, 230)

This resistance explains at least part of the often-noted lack of reality in Stevens's characteristic poetry. In a way quite similar to the way he resisted "objective" poetry, Stevens uses seemingly unrealistic descriptions of possible realities as an act of freedom and, most poignantly, as an agent of conversion.

Whether brilliant or inconsistent, the conclusion to "Notes toward a Supreme Fiction," with its Christological imagery, also anticipates what has come to be one of the greatest surprises to Stevens scholars—his apparent conversion to Roman Catholicism on his deathbed. [24] In this regard, what appears to have been an unplanned introduction to "Notes" (an introduction of a very different metrical pattern from the rest of the poem) may show Stevens's having achieved in the course of writing this poem a far closer convergence with Dante's vision than he had originally intended. When finally published in 1942, the poem begins with these additional lines, placed on a separate page before section 1:

> And for what, except for you, do I feel love?
> Do I press the extremest book of the wisest man
> Close to me, hidden in me day and night?
> In the uncertain light of single, certain truth,
> Equal in living changingness to the light
> In which I meet you, in which we sit at rest,
> For a moment in the central of our being,
> The vivid transparence that you bring is peace.
> (CP, 380)

So Dante asserted centuries before through *The Divine Comedy*, though (perhaps) with a more easily found conviction in the "single, certain truth" that could redeem both the mutability of his words and his own troubled times. Ultimately, and in ways that are not merely ironic, "Notes toward a Supreme Fiction" evokes a feeling, if not a faith, that Stevens suggests "Must Be Renewed," however much it must also "Be Changed" to accomplish that goal.

Despite his sustained attempts throughout the war years to create in poetry an imaginative space in which "we can survive," Wallace Stevens may have inadvertently encouraged his contemporaries' judgment that his poetry was socially unaware by saying that the poet does not owe "any more as a social obligation than he owes as a moral obligation" (NA, 27). Yet Stevens carefully qualified that statement with this important explanation: "The truth is that the social obligation so closely urged is a phase of the pressure of reality which a poem . . . is bound to resist or evade today" (NA, 28). In other words, with great consistency, Stevens opposes both propagandistic and "realistic" poetry, poetry in which the words are taken, naively, for the "things themselves," just as he opposed "objective" poetry. Such opposition certainly does not preclude "social" involvement but rather increases the poet's (or any person's) responsibility in achieving "conversion" of our circumstances.

The possibility of such "conversion" is intimated by his "Prose statement on the poetry of war," originally included in *Parts of a World* as "Poetry and War" though not reprinted in *The Collected Poems*. In it Stevens concludes that "[n]othing will ever appease" the desire for war—equivalent, there, to "the desire to move in the direction of fact as we want it to be" and to do so "quickly"—other than "a consciousness of fact as everyone is at least satisfied to have it be" (OP, 242). In other words, what will "satisfy" is not necessarily changed *facts* but converted *consciousness*. This is an "act of the mind" that can be achieved only through the power of language—a power that must, at the same time, destroy the "old descriptions" of the world, particularly the notion that the old descriptions are objective, valuable, or inevitable. It is, at least in part, this terribly ironic conjunction of aesthetic and political concerns that appears to have been the initial step in transforming, in a nearly explosive way, an already remarkable poet into the great master of his later years. From this perspective, there is an intensely ironic but also urgent political impetus behind his imperatives for the "Supreme Fiction"— "It Must Be Abstract," "It Must Change," "It Must Give Pleasure." However, "Notes toward a Supreme Fiction" is itself temporary, perhaps mutable, and certainly historical. As Elizabeth Bishop notes in "At the Fishhouses," all "our knowledge is historical, flowing, and flown."[25] And the actual historical events over the next two years seem to have almost overwhelmed Stevens, producing a very different poetic response to the war, first in the form of "Esthétique du Mal" and, subsequently, in a different form, "Description without Place." In fact, the next three years of the war produced in Stevens a vigorous poetic debate over the proper modes of addressing, even redressing, the growing catastrophic violence of the times.

CHAPTER FOUR

THE POET IN/UNDER HISTORY

Since the preceding chapter places so much political weight on and finds so much moral courage in the aesthetic resistance to the catastrophic violence of World War II that Wallace Stevens achieved in composing "Notes toward a Supreme Fiction," it becomes critical here to discuss why I am partially overriding the way Stevens himself ordered the poems of *Transport to Summer* by discussing in this and subsequent chapters certain seminal poems of that volume in the order in which Stevens composed them rather than in the order they ultimately appeared in the 1947 publication. Put succinctly, to fully document Stevens's evolving sense of the relation between words and war, it is necessary to consider the great three poems of *Transport to Summer*—that is, "Notes toward a Supreme Fiction" (1942), "Esthétique du Mal" (1944), and "Description without Place" (1945)—not only in the context of his other wartime poems but also in the chronological sequence of their composition. As Henri Focillon notes in *The Life of Forms in Art*, a book Stevens appears to have read during this period,

[w]henever we attempt to interpret a work of art, we are at once confronted with problems that are as perplexing as they are contradictory. A work of art is an attempt to express something that is unique, it is an affirmation of something that is whole,

complete, absolute. But it is likewise an integral part of a system of highly complex relationships. A work of art results from an altogether independent activity; it is the translation of a free and exalted dream. But flowing together within it the energies of many civilizations may be plainly discerned.[1]

While I may be somewhat more skeptical about the artistic "independence" Focillon exalts in this passage, his warning about critical complexity applies well not only to individual poems Stevens wrote during the period of war but also to collective compositions, including the aesthetic arrangement of *Transport to Summer* that masks—or perhaps transmogrifies—the actual stages Stevens went through. By placing "Notes toward a Supreme Fiction" at the end of the volume rather than at the beginning, Stevens initially obscures both the chronological composition of this major poem and, more importantly, the following changes he made in his aesthetics after the writing of "Notes," since subsequently his poetry became ever increasingly a rhetorical questioning of the very tenets first proffered in that poem. Thus, while it may be possible to regard the volume as an entity ("unique," "whole," and "complete"), it is equally possible to discern in this volume, if examined in its actual chronological production, different facets of Stevens's response to the relation of war and words during this period, including some sustained and intense responses that fundamentally undermine the faith in aesthetic resistance discussed in the preceding chapter.

In fact, the relative lack of discussion about Stevens's aesthetic *ordering* of *Transport to Summer* constitutes the single largest oversight of most critical discussions of this pivotal volume. For example, in her otherwise sterling book, *Poetry, Word-Play, and Word-War in Wallace Stevens*, Eleanor Cook rightly notes that

> Stevens arranged the poems of *Transport to Summer* in approximate chronological order, except for the greatest, *Notes toward a Supreme Fiction*. This poem, first printed privately in 1942, closes *Transport to Summer*, a collection written between 1942 and 1947.
>
> What is Stevens doing in this poem? To put it oversimply, *Notes toward a Supreme Fiction* is a poem that rewrites "supreme" writing, that is, our sacred scriptures; or points toward ways of rewriting them.[2]

Certainly, this most well-known poem of Stevens "rewrites 'supreme' writing," though, I would argue, it rewrites the "supreme writing" of Dante rather than of "sacred scriptures." However, Cook's observation either misses or minimalizes the fact that the actual placement of a poem written in 1942 at the end of a volume published in 1947 totally rewrites the important poetic process Stevens went through during this period. In particular, it ignores the next crucial stage in Stevens's developing poetics as he begins to wonder whether, in the face of escalating violence in the actual world, the poet should continue to "resist" that violence through aesthetic form or begin to "witness" to it. Equally important, Cook's summary misses altogether the redemptive possibility Stevens subsequently describes for himself and for the future in the writing of "Description without Place"—a possibility that he then initially appears to obscure by placing that poem near the middle of *Transport to Summer* and "Notes toward a Supreme Fiction" at its end. However, as a later chapter will suggest, by the end of the war Stevens had himself reinterpreted the poem's "formal resistance" as one possibly open to new calls for redemption.

The inside cover of *Transport to Summer* itself calls attention to the chronological displacement by noting that " 'Notes toward a Supreme Fiction' is the earliest of the poems contained in this book. Otherwise the poems are arranged in the order in which they were written."[3] A far more revealing note could have informed us that the opening poem of the volume, "God Is Good. It Is a Beautiful Night," was written in the same year Stevens composed "Notes toward a Supreme Fiction" with a similar desire to resist political violence; that "Esthétique du Mal" was written in 1944 as the war continued to escalate; and that "Description without Place" was written near the end of the war, as Stevens worried about what the future would be after the increased escalation of violence against the Japanese.[4] Within the context of this somewhat simplified account of Stevens's changing responses to World War II, the placement of "Notes" at the end of the volume becomes a crucial aesthetic and political gesture, transforming, as it does, a poem written primarily in *resistance* to war into one offered years later as one of *restitution*, even as Stevens—and entire cultures—tried to recover some semblance of normalcy. The desire to recover normalcy—a desire experienced after the war not only by Stevens but by many other writers as well—accounts for such late poems in *Transport to Summer* as the 1946 "Attempt to Discover Life" and certainly for subsequent poems in *The Auroras of Autumn*, most particularly the 1949 "An Ordinary Evening in New Haven," to which I will return in a following chapter.

Between the time he composed "Notes toward a Supreme Fiction" and the time he included it as the "supreme word" of *Transport to Summer* (calling it "the most important thing in the book" [L, 538]), Wallace Stevens had developed both as person and as poet in critical ways that we should not ignore. However moving we may find "Notes toward a Supreme Fiction" to be, within the larger aesthetic/political climate, such fictional "consolations" as Stevens offered aesthetically (in the form of the poem and overtly in both its prologue and coda) do not, as the poet well knew, stop the actual pain of war, a fact reflected or, more accurately, debated with great intensity in several of his subsequent poems. As much as he may have wished that "Notes" could provide the kind of consolation that Dante seems to have found in his *Comedy*, subsequent poems written during World War II, such as "Dutch Graves in Bucks County" and "Gigantomachia," provide their own kind of critique of the very aesthetic "crystal" that "Notes" attempts to inscribe. (As Charles Altieri notes in a slightly different context, "One measure of Stevens's greatness is the fact that he did not need other people to point out his problems.")[5] Of the poems written after "Notes" during World War II, "Esthétique du Mal" most fully demonstrates the degree to which Stevens's response progressed (or regressed, depending upon perspective) from active resistance to near despair. However, this change in Stevens's poetic response to his climate begins almost immediately after completing "Notes toward a Supreme Fiction," constituting a crisis in his evolving poetics as to whether aesthetic formulations amount to freedom or misleading ceremonial repetition.

Perhaps most acutely (because of its nominal placement within American shores), "Dutch Graves in Bucks County," written in 1942 and published the following year, makes it clear that it is war—not any semblance of order or of an ordering fiction—that is taking dominion everywhere.[6] As in the earlier "Examination of the Hero in a Time of War," Stevens once again evokes modern technological warfare. But the disturbing implication in "Dutch Graves" is that these "[a]ngry men and furious machines" are in Bucks County, in America, either actually swarming across the skies or invading the "great blue" of the imagination:[7]

Angry men and furious machines
Swarm from the little blue of the horizon
To the great blue of the middle height.
Men scatter throughout clouds.
(CP, 290)

If we return to the historical reality surrounding the composition of this poem, we are reminded that this was, in fact, a time when American children were receiving fighter-plane identification cards when they bought a Coke at the drugstore and when American cities were engaging in nightly blackouts. The *felt* experience during this period of being actually threatened on American soil extended from the earlier fear (previously discussed) of the "yellow horde" to a more insidious one signaled by the essay "Hitler's Guerillas over Here," published in the *New Republic*.[8] Thus, as the war continued and expanded, it became increasingly difficult for Stevens to accept as valid or even as efficacious the kind of aesthetic resistance figured in the architectonics of "Notes toward a Supreme Fiction."

More importantly, perhaps, in "Dutch Graves" Stevens names this military and psychic state of affairs as specifically "evil" (a word that his friend Van Geyzel attributed to *both* sides of the war) and not as merely violent.[9] As Eleanor Cook notes, the history of Stevens's use of the word "evil" is quite revealing: in his early work the word is used ironically, but by the middle of World War II Stevens begins to use the word more seriously, "at first concerned to balance evil with good, and equally not to imply a Christian metaphysics of evil," but later, as in "Esthétique," "to acknowledge fully the seriousness of evil."[10] If we look at the actual historical events of this period, we find that early in the year that Stevens produced "Dutch Graves," Hitler had made it clear that he was calling for the "extinguishing" of all "traitors," including Jewish, European, and even Aryan dissenters. As subsequently reported in the 8 March 1943 issue of the *New Republic*, Hitler intends that there will be "no halt in the wholesale massacre of Jews" and, furthermore, that he "will destroy the culture and the very life of Western Europe before he surrenders."[11] In another article of the same issue, it is speculated that "the Jews of Europe are being systematically murdered at the rate of at least seven thousand a day, and perhaps much more rapidly still. How many non-Jews are also being eliminated no one dares to guess."[12] As Stevens wrote to Henry Church toward the end of the war, "People in Germany must be in an incredible predicament, in which even correctness is incorrect" (L, 494), and here I think he means specifically the ethical "correctness" in resisting German occupation and the slaughtering of millions. In addition, only one month after these disturbing articles about Hitler's atrocities appeared in the *New Republic*, another writer raises serious question about the ethics of Americans bombing European cities, where "large numbers of innocent civilians are being killed."[13] I find it no wonder that Stevens would later write, in what seems to be a factual rather than a farcical statement, "A little of THE NEW REPUBLIC goes a *long way with me*" (L, 511, my emphasis).

It is in the midst of this grim reality that Stevens writes the following moving stanza in "Dutch Graves in Bucks County," part of which proves grotesquely prophetic:

> An end must come in a merciless triumph,
> An end of evil in a profounder logic,
> *In a peace that is more than a refuge,*
> *In the will of what is common to all men,*
> Spelled from spent living and spent dying.
> (CP, 291, my emphasis)

As he had argued in his "Prose statement on the poetry of war," originally included in *Parts of a World*, "in war, the desire to move in the direction of fact as we want it to be and to move quickly is overwhelming. Nothing will ever appease this desire except a consciousness of fact as *everyone* is at least satisfied to have it be" (OP, 242, my emphasis). Though obviously opposed to Communism in the economic sense, throughout this period Stevens consistently appeals to a different "common" good as the only possible (even "supreme") cure for the actual, universalized "spiritual violence" afflicting the world. This is a complicated point that should give us some pause before continuing to examine "Dutch Graves in Bucks County."

Although Stevens would say that he was specifically not one of the "so-called social revolutionists" within a letter in which that term is synonymous with "communists" (L, 350–51), Margaret Dickie is right in asserting that Stevens was basically aligned with Communist theory from as early as the mid-1930s.[14] As he explains in this letter written to Hi Simons in January 1940, "What really divides men into political classes in respect to these things [such as how to improve the condition of workers, the possible power and freedom that stem from education, even the public ownership of public utilities] is not the degree to which they believe in them but the ways and means of putting their beliefs into effect" (L, 351).[15] Although Stevens would humorously distance himself from the growing public distrust of Communism by 1945 (writing to Henry Church almost precisely at the end of World War II that he used to read "Turgeniev . . . in college" and that "that was when Russia was still a part of Europe, and when a Russian novelist was still a normal creature, concerned with other normal creatures" [L, 509]), as early as "Dutch Graves" Stevens was concerned with the immediate "fatalism" and even "sense of helplessness" (L, 350) not only that the world was experiencing but that most Americans were experiencing. Most Americans were witnesses to, if not actual participants in, the many theaters of war of the time, including the growing anxiety noted about the possible invasion of American shores. As a consequence, Stevens appeals to the desire for "a peace" that is "the will of what is common to men" in "Dutch Graves," but at the same time he writes, "There are circles of weapons in the sun," and

> The air attends the brightened guns,
> As if sounds were forming
> Out of themselves.
> (CP, 290)

This is a somewhat apocalyptic, or at least very ominous, image that thoroughly dismantles the "diamond globe" (CP, 251) of the earlier "Asides on the Oboe." Once again, Stevens addresses here the horribly ironic historical conjunction of war, words, and weapons.[16]

However much Stevens may have wished to believe in either a Nietzschean hero or a new generational and collective "hero," he articulates an unmistakable irony toward our inherited notions of "heroes" near the end of "Dutch Graves": "And you my semblables, behold in blindness / That a new glory of new men assembles" (CP, 292). Whatever "new glory" is being created in this global catastrophe, it is one beheld not by heroes but by "violent marchers," "in blindness." The irony becomes replete in the concluding lines of the poem:

> These violent marchers of the present,
> Rumbling along the autumnal horizon,
> Under the arches, over the arches, in arcs
> Of a chaos composed in more than order,
> March toward a generation's centre.
>
> Time was not wasted in your subtle temples.
> No: nor divergence made too steep to follow down.
> (CP, 293)

The distance between this poem and "Notes toward a Supreme Fiction" is made clear by noticing that thematically the conclusion here has far more in common with the "ambiguous undulations" of the ending of "Sunday

Morning" (written, not insignificantly, during World War I) than it does with the ending of "Notes." In these lines Stevens suggests that it is far more than a mere possibility that the new "generation's centre" will not be a positive transformation at all but an explosive chaos genuinely turned "downward toward darkness." From this perspective, "Dutch Graves" engages in something close to a debate as to whether words during war should resist or bear witness, about whether that movement "*toward* a generation's centre" (my emphasis) should be toward an imagining of a supreme fiction or toward a registering of a felt apocalyptic end. Though Stevens would subsequently call upon our responsibility to create a better world precisely through our powers of "description" (in the 1945 poem "Description without Place"), in this poem Stevens undermines such hope, suggesting that the "lost generation" (that term of Gertrude Stein made so popular by Hemingway in the 1920s) was once again being made the victim of a deadening and reductive rhetoric that had spawned yet another global war that could, in all likelihood, spell the end of the world as we know it.

Many of the poems written during this period graphically illustrate the internal debate Stevens felt between the need to resist and the need to witness to the violence of the actual world. For example, "Chocorua to Its Neighbor" (1943) engages in two kinds of rhetoric: the swarming and somewhat grotesque rhetoric of the armies in section 2 of the poem, in which "The armies are forms in number, as cities are" (CP, 296), and the idealized "external majesty" (CP, 299) of section 14, which inscribes the fictional yet still desired hero of the majority of the poem. However, "Gigantomachia," a poem rarely discussed in Stevens criticism, proves even more revealing in this regard. Alan Filreis—rather curiously, given his subject of his book—mentions the poem not at all; Harold Bloom also omits it from *The Poems of Our Climate*; and Eleanor Cook dismisses it in favor of "The Motive for Metaphor," saying that "Gigantomachia" is "a rather weak poem, for all the bluster of its title" and that "[i]t is 'The Motive for Metaphor' that we think of as Stevens's chief poem on the subject of metaphor."[17] However, "Gigantomachia," placed immediately *after* "The Motive for Metaphor" and *before* "Dutch Graves in Bucks County" in *Transport to Summer*, is not so much a poem on the subject of metaphor as it is a poem demonstrating Stevens's continuing theoretical debate as to the proper use of language in general and of metaphor in particular during a time of war.[18]

The "blustering" title, which actually alludes to the Greek myth of the same name, serves itself as a kind of involucrum in the text, inviting us to question from the outset whether this poem will be about something of significance or much ado about nothing. We are not, however, given an unequivocal answer to that question in the text of the poem; rather, the poem (cited in full below) displays over the course of its three stanzas a subtle but serious questioning of the rhetoric of poetic consolations:

> They could not carry much, as soldiers.
> There was no past in their forgetting,
> No self in the mass: the braver being,
> The body that could never be wounded,
> The life that never would end, no matter
> Who died, the being that was an abstraction,
> A giant's heart in the veins, all courage.
>
> But to strip off the complacent trifles,
> To expel the ever-present seductions,
> To reject the script for its lack-tragic,
> To confront with plainest eye the changes,
> That was to look on what war magnified.
> It was increased, enlarged, made simple,
> Made single, made one. This was not denial.
>
> Each man himself became a giant,
> Tipped out with largeness, bearing the heavy
> And the high, receiving out of others,
> As from an inhuman elevation
> And origin, an inhuman person,
> A mask, a spirit, an accoutrement.
> For soldiers, the new moon stretches twenty feet.
> (CP, 289)

In contrast to an authentic "common good" evoked in "Dutch Graves," this poem undermines, even ridicules, any sense of unity as being reductive and even "inhuman." In particular, the Nietzschean sense of the hero Stevens so clearly embraces at other times becomes subject to "perspectivist reaction."[19] The first two and a half lines tell us specifically "how poor" the soldiers are: they have no sense of tradition, no sense of identity (as men), no sense of the possible hero in this modern war. In addition, as opposed to the gigantic heroes of the Greek myth (including Zeus, Heracles, Poseidon, and occasionally Athena), they are nameless and merely mortal soldiers. Immediately thereafter, Stevens introduces the traditional and fictional "abstraction" of the "braver being" who supposedly should compensate for the soldiers' actual experiences. However, the second stanza critiques that verbal maneuver by intimating that a real look at war—not at the rhetoric of war—would of necessity "strip off" the minor, the seductive, the inherited "script" and expose a horrifying sense of the largeness, the *totality* of the Second World War, the poetic recognition of which Stevens overtly insists is "not denial."

If the first two stanzas imply that modern soldiers cannot continue to carry or to believe in the heroic tradition when confronted with the reality of modern war, the last stanza begins to ridicule that older tradition, what me might call the machismo tradition, as being ultimately inhuman and inhumane—a mask or mere "accoutrement." Significantly, the rhetorical strategy of the last stanza anticipates that of the seventh canto of "Esthétique du Mal" as being an *excoriation*, particularly an excoriation of a rhetorically false tradition, by reminding us abruptly in the last line that actual soldiers, in reality, experience nothing of that false rhetorical "light."[20] Notably, the "new moon," which is also notably black, "stretches twenty feet" for soldiers, as if they were walking in a void. The effect of this unexpected denouement is to collapse utterly any fictional consolation of largeness or elevation in war, including exhortations to war.[21] Thus, in "Gigantomachia" we see Stevens demonstrating that, if taken to extreme, resistance can turn into rhetoric, metaphors into mere masks.

A passage from "The Noble Rider and the Sound of Words" serves as an excellent gloss here, at least in terms of articulating this felt sense of the totality of war:

> The defeat or triumph of Hitler are parts of a war-like whole but the fate of an individual is different from the fate of a society. Rightly or wrongly, we feel that the fate of a society is involved in the orderly disorders of the present time. We are confronting, therefore, a set of events, not only beyond our power to tranquilize them in the mind, beyond our power to reduce them and metamorphose them, but events that stir the emotions to violence, that engage us in what is direct and immediate and real, and events that involve the concepts and sanctions that are the order of our lives and may involve our very lives; and these events are occurring persistently with increasing omen, in what may be called our presence. These are the things that I had in mind when I spoke of the pressure of reality, a pressure great

enough and prolonged enough to bring about the end of one era in the history of the imagination. (NA, 22)

However, as already noted in the previous chapter, when he wrote that essay, Stevens was still committed to the idea that we should "resist" that pressure in poetry. "Gigantomachia," written the following year, suggests that we must confront that pressure, not merely resist it.

Obviously, this kind of poetry or "thinking about war" is totally different from realistic wartime poems such as Randall Jarrell's "Death of the Ball Turret Gunner." However, I would argue that in terms of expressing the actual feeling of the war, especially the feelings of Americans still at home, Stevens's supposedly aesthetically irresponsible poems prove ironically quite accurate in articulating the changing response to the Second World War in reality. For example, in another poem of 1943, "No Possum, No Sop, No Taters" (a poem with a problematically and singularly American name), Stevens self-consciously describes that changed weather by evoking, first, the old order in the figure of the sun and then substituting it with a new and very distressing "finality":

He is not here, the old sun,
As absent as if we were asleep.

The field is frozen. The leaves are dry.
Bad is final in this light.

In this bleak air the broken stalks
Have arms without hands. They have trunks

Without legs or, for that, without heads.
They have heads in which a captive cry

Is merely the moving of a tongue.
(CP, 293–94)

Although Alan Filreis has helpfully remarked that the old trees "are subtly and ominously likened to horribly wounded, captive men, trying to cry out the story of their own version of wintriness," he somewhat reductively regards this poem as a "brilliant wartime rewriting of 'Farewell to Florida,'" motivated by Stevens's combined fear of being literally frozen in the "frightful winter of 1942–1943" due to oil restrictions and his frustration against prohibitions against unnecessary travel.[22] While it may well be true that the fear of living through a New England winter without enough heating oil to warm his home may be part of the specific provocation of the poem, in its finished form "No Possum, No Sop, No Taters" speaks much less to personal anxieties than to an entire cultural change in mood (and metaphysics). If, for example, the "old sun" (with the pun on "Son") represents the Christian belief system (including the inevitable triumph of "good over evil"), it is not surprising that Stevens would write, "He is not here"—Stevens had been making that pronouncement in various ways since "Sunday Morning." What *is* surprising, given the title, is precisely the subtle introduction of those "horribly wounded, captive men" noted above and, equally, the ominous tone.

Here I disagree completely with Filreis's conclusion that in the last half of the poem Stevens is in "agreement with reality in the war's second phase" and evokes "a poetry of national redemption, a moral sustenance that is discovered only by standing at a distance from what was once considered fertile."[23] It may well be that the "old sun," for which there is considerable nostalgia in this poem, is less the old Christian order than the human-centered, pagan, and earth-bound "devotion to the sun" Stevens had preferred at the end of "Sunday Morning" (including, notably, "wakened birds" and "casual flocks of pigeons"). If so, this poem represents an acute disillusionment on Stevens's part. Furthermore, it is not insignificant that Stevens chooses to write "[b]ad is final in this light" rather than the more predictable "[e]vil is final in this light." "Bad," with its Nietzschean associations with the oppressed, the poor, and the weak, speaks again to a sense of vulnerability and emasculinization that was more and more the felt cultural experience of people in the twentieth century's monstrously mechanized wars. Certainly, this is the feeling evoked by the subjective (not objective) correlative of the surrealistically figured handless, legless, headless captives and by the grotesque image of the inarticulate moving tongue. It is true that Stevens offers one redemptive moment toward the end of the poem: the coming of "this bad," Stevens writes, has the ambiguously described and nostalgic consequence of allowing us to "reach / The last purity of the knowledge of good." But the implication here is that such purity and goodness are in fact gone and that such knowledge is horribly belated even if never more desired. The poem then turns in its conclusion to a very ominous image that suggests that there has been a total and horrifying switch in our sense of reality and in the mythology through which we describe that sense of reality:

The crow looks rusty as he rises up.
Bright is the malice in his eye . . .

One joins him there for company,
But at a distance, in another tree.
(CP, 294)

In the place of the "old sun," bright malice? This may not be a "war poem" as such, but it is certainly responsive to the war, registering in that malice just what it means at that time to be in a world at war. While I agree that Stevens is describing a distancing from "what was once considered fertile," as Filreis notes, I find no nationalist redemption in the poem's conclusion. As in "Gigantomachia," the final image subverts any such attempt at easy consolation, including, here, the consolation of the "last purity of the knowledge of good." For whatever it replaces under the old sun, whether the Christian dove, the "absolute bird" of William James, or the physical birds of this earth in "Sunday Morning," this rising, rusty crow, with "malice in his eye," is hardly a figure to join for redemption. If, in fact, one does join "him there for company, / But at a distance, in another tree" (my emphasis), it is from the pain of having to witness to the growing madness of the war and from no longer trying to resist that reality with poetic (or nationalist) consolations. Indeed, in "Crude Foyer," a poem that appears in Transport to Summer only eight poems later, we are specifically told that even "Thought" itself is "false happiness," since "[w]e are ignorant men incapable / Of the least, minor, vital metaphor" (CP, 305). The very next poem, "Repetitions of a Young Captain," actually asks that we let "pathetic magnificences" (which I also read as poetic magnificences) "dry in the sky," exhorting a "civil nakedness" in which

> to bear with the exactest force
> The precisions of fate, nothing fobbed off, nor changed
> In a beau language without a drop of blood.
> (CP, 310)

Here, Stevens is not only beginning to reject the aesthetic consolations of previous writers such as Dante, whose work he had specifically tried to revise into forms more amenable to modern consciousness, but also starting to question even the "beau language" of his own "Notes," precisely for its failure to reflect the spilled blood of actual war.

"Esthétique du Mal," the next great poem Stevens wrote after "Notes toward a Supreme Fiction," testifies to the degree that Stevens's aesthetics in relation to war had changed by 1944 and to the degree to which that change was painful, even threatening to himself. As Joan Richardson notes of this period of time, "The idea" that Stevens's "imagination now seized on was one that he had had most difficulty with his whole life: pain." [24] In this context, "Esthétique du Mal" (which Cook discusses as if it were written before "Notes toward a Supreme Fiction") represents a huge change in Stevens's sense of poetic purpose. "Esthétique du Mal" proves to be the climax (though a climax that is actually a marked deflation) for Stevens in turning away from the desired consolations of the earlier "Notes" toward the troubling awareness that, if it is to be a "modern poetry" speaking to men and women of the time, poetry must after all not only "think about war" but bear witness to its atrocities, evils, pain, and despair.

The entirety of "Esthétique du Mal" (and, I would argue, not just section 7, where the "soldier" is overtly mentioned) should be read as a *poetic* statement on the poetry (or aesthetics) of war, specifically, the evil that defined this war, and with a very different relation to war than posited in "Notes toward a Supreme Fiction." As Stevens wrote to John Crowe Ransom, "The title is not quite right in the sense that anything of that sort seems to be not quite right now-a-days" (L, 469). Rather than alluding primarily to Baudelaire or to some abstract sense of evil, the "Mal" signals the war—and the whole mentality that had come to be the constant—but at a far and painful remove from the "diamond globe" (CP, 251) he had naively wished for in the 1940 "Asides on the Oboe." In "Esthétique du Mal" Stevens recants that wish, noting acerbically that

> Life is a bitter aspic. We are not
> At the centre of a diamond. At dawn,
> The paratroopers fall and as they fall
> They mow the lawn. A vessel sinks in waves
> Of people.
> (CP, 322)

It is with something closer to desperation, if not despair, than to clownish levity that Stevens then writes (in lines that I believe have been consistently misread in Stevens criticism), "Natives of poverty, children of malheur, / The gaiety of language is our seigneur" (CP, 322). The next lines of the poem reiterate this position:

A man of bitter appetite despises
A well-made scene in which paratroopers
Select adieux; and he despises this:
A ship that rolls on a confected ocean,
The weather pink.

(CP, 322)

Although Stevens would wish to resist becoming a "man of bitter appetites," these lines make clear that such a man is far preferable in this actual time to that student of the sublime who would literally sugarcoat the violent reality with pink confections, however sublime.

Earlier criticism of this poem overaestheticized—or anesthetized—the content and purpose of "Esthétique du Mal." In one of the better-known summaries of the poem, Joseph N. Riddel, for example, dismisses the historical specificity prompting Stevens's meditations by saying, "The *mal* of his time was simply the intensified *mal* of all time."[25] After saying that for "modern man" not only had faith vanished but "metaphysical evil had disappeared with the old beliefs" as well, Riddel then asserts the following: "What modern man had was not imaginative forms of explanation, but imagination, not the old mythologies, but the human power that created them and gave them life. Whatever had passed, there remained the human and its commitment to order, to aesthetic. Thus 'Esthétique du Mal' and its commitment to order, to aesthetic." However, by the time Stevens wrote this poem, his concerns had gone far beyond mere aesthetic concerns with the "poems of our climate" to an overwhelming concern with how poems should witness to a changed and violent climate. Thus, it seems to me that "Esthétique du Mal" is a poem that acutely needs to be read in its historical "moment"—and perhaps not merely for tracing Stevens's own poetic/political development but also for capturing a sense of the changing aesthetic sensibility of many writers in those politically turbulent times.[26] As Stevens wrote in his *Adagia*, "*Esthétique* is the measure of a civilization: not the sole measure, but a measure" (OP, 197).

Admittedly, Eleanor Cook does in fact devote an entire chapter of *Poetry, Word-Play, and Word-War in Wallace Stevens* to "Esthétique du Mal" and its particular relation to World War II, as does Charles Berger in *Forms of Farewell*; and both James Longenbach and Alan Filreis have offered extensive contextual evidence for the provocation of this poem, including an actual soldier's complaint to the editor of the *Kenyon Review* that the poetry being published, even the "war poetry," was not dealing directly enough with the reality of pain. [27] However, none of these critics suggests the fact that this poem is pivotal in tracing Stevens's changing ideas about the relation of words and war between "Notes toward a Supreme Fiction," written before, and "Description without Place," written after. For the precise provocation of "Esthétique," it is useful to remember not only that an actual soldier wrote a complaint to the *Kenyon Review* but also that Stevens began this poem only a few days after D day in June 1944, at a time of extraordinary emotional confusion. As Ernest Hemingway would note a month later in *Collier's* when recounting his own experience of being among those who gained Fox Green beach at the same time on D day, "Real war is never like paper war, nor do accounts of it read much the way it looks." [28] The historical specificity surrounding this questioning of allegiance to "aesthetic" orderings at this time cannot be stressed enough.

Whereas Riddel says that the "poem opens with the poet at Naples, in- volved paradoxically in activities both mundane and intellectual," Cook of- fers a form of a "new historical" corrective by noting that Stevens begins "with a natural example of mal, the erupting volcano Vesuvius," which she also notes erupted in 1944.[29] She persuasively argues that the volcanic eruption is intimately connected in Stevens's poem to the Second World War:

> When Stevens wrote the poem, then, Naples had just passed into Allied hands and Vesuvius had just repeated the geological phenomenon known to ancients and moderns alike. The place and time seem made to order for a war poet about an aesthetics of pain. . . . More than one observer of Vesuvius in eruption compared the sight and sound to the guns of war. Quite apart from war, volcanoes are places of terror, where warlike language sounds appropriate. They are conceived as mouths of hell, again an appropriate wartime metaphor. [30]

However, most of Cook's discussion of the poem actually traces echoes from other literatures and traditions, particularly, the traditional concept of the sublime rather than exploring the *mal* as the evil of war and the poet's difficult relation to it. Toward the end of her discussion of the poem, Cook says, "I began by connecting Stevens's word-play and word-war in *Esthétique du Mal* with actual war. That is where I shall end, though the connection I want to make is different. It is best put by a question: what have the theories of the sublime to do with war?" Imagining that a soldier, reading this (1944) poem, would be asking such a question, Cook then concludes that for Stevens's "sense of the sublime, we should turn to his essay, 'The Noble Rider and

the Sound of Words' "(first published in 1942), as if the essay were something to be written by Stevens and read by that soldier *after* the questioning
"Esthétique du Mal" would have engendered. She then introduces "Notes
toward a Supreme Fiction" by saying, "It takes some time to see the strength
of Stevens's title ["Notes toward a Supreme Fiction"] and the scope of his
answer to the soldier of 1944. I hope that soldier also saw it,"[31] as if "Notes"
were next in Stevens's poetic responses to the political realities of his time
and one that she hopes the soldier would have been able to read in the
future.

"The Noble Rider," however, was written well before the composition of
"Esthétique du Mal" and the imagined soldier's questioning. In fact, the
essay was written the year before Stevens composed "Notes toward a Supreme
Fiction"—that poem that Cook then turns to in her text as the subject of
the chapter *following* her discussion of "Esthétique du Mal."[32] I am stressing
this point because by the time he wrote "Esthétique du Mal," Stevens no
longer believed in the same way in the consoling power of poetic and formal
"resistance" offered in "The Noble Rider and the Sound of Words" and
"Notes toward a Supreme Fiction." Instead, he was struggling with developing
a different aesthetic relation to war, one that would accurately address the
reality of pain and poetry's place within it. In this sense, Cook's remark that
the "student of aesthetics" (with whom Stevens opens "Esthétique du Mal")
"may be composite, something of a self-parody whose purpose is to make us
question our own way of thinking about the sublime" is one that proves to
be precisely to the point, though not in the way Cook intends.[33] That is, the
"student of aesthetics" could be regarded as a parody not only of the "ephebe"
of the earlier "Notes toward a Supreme Fiction" but of Stevens himself and
his attempt to create an aesthetically sublime (even if terrestrially bound)
consolation in that 1942 "Fiction."

While certainly not "realistic," for a number of obvious reasons, including
Stevens's remaining in America throughout the war, "Esthétique du Mal"
records Stevens's courageous act of attempting to register this new evil and
global thought. This is both a poetically and psychologically risky move for
Stevens, full of the potential of leaving him (like his "firm stanzas") hanging

> like hives in hell
Or what hell was, since now both heaven and hell
Are one, and here, O terra infidel.
(CP, 315)

Specifically, the first canto of "Esthétique du Mal" introduces a student of aesthetics who, in a very escapist fashion, is writing letters and reading paragraphs precisely on the "sublime"—that subject so central to the concerns of "Notes toward a Supreme Fiction." But, in contrast to the last section of "Notes" ("It Must Give Pleasure"), the first canto of "Esthétique" ominously concludes, "The volcano trembled in another ether, / As the body trembles at the end of life." Not trembling in a sublime ether but in the ether of actuality, the volcano trembles in a totally apocalyptic way. The student then tries (but fails) to sublimate the evil of the times with the glib remark that "[p]ain is human," that "except for us, / The total past felt nothing when destroyed" (CP, 314).

However, the second canto of the poem exposes the shallowness of such clichés, introducing a nonhuman moon, the force of which cannot be subsumed or integrated into his aesthetic musings. Far from being a symbol of perfection, the "moon was always free from him," or rather always free from humanity, and specifically free from the violent script of its history and historical script of violence. Synecdochically, the moon reflects in its very indifference and otherness the ironic fact that "evil" is not natural but precisely human. Nature then serves in this canto as a force that undermines the escapist tendencies of canto 1:

> Warblings became
> Too dark, too far, too much the accents of
> Afflicted sleep,

ironically communicating the "intelligence of his despair" (CP, 314) as it does in another poem of the same time, "Less and Less Human, O Savage Spirit": "It is the human that is the alien, / The human that has no cousin in the moon" (CP, 328).

More importantly, the third canto of "Esthétique du Mal" (with its obvious gesture toward Dante) self-referentially and even bitterly notes, "His firm stanzas hang like hives in hell" or, more accurately, given the actual reality of 1944, that they hang in a "terra infidel" rather than being those "firm stanzas" that Stevens had earlier felt could construct if not create a terrestrial paradise. The rest of canto 3, which rejects Christian consolation and belief, attempts to argue that if we have lost our belief in God (and therefore also in Satan), hell and pain should disappear, that in the subsequent "health of the world" we will be "sure to find our way" (CP, 315–16). But, just as in "A Dish of Peaches in Russia," where "peace" evokes its opposite, "war," the word "health" (held off in a subjunctive clause) reminds us of the actual sickness, the actual evil spreading over the entire world at the time, just as the phrase "as if we were sure to find our way" harks back to the opening line of Dante's *Inferno*, in which the pilgrim Dante tells Virgil that he has lost his way and has little hope of being led back to safety.[34]

Canto 4 ridicules the "sentimentalist," who tries to introduce meditations on various aesthetics, and then sweeps all such fictitious consolations away with these startling and ominous lines:

> The genius of misfortune
> Is not a sentimentalist. He is
> That evil, that evil in the self, from which
> In desperate hallow, rugged gesture, fault
> Falls out on everything: the genius of
> The mind, which is our being, wrong and wrong,
> The genius of the body, which is our world,
> Spent in the false engagements of the mind.
> (CP, 316–17)

In contrast to the romantic or sublime notion of poetic genius, here Stevens clearly evokes the idea of a mind that is evil, from which "fault" is now falling "out on everything"—an accurate sense of how many regarded World War II and perhaps Hitler's particular place in it. Against that disturbing reality, canto 5 offers one of the most intimate passages in Stevens's corpus, in which a deep familial warmth and unity is (secularly) consecrated with the lines "Be near me, come closer, touch my hand, phrases / Compounded of dear relation" (CP, 317). Much like the "violence from within that protects us from a violence without," these phrases are admittedly reminiscent of what Stevens calls in this same canto the "in-bar" protecting us against the "suns / Of ex-bar." But the words "in-bar" and "ex-bar" point to an acknowledged artificiality—or at least to a potential for a distorting artificiality—not seen in "The Noble Rider and the Sound of Words."

Structurally, then, it is no accident that the next canto offers a genuinely ominous vision of what is occurring out there in "ex-bar," that is, a bony bird with an insatiable appetite pecking at an imperfect sun:

> A big bird pecks at him
> For food. The big bird's bony appetite
> Is as insatiable as the sun's.

Though not objectively reflective of any particular war atrocity, this vision (which extends the vision of the crow with "malice in his eye" from an earlier poem) is a nearly perfect "subjective correlative" for the experience of the pervasive *mal* of World War II. The anthropomorphic nature of this image is reinforced by the following "point of redness":

> The bird
> In the brightest landscape downwardly revolves
> Disdaining each astringent ripening,
> Evading the point of redness.
> (CP 318)

In fact, canto 6, in which the bird curiously avoids the "point of redness," constitutes what we might call an extended example of ineffective "in-bar" distortions:

> These are within what we permit, in-bar
> Exquisite in poverty against the suns
> Of ex-bar, in-bar retaining attributes
> With which we vested, once, the golden forms.
> (CP, 317)

As such, I regard the bird with the "bony appetite" to be an example of that "ex-bar" we have traditionally tried to keep out of consciousness and certainly out of "high poetry."[35]

The real center or touchstone of the poem appears two cantos later, with "[p]anic in the face of the moon" (CP, 320), a phrase encapsulating Stevens's actual response to "evil." In between, the "logic" of canto 8 prepares us for such "panic" by asserting, "The death of Satan was a tragedy / For the imagination" (CP, 319). But, we must surely ask, why? As Stevens argues in this poem, in a new time of global violence and escalating human evil, without Satan as the motivator for evil, the evil in life cannot be condensed or ordered, much less redeemed, not even by the "red rose" of a "soldier's wound" of canto 7 (a problematic canto to be discussed at length in chapter 7). Stevens even speculates that the "tragedy" may have begun from the desire for an absolute—

> In the yes of the realist spoken because he must
> Say yes, spoken because under every no
> Lay a passion for yes that had never been broken.
> (CP, 320)

—and the corollary possibility of trying to impose order. Here, as we have seen before, Stevens specifically rejects the kind of absolutist stances of rhetoric that led to the increasingly horrific realities of his time, resulting perhaps in nothing more than a choice between two "evils." Whatever reasoning or rationalizations about the actual *mal* may fuel the student of aesthetics, the feeling of "panic" is the most pervasive feeling of the poem as Stevens has written it. Recalling the frightening moon of canto 2 and anticipating the "logical lunatics" of canto 14 (in which "lunatics," we should remember, derives etymologically from "lunar"), the "panic" in canto 9 noted above underscores, even as it exposes, the Pan-like chaos—the inexplicability of evil—that defies the student's futile and fallacious attempts to order actual chaos with appeals to the sublime.

In fact, canto 14 suggests that such appeals to the sublime are, in the midst of World War II, mere *sublimation*. "Revolution / Is the affair of logical lunatics," in which such a misguided "believer" (my word)

> would be the lunatic of one idea
> In a world of ideas, who would have all the people
> Live, work, suffer and die in that idea
> In a world of ideas. He would not be aware of the clouds,
> Lighting the martyrs of logic with white fire.
> His extreme of logic would be illogical.
> (CP, 324–25)

In this way only "Esthétique du Mal" confirms the ending of "Notes toward a Supreme Fiction," that we will be pleased one day to discover that the "rational" is "irrational." But in tone and actual consequence, "Esthétique du Mal" suggests such an ironic pleasure will be significantly different from the one offered at the end of that "sublime" poem. Canto 14 thus implies that an aesthetics of the sublime (even if reconfigured as an "evil" absolute) is impossible, thus preparing us for the final canto, in which

> The greatest poverty is not to live
> In a physical world, to feel that one's desire
> Is too difficult to tell from despair.
> (CP, 325)

These lines finally articulate the emotion motivating this poem.

Toward the middle of the last canto, the poet (rather than the student of aesthetics) then writes of "the rotund emotions, paradise unknown," concluding (approvingly, it seems), "This is the thesis scrivened in delight, / The reverberating psalm, the right chorale" (CP, 326). But—and this is important —the rather "supremely fictional" ending just cited is then totally deflated with the following four lines, which, at least to me, expose Stevens's final attitude in this poem on the attempt to aestheticize evil:

> One might have thought of sight, but who could think
> Of what it sees, for all the ill it sees?
> Speech found the ear, for all the evil sound,
> But the dark italics it could not propound.
> (CP, 326)

The temptation to "despair," the emotion named at the beginning of this canto, is clear enough here. Taken as a whole, then, "Esthétique du Mal" consistently questions, even undermines, the aesthetic "resistance" Stevens had so eloquently articulated two years earlier in "Notes toward a Supreme Fiction." It is a brutally honest self-examination of Stevens's earlier poetics with an enormous potential for despair and retraction.

In this context, it is all the more remarkable that four years later, in 1948, Stevens would be talking about the importance of the imagination in recognizing the "normal" and defending that importance against people who "insist on the solitude and misery and terror of the world. They will ask of what value is the imagination to them; and if their experience is to be considered, how is it possible to deny that they live in an imagination of evil?" (NA, 154). However, in 1944 Stevens was himself quite capable of imagining "the solitude and misery and terror of the world" in the panic-stricken "abstractions" of

"Esthétique du Mal." Far from being a poem that insists that poetry, particularly the sounds of it, helps people to live their lives, "Esthétique du Mal" suggests that poetry—and especially the fictions of the sublime—may be irrelevant, perhaps even actually destructive, to our lives. In fact, the overall experience of "Esthétique du Mal" is not one of intellectual or aesthetic ordering or of "sublime" or "romantic" consolations but one of confusion and chaos. With a pervasively brooding, ominous mood, "Esthétique du Mal" continually suggests that this earth is truly "imperfect" but without the positive connotations associated with the imperfect in "The Poems of Our Climate." As such, Stevens's most difficult and perhaps most personally painful poem deliberately raises in its first canto the traditional desire of a "student-poet" to enter a shattered landscape and transform it into poetic patternings that will suffice to invoke (as Stevens once had) a "violence from within" that would protect us from a "violence without." But ultimately, as the rest of the poem demonstrates, this desire proves to be more than tinged with the suspicion of failure, at least for Stevens as well as for that student he so ruthlessly exposes as naively desiring the kind of transcendent (however "terrestrial") consolations Stevens had himself offered in his earlier "Notes toward a Supreme Fiction." However, looking forward to the next chapter, such acute malaise on Stevens's part proved temporary, though it remains a crucial stage in his ever-evolving poetics, which would next seek a "return" to "normalcy" but with an altered sense of the place and importance of poetry in the experienced political world.

CHAPTER FIVE

A SLOW (RE)TURN

Other poems written immediately after "Esthétique du Mal" testify to the degree Stevens was tempted to despair—at times, perhaps, personally about the efficacy of his preferred vocation but primarily about the fallacy of language in general and of poetic/aesthetic constructs in particular, especially when they attempted to respond to the actual world. A second-order level of possible despair, already intimated in "Esthétique du Mal," that haunted Stevens at the time is that human beings in general, including all their constructs (whether poetic or political), are contaminated and contaminating, a source of "evil" totally alien to the natural (rather than "actual") world. Such is the ominous suggestion of the poem aptly entitled "Less and Less Human, O Savage Spirit," also written in 1944. There, having postulated that "it is the human that is the alien, / The human that has no cousin in the moon," Stevens goes on to imply that human nature is so distorted that it would be preferable that no god (if there were a god) would even respond to tainted human speech:

> It is the human that demands his speech
> From beasts or from the incommunicable mass.

If there must be a god in the house, let him be one
That will not hear us speak.
(CP, 328)

As opposed to the coda of "Notes toward a Supreme Fiction," this poem, which could itself be regarded as a coda to "Esthétique du Mal," rejects "faithful speech," all Christological imagery, and potentially both poet and soldier alike.

Similarly, "Paisant Chronicle" satirizes all men, all nations, the human race itself—and even the idea of "major man" (CP, 334–35). However, it is "The Bed of Old John Zeller" (cited in full below), the poem that appears between "Esthétique du Mal" and "Less and Less Human" in *Transport to Summer*, that displays Stevens's most acute anxiety at this time—the primary anxiety mentioned above that appears to turn back precisely to Stevens's initial resistance to objectivist poetry with which this study began. However, in contrast to his initial confidence in having "things to say" beyond mere objects in space, Stevens now appears to undermine that position, suggesting such a position is entirely self-indulgent, even facile:

This structure of ideas, these ghostly sequences
Of the mind, result only in disaster. It follows,
Casual poet, that to add your own disorder to disaster

Makes more of it. It is easy to wish for another structure
Of ideas and to say as usual that there must be
Other ghostly sequences and, it would be, luminous

Sequences, thought of among spheres in the old peak of night:
This is the habit of wishing, as if one's grandfather lay
In one's heart and wished as he had always wished, unable

To sleep in that bed for its disorder, talking of ghostly
Sequences that would be sleep and ting-tang tossing, so that
He might slowly forget. It is more difficult to evade

That habit of wishing and to accept the structure
Of things as the structure of ideas. It was the structure
Of things at least that was thought of in the old peak of night.
(CP, 326–27)

With biting irony, the opening stanza rejects the kind of "structure of ideas" associated with his own "Notes" and Dante's *Divine Comedy*, concluding that they add only "disorder to disaster" and make "more of it." With the obvious etymological roots and puns in "dis-order" and "dis-aster," the self-consciously derisive evaluation of poetry articulated here appears to cut back all the way to such early poems as "Sunday Morning" and "The Idea of Order at Key West." Indeed, "The Bed of Old John Zeller" goes on to charge that "[i]t is easy to wish for another structure / Of ideas" and "to say as usual" that it must be "luminous." More biting, perhaps, is the suggestion that, as opposed to the "modern" sensibility Stevens always wished to have, such a "habit of wishing" for luminous aesthetic structures is not only "easy" but antiquated, "as if one's grandfather lay / In one's heart." Yet the most personal index of pain in the poem is the conclusion, which suggests that, as opposed to his aesthetic position only six years before, "[i]t is more difficult" to abandon the "structure of ideas" and to "accept the structure / Of things as the structure of ideas." No ideas but in things. But, as we have seen, the "things" that constituted both his and Williams's world in 1944 were unthinkable in 1938, when Stevens wrote "The Poems of Our Climate," and the ideas to which these things had given rise were evil beyond the mind's previous last extensions.

Collectively, then, "Esthétique du Mal" and these other short poems constitute a sort of poetic confession and consequently account, at least in part, for Stevens's writing Oscar Williams only a few months later that a "*prose* commentary on War and Poetry is out of the question" (L, 479, my emphasis). In part, Stevens's refusal to write a prose commentary (when he had been willing to write a "Prose statement" only two years before) as well as his previously cited concern in the same letter with the economic conditions of the future rather than with the actual war may also be explained by the generalized feeling growing throughout 1944 that the war *was* virtually over. As early as 22 May 1944 George W. Norris was already writing about "Germany after Defeat."[1] And yet, just as victory seemed imminent, the *New Republic* introduced the possibility, even probability, of cartels in a special issue entitled "CARTELS: The Menace of Worldwide Monopoly" (27 March 1944).

The very first paragraph of this twenty-page section begins by noting that although "[p]eople in all countries have been talking about an international government after the war," in reality "there was before this war, there is now, and there bids fair to be on an even greater scale after it, an international government of a different kind." The rest of this essay goes on to give an ominous description of Hitler-like economic rulers who have been and will be controlling the world through "influencing the few rather than by giving an account to the many": the natural rubber cartel, the chemicals cartel, the diamond cartel, and others in tin, in steel.[2] Though Stevens's fear of the "leftist" labor movement toward the end of the war may seem perversely right wing after this issue, I think his sense of future *economic* chaos as the controlling future reality was genuine and something felt by many people at the time, especially after having already witnessed economic disaster in the form of the Great Depression following the Great War. As Stevens reconsidered the position of the poet in the face of this impending future, we once again see a continued vacillation (now in increasingly quickening swings) between his distrust in the power of language and his faith in its (and the poet's) power as a necessary, even redemptive force. However, despite the nearly total malaise of "The Bed of Old John Zeller," Stevens never doubts that words (and poetry) are a constitutive force in the world. The question becomes whether that force is a destructive or a constructive one. Stevens's growing sense that the future depends upon a collective agreement—or, as already cited, "a consciousness of fact as everyone is . . . satisfied to have it be" (OP, 242)—directly leads to "Description without Place," a poem that I regard as Stevens's finest antiwar poem as well as his greatest expression of the ethical responsibility we have in how we choose to order our words.

It is quite consistent that Stevens should again incorporate his subtle "resistance" to "objective" poetry in his own attempt to describe "Description without Place." In the opening section of the poem Stevens turns to the figure of the sun (with which he opened "Notes toward a Supreme Fiction" in 1942): "It is possible that to seem—it is to be, / As the sun is something seeming and it is" (CP, 339). Perhaps with Williams in mind, this affirmation is placed in opposition to "objective" descriptions of the world, for in contrast to such seemingly realistic statements as William Carlos Williams's "[g]reen is green,"[3] Stevens here describes the "vacancy" inherent in linguistic description:

> This green queen

> In the seeming of the summer of her sun
> By her own seeming made the summer change.

In the golden vacancy she came, and comes,
And seems to be on the saying of her name.
(CP, 339)

As in "The Poems of Our Climate," these lines engage in an argument with
the "realistic" assumptions about language that Stevens felt presumed in
"descriptive" or "objective" poetry. It is an argument, however, designed not
to denigrate language but rather to reaffirm the power of the word. As he
insists later in the poem,

Description is revelation. It is not
The thing described, nor false facsimile.

It is an artificial thing that *exists*,
In its own seeming.
(CP, 344, my emphasis)

The quasi-religious didacticism of this argument reaches its fullest expression a few lines later: "In description, canon central in itself / The thesis of
the plentifullest John" (CP, 345). The potential didacticism of this theory
of description is tempered, however, by its own playful allusion to (and description of) this *scripture* as well as by its own serious examination into
the possibilities and the limitations of "description" itself. Yet with equal
urgency, Stevens also insists in "Description without Place" that in spite of
the limitations of language and its inherent deviation from reality, language
still is powerful in reality. The references to historical figures such as Calvin,
Queen Anne, Neruda, Nietzsche, and Lenin demonstrate the power of people's visions or "descriptions" of the world to become precisely "[s]eemings
that it is possible may be" (CP, 342). Thus, the colors of the world become
"discolorations" in Nietzsche's mind, and "his thoughts" in turn become the
"colored forms" (CP, 342).

Ultimately, however, Stevens's greatest explanation of this "theory" lies not
in his theorizing about poetry but in its practice, as in the concluding lines
of "Description without Place." The "theory of description matters most,"
he says, because

everything we say
Of the past is description without place, a cast

Of the imagination, made in sound;
And because what we say of the future must portend,

Be alive with its own seemings, seeming to be
Like rubies reddened by rubies reddening.
(CP, 345–46)

Perhaps again in contrast to the "delineating" way that Williams uses color in poems such as "The Red Wheelbarrow" and "The Red Lily," Stevens deliberately combines a static image (the red rubies) with an act of the mind ("rubies reddening") that is obviously created through an act of language—*through description itself.* This conjunction is, as we know, not an object in reality, yet even as they expose the gap between meaning and the world, these words prove the power of description to create meaning. In fact, part of the success and even humor of the last line lies in the fact that the word "red" and the word "ruby" stem from the same Latin root. The discrimination we therefore "see" in reality—the intensification of color by other colored objects—is ultimately a linguistic discrimination that nonetheless comes to describe reality. Instead of "no ideas but in things," the ending of this powerful poem embodies the suggestion of "no things but in ideas" when "ideas" mean the verbal descriptions with which we construct (or destroy) the world. Such is the power of the word, one that Stevens feels we cannot repress and should not dismiss.

In terms of this larger artistic perspective, it is worth noting that the concluding image of "Description without Place" may have had its own aesthetic precursor in Picasso's verbal description of his artistic process:

Auparavant les tableaux s'acheminaient vers leur fin par progression. Chaque jour apportait quelque chose de nouveau. Un tableau était une somme d'additions. Chez moi, un tableau est une somme de destructions. Je fais un tableau, ensuite je le détruis. Mais à la fin du compte rien n'est perdu; le rouge que j'ai enlevé d'une part se trouve quelque part ailleurs.[4]

[Formerly, paintings would move toward their end by progression. Each day brought something new. A painting was a sum of additions. With me, a painting is a sum of destructions. I do a painting, then I destroy it. But in the end nothing is lost; the red I have removed from one place is to be found someplace else.]

This description of the artistic process, which Stevens appears to have read, reinforces the suggestion that ultimately for Stevens "the theory of description matters most" *not* because language (or art) accurately reflects the world but because, no matter how much we destroy it with the recognition that language is ultimately representation and not the "thing itself," its "stubborn sounds" still remain an active force in the world. The "rouge"—what years later Jacques Derrida might call a "trace"—remains, representing no longer the wound of war but the power through which, Stevens feels, we can "convert" our circumstances.[5] It seems to me that this "supreme" possibility is precisely the sense that Stevens may have meant to convey earlier in "Notes toward a Supreme Fiction" by the "possible red" (CP, 393), the "[r]ed-in-red repetitions never going / Away, a little rusty, a little rouged" (CP, 400), though without the sophistication achieved in these terms in "Description."

And yet it seems necessary to literally contextualize "Description" once again, especially as this poem figures as a climax to one of the stages of Stevens's poetics described thus far. Despite the almost uncanny way Stevens's "Description without Place" meshes with the subsequent ethical imperatives voiced by journalists after the dropping of the atomic bomb about our responsibility in choosing how we will describe the future world, we should note that the bomb had not yet been dropped when Wallace Stevens was writing the poem. Yet, as Stevens wrote in June 1945, the week he delivered this poem as the Phi Beta Kappa speech at the graduation exercises for Harvard, "The ordinary state of mind seems to be one of suspense. Shortly, when the Japanese war begins to mount in fury, we shall feel differently. . . . [T]he truth about Japan seems to be difficult for most of us to grasp. From our point of view here at home, America has never been on the make, or on the grab, whatever people may have said of us elsewhere. The Japanese war is likely to change all that" (L, 506–7). And not just for this generation, Stevens laments, but for the next generations as well (L, 507). Six weeks after Stevens's letter, the first atomic bomb exploded over Hiroshima.[6] In this regard, "Description without Place" can be seen as a prophetic manifesto, attempting to shape ahead of time an ethical vision for America that would be sorely needed (and, we might note, not entirely achieved) after what Stevens (and others) felt to be a palpable escalation against Japan in toto.

However much this poem may have expressed the growing anxieties of the time, an additional and I think conscious provocation for "Description without Place" may well have been the various maps published in the *New Republic* (and other journals as well) in 1944 and 1945 that kept attempting to describe agreeable boundaries for a future Poland. It was exactly that dispute that prefigured the war, as Germany and Russia variously described "Poland" in different ways. And at what appeared to be, and was, the end of the war, the world had still not settled upon a "satisfactory" description of Poland. Other maps showed the extent or retreat of various countries' boundaries changing every week. Underneath one map of eastern Europe entitled "On the Borders of the Empire," we find, "Because we consider Germany as having a different set of boundaries, we ought not to overlook the fact that Hitler's own Germany follows the limits of the old German Empire before 1648."[7] It was in this historical context as well as within the realized increasing fury of technological warfare that Stevens wrote to Henry Church on 4 April 1945, just prior to composing the poem, that "[i]t seems to me to be an interesting idea: that is to say, the idea that we live in the description of a place and not in the place itself, and in every vital sense we do" (L, 494). Immediately after exploring this "interesting idea," Stevens attempted to articulate it further in poems such as "Attempt to Discover Life" and "Credences of Summer," both written in 1946. Certainly, Stevens was not imaginatively prepared (nor was most of the world) for the atomic bomb. And yet the bomb was dropped, and Stevens continued to wrestle with the position of the poet in a torn world. Specifically, "Two Tales of Liadoff," written just after the bomb had been dropped and the war had ended, indicates Stevens's continued responses to this moment in history, as does the subsequent "Burghers of Petty Death," published in a very brooding group of poems entitled *More Poems for Liadoff.*[8]

The "Two Tales of Liadoff," published in the journal *Pacific* only three months after the bombs were dropped on Hiroshima and Nagasaki, have as their context not only the many bombs that had so gruesomely characterized this war, including the "blockbusters," the long-range rockets being developed at the end of the war, but possibly the bomb itself.[9] The first "tale" begins with what appears to be a recasting of reality into a "more amenable circumstance" (OP, 230):

Do you remember how the rocket went on
And on, at night, exploding finally
In an ovation of resplendent forms—

Ovation on ovation of large blue men
In pantaloons of fire and of women hatched,
Like molten citizens of the vacuum?
(CP, 346)

In addition to the specific reference given in the title to a contemporaneous composer, Stevens may also be referring to the "ovation" we have given to "the rocket's red glare," the celebration of "bombs bursting in air" in the form of more amenable fireworks. That *was* our tale, one that envisioned military victory as freedom, something to be celebrated with fireworks, for "the home of the brave" as well as the many other rhetorical war poems discussed, as a long tradition, before. But the second tale begins quite differently: "The feeling of Liadoff was changed," much as the "theater" and the "classic" hero had changed. But *this* particular change, published in November 1945, describes a fundamental revision of both the self and the public, of the poet and how Americans would see themselves, as a consequence of escalating violence. Even Liadoff (who stands for the poet) was changed:

> It is
> The instant of the change that was the poem,
> *When the cloud pressed suddenly the whole return*
>
> *From thought, like a violent pulse in the cloud itself.*
> (CP, 347, my emphasis)

What *was* the poem is no longer possible after this thought, which has returned on itself in such violence. The poem goes on to say that both "the town" and he, himself, now seek the sounds that would "soon become a voluble speech," concluding that such speech, if possible, will be "[v]aluable but archaic and hard to hear" (CP, 347). Perhaps also barbaric and hard to bear.

The possibility of this militaristic as well as the more obvious musical or aesthetic context becomes even more clear in "Burghers of Petty Death," published the following year within a series of twelve poems entitled *More Poems for Liadoff,*[10] in a poem in which I think Stevens clearly refers to the mushroom cloud of the atomic bomb:

> The grass is still green.
>
> But there is a total death,
> A devastation, a death of great height
> And depth, covering all surfaces,
> Filling the mind.
> . . . .
> Of great height and depth
> Without any feeling, an imperium of quiet,

In which a wasted figure, with an instrument,
Propounds *blank final* music.
(CP, 362, my emphasis)

This is neither aesthetic detachment nor the transformation of a painful reality into a merely metaphoric or placebic "crystal." The first part of this quotation, the "death of great height / And depth, covering all surfaces, / Filling the mind," would have been immediately recognizable in 1946 as an accurate description of the first atomic bomb and of its immediate impact not only on the Japanese who died but on the rest of the world who survived. The second part makes it clear that this new, devastating reality is a function of the imagination, that is, of the mind or minds that first thought of and then created this *catastrophic instrument*. (It is no wonder that Stevens would have written down as the possible title of a poem "Why the Poet Doesn't Smile" a couple of pages after "Words about Death" as well as "Poetry as the Switzerland of the Mind.") [11]

The most negative statement about the place of poetry in the world appears in the short poem of 1946 entitled "Men Made out of Words," cited in full:

What should we be without the sexual myth,
The human revery or poem of death?

Castratos of moon-mash—Life consists
Of propositions about life. The human

Revery is a solitude in which
We compose these propositions, torn by dreams,

By the terrible incantations of defeats
And by the fear that defeats and dreams are one.

The whole race is a poet that writes down
The eccentric propositions of its fate.
(CP, 355–56)

Here, however, our "defeats" (and "the fear that defeats and dreams are one") are not the product of a singular poet—whether "virile" (as in his earlier essay) or ironically "casual" (as in "The Bed of Old John Zeller"). Instead, "The whole race is a poet" that writes its possibly "eccentric" or destructive fate.

I should stress that although some journalists referred to the bomb as the "miracle of Manhattan" (as in Bernard Jaffe's "How the Bomb Came to Be"),[12] the immediate response to the bomb even in 1945 was not necessarily the victorious celebration of the end of World War II, as it has often been presented in films, but a pervasive sadness and anxiety, at least among the writers for the *New Republic*, as several articles in August 1945 testify. Only two weeks after the first atomic bomb was dropped, one reporter writes:

> The terrible moral decision to use the atomic bomb was made by a few people. I suppose its use was inevitable. Once you invest two billion dollars in a firecracker you have to light it. Personally, I am sick and tired of decisions like this being made in secret, including those at Potsdam. . . . For the atomic bomb, it could justly be argued that in the short-range view it shortened the war and saved lives, though from the longer view we may all regret that it was ever employed. . . . Among my friends I find a curious new sense of insecurity, rather incongruous in the face of military victory.[13]

Or, as Bruce Bliven puts it, "A report from Washington said the people of the capital have been plunged into gloom" by the "news of the atomic bomb." More ominously, he concludes, "Candor compels us to admit that nothing in the history of humankind justifies the hope that we shall be able to master this new weapon and exploit its possibilities for good and not for evil." With an earnestness and an ethical appeal that match almost exactly Wallace Stevens's "Description without Place" (written only a few months before), Bliven introduces his article, "The Bomb and the Future" (which was also published only two weeks after the first was dropped), this way: "The coming of the atomic bomb is an event of such tremendous importance that all responsible persons will weigh their words in speaking or writing of its consequences."[14]

Given how powerful "descriptions" had proven to be, in reality, given that they can determine a place and, by dissent or consent, start or end an atrocious war, it seems to me that Stevens is ethically correct (rather than escapist) when he would subsequently say that he finds it impossible to believe that he is living in the "atomic age" and that he thinks it nonsense to try to do so. Accepting the description of our world as "atomic"—or "nuclear" or now "terrorist"—is suicidal. "Thought is an infection," Stevens writes in his *Adagia*: "In the case of certain thoughts it becomes an epidemic" (OP, 185). As Stevens repeatedly makes clear, even as early as 1936, when a large portion of the world was predicting and fearing the coming of a second world war, we must "resist" such epidemic thoughts or descriptions through stances and stanzas, political as well as poetic: "We have a sense of upheaval. We feel threatened. We look from an uncertain present toward a more uncertain future. One feels the desire to collect oneself against all this *in poetry as well as in politics*" (OP, 229, my emphasis). Collecting oneself "against all this" is "resistance." And, expanding on his earlier attempt to explain the importance of poetry in helping people to live their lives, he finally states, "Resistance is the opposite of escape. The poet who wishes to contemplate the good in the midst of confusion is like the mystic who wishes to contemplate God in the midst of evil. There can be no thought of escape" (OP, 230). After World War II, however, "resistance" seems to have changed for Stevens from the *formal* resistance of "Notes toward a Supreme Fiction" (i.e., aesthetic consolation) as well as from the need to bear witness of "Esthétique du Mal" to something far more active, even revolutionary—an ironic call for the poet to change the world through the "spelling" of proper words.

Specifically, while Charles Berger has suggested that " 'The Auroras of Autumn' is a specific reaction to the dropping of the Atomic Bomb" (an interpretation praised at length by Joan Richardson), this poem was, in fact, written well after this literal cata-strophe (in 1947) during a later time when Stevens, like most of the country, was trying to find and describe a new sense of normalcy.[15] As opposed to Berger's interpretation that the aurora borealis of this poem represents the sights and effects of the atomic bomb, I find that this poem uses the unexpected visual pleasures of the aurora as a metaphor for Stevens's continued examination of what it would mean to find a poetry "that would suffice" in a time that, despite the end of the actual war, was still characterized by tremendous cultural upheaval. The first section of "The Auroras of Autumn" dismisses the temptation to believe in and espouse the place where "the serpent lives" (CP, 411), a dismissal that contradicts (while being prefigured in) "Esthétique du Mal." Subsequently, the poem says "farewell" to many other cultural rhetorics of actual or unconscious beliefs. Canto 2 says, "Farewell to an idea . . . A cabin stands / Deserted on a beach," with a possible allusion to Thoreau's somewhat deceptive call for individuality and a "sublime" recourse to nature. Canto 3 says farewell to another "idea. . . . The mother's face" (ellipses in original) and to the idea that he had once entertained, especially in "Notes toward a Supreme Fiction," that it is the earth alone that is truly nurturing. Canto 4 then rejects the "father" and that whole patriarchal system Stevens had earlier supported with his emphasis on the "masculine" and "virile" poet as yet another debilitating and even belittling tradition:

> The father sits
> In space, wherever he sits, of bleak regard,
>
> As one that is strong in the bushes of his eyes.
> He says no to no and yes to yes. He says yes
> To no; and in saying yes he says farewell.
> (CP, 414)

And yet near this poem's conclusion Stevens reinscribes a new faith in poetry itself, advocating (as he would with other poems of this postwar period) a profound sense of the power of words to construct a better world:

> There is or may be a time of innocence
> As pure principle. Its nature is its end,
> That it should be, and yet not be, a thing
>
> That pinches the pity of the pitiful man,
> Like a book at evening beautiful but untrue,
> Like a book on rising beautiful and true.
> (CP, 418)

As the next lines insist and insist again,

> It is like a thing of ether that exists
> Almost as predicate. But it exists,
> It exists, it is visible, it is, it is.
> (CP, 418)

As a consequence, the aurora borealis evokes less the repetition of an old despair than an invitation to the surprising but "necessary" reconfigurations of a better world to come after the doubled tragedies of war in the first half of the twentieth century. In this way, "The Auroras of Autumn" comes to confirm Berger's larger ideas about Stevens's poetic sensibility at this time (though not his particular reading of the poem as "apocalyptic"), that is, that soon after the war, Stevens was committed to writing "Poems of Peace."[16]

Such a change on Stevens's part as I have sketched here—from an initial and even confident aesthetic resistance to World War II, to the felt need eventually to register rather than resist its horrors, to a more humbly realized call for ethical responsibility in how we choose to describe our world—may account for the seemingly inconsistent placement of "Notes toward a Supreme Fiction" as the last word, as it were, of *Transport to Summer*. Rather than simply configuring a formal pattern of resistance akin to that of Dante, as it clearly did in 1942, by 1947 the same poem, which begins with "love" and concludes that the soldier's and poet's wars "are one," may well reaffirm a renewed faith in the power of words and of poetry in particular that Stevens had come to question in the intervening years. However, as we shall see in the following chapters, this "reaffirmation" is of a significantly different order from his earlier "rage to order" (CP, 130). As Stevens writes in his *Adagia*, "Politics is the struggle for existence" (OP, 188), and "[w]ar is the periodical failure of politics" (OP, 191). In that "unbelievable catastrophe" (L, 343), the strophes of poetry must offer themselves not only as a means of resistance but also as "a means of redemption" (OP, 186).

The critical change in Stevens's aesthetics that occurred during World War II, from a relatively private poet to one with a public voice and conscience, can most clearly be seen by comparing Stevens's statement in "The Situation in American Writing" (1939) to a relatively long letter of 1946, written only eight months after World War II had ended. In the first, as already cited, Stevens writes that the writer's role in a time of war would be the same as any other time, only "concentrated and intensified," by which it appears that he means validating personal experience. (This is also the article in which he had stated that "war is a military state of affairs, not a literary one," a statement that his subsequent poetry comes to contradict.) However, in the later letter of 1946, we find a Stevens with a deepened sense of the crucial, and even political, necessity of the poet, insisting that the social role of the poet had never been more urgent. In contrast to his offering a *private* sanction, Stevens argues at the end of the war that poetry (and the poet) very much offers a *public* sanction. It is consistent with his own rejection of what might be called propagandistic or dogmatic poetry that in the same letter Stevens rejects the political domination of the world, noting ironically, "Today, in America, all roles yield to that of the politician" (L, 526). He continues to assert that the poet "must remain individual," by which he also means that the poet "must remain free." He goes so far as to pit the poet *against* the politician: "The poet absorbs the general life: the public. The politician is absorbed by it. The poet is individual. The politician is general" (L, 526). But then he clarifies that "[t]his does not mean" that the poet is "a private figure":

> If people are to become dependent on poetry for any of the fundamental satis-
> factions, poetry must have an increasingly intellectual scope and power. This is a
> time for the highest poetry. We never understood the world less than we do now,
> nor as we understand it, liked it less. We never wanted to understand it more or
> needed to like it more. These are the intense compulsions that challenge the poet
> as the appreciatory creator of values and beliefs. *That, finally, states the problem.*
> (L, 526, my emphasis)

From my perspective, that makes the poet—and the critic—intensely political, though not politicians.

The "high poetry" that Stevens wrote after 1946—from "The Auroras of
Autumn," to "An Ordinary Evening in New Haven," to "The Rock" and the
stunning lyrics from "Angel Surrounded by Paysans," "Final Soliloquy of the
Interior Paramour," and "A Quiet Normal Life"—testifies to his persistent
and successful attempts after World War II to "satisfy" this role, one that
is finally committed less to the polis per se than to the cosmos-polis. The
world "we make" "[o]ut of this same light, out of the central mind" (CP,
524) is a world that makes far more *sense* to me than the atomic age, the
age of the cold war, or the age of terrorism. This is one of the many reasons
that we are drawn so intensely to Stevens, despite his obvious and growing
list of human failings. There is something of a satisfaction, even a religious
sanction, in his finest verse. Well before the end of the Second World War,
Stevens's attitude seems akin to Psalm 50, in which God promises salvation
to "him that ordereth his conversation aright." For Stevens, there remained
the belief—and this, finally, was not a fiction—that we can save the world if
he or rather we can order our words aright.

If we must have a more secular ending to this phase of his critical transfor-
mations in poetics, Stevens has given us that as well in the essay appropriately
entitled "Imagination as Value" (1948). As opposed to the impoverished possibility of "Chaos in Motion and Not in Motion" that reality has been reduced
to "[a]ll mind and violence and nothing felt" (CP, 358), in that essay Stevens
writes, "My final point, then, is that the imagination is the power that enables
us to perceive the normal in the abnormal, the opposite of chaos in chaos"
(NA, 153). The same point had been made by W. P. Southard two years before,
only one year after the end of the war, in "Escape to Reality." Asking, again,

what should the modern writer write about now, Southard remarks, "About love," explaining that "this would be simply the escape from the irremediably diseased to the relatively normal—escape to reality."[17] Just before the war began, William Carlos Williams had written that great art "liberates while it draws the world closer in mutual understanding and tolerance." [18] We come back to something like truth and beauty after all. That both Stevens and Southard could, after the horrors of World War II, sound so much like Williams before the war began is yet another facet, even fact, of our history that we should not cease to describe.

CHAPTER SIX

OPENING THE FIELD

It is important to note that in the poems of his later years Stevens would use different means, though not essentially different assumptions, to explore his "theory of description." Although the Second World War had finally ended, the "pressure of reality" became increasingly for Stevens a "poverty" (CP, 533) in reality that needed *compensation* rather than resistance. This is not to say that the dominant concerns of his middle period disappear altogether in the late poetry. In the 1947 "Someone Puts a Pineapple Together," for example, Stevens playfully and quite self-consciously calls his twelve highly imaginative descriptions of a pineapple "casual exfoliations," "[a]pposites, to the slightest edge, of the whole / *Undescribed* composition of the sugar-cone" (NA, 86, my emphasis). And in "The Bouquet," which Stevens tried to publish in 1948 (see L, 609), he combines an image quite reminiscent of that from "The Poems of Our Climate," that is, the "bouquet" itself, with the figure of a soldier. This poem is particularly intriguing, for it shows Stevens in his most cynical of moods when perhaps his own measure of resistance was weary. While the bouquet "stands in a jar, as metaphor" (CP, 448), leading through the course of the poem to a discourse on "meta-men" and "para-things," in the last section

A car drives up. A soldier, an officer,
Steps out. He rings and knocks. The door is not locked.
He enters the room and calls. No one is there.

He bumps the table. The bouquet falls on its side.
He walks through the house, looks round him and then leaves.
The bouquet has slopped over the edge and lies on the floor.
(CP, 452–53)

Here the "pressure of reality" seems to overcome the claims of metaphor
quite emphatically, although with obvious irony, since this outcome is created
precisely through the metaphors of Stevens's poem.

Nevertheless, in the majority of his later poems, such as "Credences of
Summer," "Angel Surrounded by Paysans," and "An Ordinary Evening in New
Haven," Stevens consistently evokes a sense of reconciliation between the
self, language, and the objective world. The best of his late poems are gathered
in *The Rock*, the title of which, with its singular subject and definite article,
suggests a fundamental change from the earlier poems gathered in *Parts of
a World*. [1] In his final lyrics, the poet's reconciliation with reality, however
illusory, tends to be stronger and his poetic strategies, because less obvious,
even more critical. It is not the strategy of "The Poems of Our Climate" or
that of his middle poetry in general: the last poems are at once more deeply
private and simultaneously more universal to the human experience. But
more important, they postulate a "cure" (CP, 526) rather than a "conversion"
of reality, a redemption of rather than a "resistance" to the climate after
1945. Addressed to the "finally human," however "unaccomplished" (CP, 504),
the last poems acknowledge perhaps even more than the middle poems the
limitation of language while confirming the power of language to "help us
live our lives," to endow our lives with meaning. As he poignantly remarked
in "The Planet on the Table,"

It was not important that they survive.
What mattered was that they should bear
Some lineament or character,
Some affluence, if only half-perceived,
In the poverty of their words,
Of the planet of which they were part.
(CP, 532–33)

As Stevens had said earlier in "Extracts from Addresses to the Academy of Fine Ideas," "Time troubles to produce the redeeming thought" (CP, 257), and in poems such as "Lebensweisheitspielerei" and "Final Soliloquy of the Interior Paramour" he gave that "thought" its most moving expressions. As we can infer from his late poems, in the end Stevens's poems came to be of rather than against his climate. Or, as he also put it in his *Adagia*, "[p]oetry is a health" (OP, 200), by which he clearly no longer meant, if he ever did, a health for his poetic climate alone.

In fact, the fundamental changes described in the previous chapters were not achieved without a struggle on Stevens's part. But they were changes that, however ironically, moved a poet initially committed to a masculine voice of resistance to one increasingly open to what we may now recognize as being amenable to feminist perspectives. Although it will be necessary, ultimately, to look back to Stevens's earliest poetry and forward to the late poems of *The Rock* to trace the development discussed in this chapter, I wish to argue that the common accusation against Stevens as being unilaterally sexist ignores the fundamental changes that occurred during World War II and fails to recognize how and why Stevens's verse would be increasingly open not only to the metaphorically "feminine" within his poetry and psyche but also to feminist concerns. As we shall see, more acutely than any other place, this difficult change was enacted, albeit with almost excruciatingly ambivalence, in "The Figure of the Youth as a Virile Poet" (first read at Mount Holyoke College in 1943), with Stevens's complex introduction of that female "*sister of the Minotaur*" as a new figure for the poet.

Even though the traditional perception of Stevens as being sexist (both as a person and as a poet) has been redressed in such excellent works as *Wallace Stevens and the Feminine*, the general disapprobation of Stevens in this regard remains prevalent today.[2] Certainly, as Albert Gelpi's most recent essay on Stevens suggests, the charge against Stevens in terms of sexism remains open to current debate.[3] Just as it proves possible to mount a strong case against Stevens as being a politically irresponsible aesthete, it is equally easy to mount a case against Stevens as being not only a sexist poet but a sexist person as well. The various biographies devoted to Wallace Stevens over the last many years have all, individually and collectively, given us information about his private life, especially in relation to his wife, that makes it increasingly difficult to think of Stevens as that innocent, cherublike person that Randall Jarrell once described him as being.[4] I have in mind, for example, Stevens's effective silencing of Elsie as described by the family chauffeur to Peter Brazeau or the disturbing way in which he "scripted" her—literally made her an object of his pen, renaming her according to his needs—as seen in the previously unpublished letters to his wife included in Joan Richardson's biography.[5] In light of these facts about Stevens's personal life, it is perhaps not surprising to find the almost scathing indictment of Stevens's irresponsibility, if not moral failure, in his relationship with and to women made by Mark Halliday some years ago.[6] Put differently, when it comes to "Stevens and the 'feminine' " or, more specifically, "Stevens and sexism," it would be easy to oversimplify this complex subject as sexism *in* Stevens as a personal human being.

Yet my subject in this chapter is not sexism *in* Stevens, in the sense of Stevens's being a sexist individual, nor is it a psychoanalysis of what in Stevens's life might or might not have led to a troubled psyche, particularly concerning women. It seems almost too easy to point to Stevens's mother as a figure for the imagination, in continual conflict with his father as a figure for pragmatic action and reason. One could all too easily as well exploit the fact that Elsie Moll Stevens, who was so clearly perceived by Stevens in the early years as his muse, should be at once the girl from the wrong side of the tracks, illegitimate, and the model for the goddess of liberty on the coin, the two archetypal—and equally dehumanizing—ways of viewing women in our culture thus both being accidentally inscribed in Elsie's life.[7] Although these various facts may suggest, once again, that the personal *is* political, I want to distinguish as much as possible the subject of sexism *in* Stevens from sexism *and* Stevens, even if finally the two topics prove inseparable. What interests me here, therefore, is what happens to Stevens's poetry as he engaged in the (perhaps conscious) suppression of what *he* perceived to be his feminine voice or, more accurately, that part of his poetic voice that is feminine metaphorically, most particularly during World War II. My conclusion is that while Stevens would always suffer from a schism within himself, one that was ultimately derived from cultural biases against women (and that would affect his poetry in a number of important ways), he also came as close as it was possible for a person in his time and circumstances to "curing" himself of the "infection in the sentence" that the dominant, phallocentric structures in our culture inevitably breed.[8]

The distinction I am making between sexism *in* Stevens and sexism *and* Stevens is not meant to deny the fact that there are sexist innuendoes in Stevens's poetry. Certain sexist assumptions, including the one that denigrating women is humorous, account for a number of his earliest poems, including "A High-Toned Old Christian Woman."[9] It is not merely institutionalized religion that Stevens is mocking. "A High-Toned Old Christian *Man*" does not seem nearly as funny, and I speculate that trying to make *"widowers* wince" would not be perceived as being especially witty either. Similar attitudes also inform "Lulu Gay" (op, 44) and "Lulu Morose" (op, 45), although the first of these, in which Lulu tells the eunuchs what the barbarians have done to her, is immediately more problematic. It is probably right to the point that the males who presumably have been castrated have lost their "voice" as well—they cannot talk but can only ululate. Certainly, we find an archetypal expression of sexism in that poem with the wonderful title "Good Man, Bad Woman," in which the speaker also says, "She can corrode your world, if never you" (op, 65). In fact, such basic sexist attitudes—even if we are charitable and conclude that Stevens intends to poke fun at such attitudes—govern a variety of his early poems. There is no character in all of Stevens's poetry, for example, presented with quite the same grotesque sense of humor as the woman of "The Emperor of Ice-Cream"—dead, lying near a deal dresser with her "horned feet" protruding (cp, 64)—unless it is the "lady dying of diabetes" in "A Thought Revolved" (cp, 184). Most obviously, Stevens rejects the feminine figures of *Harmonium*, especially the figure of fecund nature in the 1936 "Farewell to Florida" (the poem, notably, with which he opened the *second* version of *Ideas of Order*).[10] There he accuses "her" of having "bound" him "round" and says that he will return to the land of the "violent mind," which is equivalent to the land of the violent men (cp, 117–18).

Yet repression of the feminine figure occurs in Stevens in more subtle and ultimately more significant ways. One of the most telling marks of Stevens's repression of the feminine is, ironically, that in his poetry female figures almost never speak. If any voice is heard at all (and that itself is a subject to take up below), it is that of a male, as in "Two Figures in Dense Violet Night":[11]

> Be the voice of night and Florida in my ear.
> Use dusky words and dusky images.
> Darken your speech.
>
> Speak, even, as if I did not hear you speaking,
> But spoke for you perfectly in my thoughts,
> Conceiving words,
>
> As the night conceives the sea-sounds in silence,
> And out of their droning sibilants makes
> A serenade.
> (cp, 86)

One exception to this generalization is the woman in "Metropolitan Melancholy," the "purple woman" with the "lavender tongue" who "[s]aid hic, said hac / Said ha" (OP, 64). Another is the quoted "*[e]ncore un instant de bonheur*," words that Stevens immediately dismisses:

> The words
> Are a woman's words, unlikely to satisfy
> The taste of even a country connoisseur.
> (CP, 157)

Here it is admittedly difficult to distinguish the repression of the feminine voice from basic sexism. Nevertheless, a glance at the *Concordance* to Stevens's poetry reveals that, surprisingly, "words" are not Stevens's most popular theme but instead "man" and "men" (appearing 507 times) and, especially, man speaking. [12] Women appear in Stevens's poetry about one fifth as frequently—a total of 106 times. But in contrast to the men, the women almost never have a voice. From the early "Primordia," in which the "voice of the wind" is "male" (OP, 25), through "A Thought Revolved," to the early essays of *The Necessary Angel*, the idea of "voice" itself is perceived by Stevens as almost exclusively masculine. But then, I think we can say, he protests too much.

One extension of this verbal "repression" is the fact that not only do the female figures in Stevens's early poetry rarely speak, they rarely move. Consider the difference between his earliest and most famous female and male characters, the complacent woman of "Sunday Morning" (1915) and "The Comedian as the Letter C" (1922). In a very disturbing way, women in his poetry remain too obviously figures—empty ciphers for masculine rumination and scripting, even de-scription. [13] The woman of "Sunday Morning" has several sisters, among them "So-and-So Reclining on Her Couch" and "Romance for a Demoiselle Lying in the Grass," in which Stevens writes:

> The monotony
> Is like your port which conceals
> All your characters
> And their desires.
> (OP, 44)

In the course of the poem this female figure is either troped to or revealed to be a guitar—Stevens closes the poem with "[c]lasp me, / Delicatest machine."

But this revelation, if we can call it that, further "objectifies" the feminine, even if metaphorically, "concealing" her behind a phallocentric and concomitantly erotic perspective that is reminiscent of the elders' view of Susanna in "Peter Quince at the Clavier" (CP, 89–92).

Nonetheless, precisely because he retained the idea of a feminine muse, Stevens's attempts to repress or silence the feminine ironically leave *him* in the position of never being able to speak, especially in the early wartime poems. Almost without exception, Stevens's greatest attempts at poetic expression, the words of that "virile poet" he so clearly desires, are instances of failures of speech, words about the words he *would* say if he could, signs, shall we say, of the failure of both logocentric and phallocentric ordering. Even in "Notes toward a Supreme Fiction," Stevens finally concludes that it is

> As if the waves at last were never broken,
> As if the language suddenly, with ease,
> Said things it had laboriously spoken.
> (CP, 387)

Thus, despite his sustained attempt in that poem to evoke—or to become— the "virile" poet, one whose words both master and are a part of what is real, that which he cannot order or master insists upon being heard, however ironically, in the very silence of the gap between "as" and "if," that is, between "order" and the "abyss," as these terms are metaphorically and sexually conceived. The white writing of such texts is perversely and subversively the trace of the repressed voice that refuses to (or cannot) coincide with the phallic and verbal structures Stevens professes to order in his words, especially in a time of war.

From this perspective, the 1934 poem "The Idea of Order at Key West" can be seen to anticipate this basic problematic in Stevens's verse rather than embodying one of his more successful figurations of women, as many critics have assumed. [14] In contrast to the other women figures of his early phase mentioned so far, the celebrated female figure of this poem is, superficially, neither mocked nor denigrated; she is also supposedly vocal and dynamic, walking and singing by the shore:

> And when she sang, the sea,
> Whatever self it had, became the self
> That was her song, for she was the maker. Then we,

As we beheld her striding there alone,
Knew that there never was a world for her
Except the one she sang and, singing, made.
(CP, 129–30)

However alluring this poem may be, we run the risk of being ruled by rhetoric if we fail to note that ultimately—and even in the narrative development of the text itself—this "woman" is simply a figure (and thus a sign or empty cipher) for Stevens himself and the way *he* sings. The clearest sign of this fact is found in the very next line, where he abruptly breaks in with "Ramon Fernandez, tell me if you know." This rupture is the most overt sign in the poem of the nature of the poetic "order" (even "rage for order") that Stevens has in mind at this point in his career. This thematic is inscribed throughout the poem: lights "master" the night, "portion" out the sea, "arrange" and "deepen" night, so that the words, in a kind of phallic "mastering," ironically create the "fragrant portals," essentially create the feminine.

But what do we hear from this feminine voice that is simultaneously created, disclosed in the portals, and repressed, silenced by the "mastering" and by the actual appropriation of the unheard feminine voice to Stevens's own? From the opening stanza, that other voice remains literally "beyond" us and ourselves:

She sang beyond the genius of the sea.
The water never formed to mind or voice,
Like a body wholly body, fluttering
Its empty sleeves; and yet its mimic motion
Made constant cry, caused constantly a cry,
That was not ours although we understood,
Inhuman, of the veritable ocean.
(CP, 128)

The need for this control—the imperative to create and to control a world in words—can be explained, at least in part, historically and culturally. The Great War, the Great Depression, and the felt menace of a second world war to come would easily give rise to the need to defend oneself against looming chaos, a fact that is amply demonstrated by the early poems of Stevens's middle period. But I think at least part of the explanation for Stevens's apparent need to break into the text—to silence this feminine figure, however lovely we may feel she may be—lies in her uncanny reflection, that *"sister of the Minotaur"* he would come to imagine during the actuality of World War II. The lovely, virtually "inhuman" woman by the sea and the somewhat unsettling "half-beast" who is yet "somehow more than human" (NA, 52) are two faces, as it were, of the same *figure*, which, precisely as "figure," also means absence and repression. Instead of the madwoman in the attic, this is a (potentially) madwoman in a maze, specifically, a linguistic maze.

The idealized version of the figure, the one who remains beyond speech, desired but controlled, together with her monstrous counterpart account for many of Stevens's more "fantastic" female characters. The idealized figure is found in "To the One of Fictive Music," in which, for example, Stevens creates a feminine trilogy of "[s]ister and mother and diviner love" (CP, 87–88), in "Infanta Marina," where "She" can make "of the motions of her wrist / The grandiose gestures / Of her thought" (CP, 7), as well as in "The Apostrophe to Vincentine" and "Bouquet of Belle Scavoir." At least in the first two of these poems mentioned, Stevens replaces the presumed masculine character of the Trinity and God's ability to create through fiat a divine incarnation with a specifically feminine power. And yet "her" monstrous counterpart is found in "The Woman Who Blamed Life on a Spaniard," where "she never clears / But spreads an evil lustre whose increase / Is evil" (OP, 66); in the fifth of "Five Grotesque Pieces" (entitled "Outside of Wedlock"), where she is figured as "an old bitch, an old drunk, / That has been yelling in the dark" (OP, 112); even in "The Common Life," where quite significantly, given the title, "women have only one side" (CP, 221). In "The Old Woman and the Statue" she has all the attributes of a witch:

> But her he had not foreseen: the bitter mind
> In a flapping cloak. She walked along the paths
> Of the park with chalky brow scratched over black
> And black by thought that could not understand
> Or, if it understood, repressed itself
> Without any pity in a somnolent dream.
> (OP, 76)

Looking forward to the ethical changes in Stevens's evolving poetics described in the rest of this chapter, it is important to note that the vast majority of the overtly sexist lines just cited are culled from his *Opus Posthumous*, suggesting, therefore, that Stevens eventually rejected them from individually published volumes as well as from his own *Collected Poems* precisely from a fundamental change that no longer meshed with that earlier and also masculine appeal to the "violence from within." Nonetheless, these rejected poems provide important markers in tracing what I see as Stevens's emerging "revolutionary" poetics.

When we find instances of apparently blatant sexism *in* Stevens, it is once again useful to remember the cultural context within which he produced his work. When Stevens first began publishing in earnest, the women's suffrage movement was well under way and was frequently the subject of essays in the magazines in which Stevens was publishing (and that he was presumably reading himself). Certainly by his middle period, the one we are concentrating on in this study, the opportunities for women in this country (and others) had expanded exponentially. Within this context, it is possible to see the ways in which Stevens's "phallocentric" perspective manifests itself in the conflicting dynamics, even the problematics of his poetry over the course of his career. His most crucial problematic may not be the conflict between imagination and reality (as has been traditionally assumed) or even the battle between competing theories of language (as I and many others have previously argued) or even the poetic battle of how to integrate aesthetics and politics in a time of war but rather a conflict between feminine and masculine expression, that is, between the male authorial voice that strives to achieve significance and control and the culturally delineated suppression or silencing of a feminine voice that struggles, nonetheless, precisely for expression. Put differently, in Stevens's work we can see the ways in which our culturally inscribed notions of male/author/authority and our culturally inscribed repression of the rest of our human voice (even within ourselves and within Stevens as well) frustrate the attempt at poetic expression itself while informing what expressions are achieved in the individual poems.

Still, it would not be accurate to reduce Stevens's poetry to reiterating endlessly this conflict within himself. If Stevens suffered (and I think he did suffer) from a schism within himself, he also seems not only to have been aware of that fact but to have tried to "cure" himself. Even as early as "Last Look at the Lilacs," he is contemptuous of that rational "caliper," that "arrogantly male, / Patron and imager of the gold Don John" (CP, 48–49). At approximately the same time, he also condemns, albeit playfully, that "[d]amned universal cock" in "Bantams in Pine-Woods" who, in a quintessentially phallocentric way, thinks that he is the center of the universe, announcing (as if by fiat), "I am my world" (CP, 75–76). To this end I see an important development between "The Idea of Order at Key West" (1934) and his well-known "Final Soliloquy of the Interior Paramour" (1950) triggered precisely by his aesthetic responses to World War II.

To understand this critical facet of Stevens's work, it is important first to stress the fact that from the rejection of the feminine figure in "Farewell to Florida" (1936) to her acceptance in "Final Soliloquy of the Interior Paramour," Stevens's poetry remains highly self-conscious about the fact that it *is* wrestling with the feminine figure and, usually in a rather Jungian fashion, specifically with the feminine figure within. Four texts, taken variously from his essays, letters, *Collected Poems*, and *Opus Posthumous* over the course of his career, reveal several critical aspects of this self-conscious struggle.

First is a letter written to Ronald Latimer in 1935 in response to Howard Baker's analysis of Wallace Stevens in the *Southern Review* ("Wallace Stevens and Other Poets") in which Baker specifically describes Stevens's poetry in Jungian terms: "There is in the last number of the SOUTHERN REVIEW or QUARTERLY, an extremely intelligent analysis of my work by Howard Baker. No one before has ever come as close to me as Mr. Baker does in that article" (L, 292).[15] This letter is important to the subject because it clarifies that Stevens thought of his own poetry, even at an early point, in somewhat Jungian terms and that, therefore, attention to the male and female figures (and hence to their voices or lack of voices) in Stevens's work is central to our understanding of it. However, as the poems of that period (including, most notably, "The Idea of Order at Key West") make clear, the "feminine" voice of his poetry was as yet unrealized.[16]

This fact leads to a second (and perhaps most important) text, the complicated essay entitled "The Figure of the Youth as a Virile Poet" included in *The Necessary Angel*. As has been often noted, this essay includes the rather remarkable if not disturbing statement: "The centuries have a way of being male" (NA, 52). In that essay Stevens also insists that the "character of the poet" must be seen as *"virile,"* otherwise, "the masculine nature that we propose for one that must be the master of our lives will be lost" (NA, 66). Since such statements must certainly sound egregious to our contemporary ears, it might be of interest to note that Ernest Hemingway, among many other writers of the time, such as William Carlos Williams and Ezra Pound, offers a useful point of comparison.[17] For instance, even as early as 1929, in a publicity blurb for Hemingway's second novel, Owen Wister obviously praises *Farewell to Arms*, concluding that Hemingway, "like Defoe, is lucky to be writing in an age that will not stop its ears at the *unmuted resonance of the masculine voice.*"[18] And as Joan Richardson intriguingly notes in her discussion of Stevens's attitude toward this desired and venerated voice, in 1940 "[t]he problem of 'Poetry and Manhood' that had begun to occupy Stevens's attention more than forty years before while he was at Harvard had not been solved," specifically comparing Stevens's anxiety about being the "virile poet" at that time with his sense that Hemingway was actually "living consistently" the life Stevens could only dream of.[19] In other words, even as (if not because) women were gaining so many rights toward the middle of the twentieth century, the preoccupation among men at the time with achieving a "masculine voice" was a large and ongoing cultural preoccupation not at all unique to Stevens and one he felt compelled to address directly at the beginning of World War II.

Within this context, the surprising move toward the "feminine" in "The Figure of the Youth as a Virile Poet" proves all the more remarkable:

> When we look back at the face of the seventeenth century, it is at the rigorous face of a rigorous thinker and, say, the Miltonic image of a poet, severe and determined. In effect, what we are remembering is the rather haggard background of the incredible, the imagination without intelligence, from which a younger figure is emerging, stepping forward in the company of a muse of its own, *still half-beast and somehow more than human, a kind of sister of the Minotaur.* The younger figure is the intelligence that endures. It is the imagination of the son still bearing the antique imagination of the father. (NA, 52–53, my emphasis)

The essentially androgynous character of this figure (since the "sister" is also the "son" of the "father") bears further study, particularly in the context of the often frustrated quest for androgynous union traced in much of the romantic poetry preceding (and anticipating) Jungian theory. Nevertheless, it seems clear here that Stevens is seriously engaged in a deliberate battle to overcome the kind of schism within himself that would give rise precisely to this kind of distortion that would figure or mark the feminine as perpetually "monstrous," thereby displacing "her" yet again.[20] Yet at least in 1943, when this essay was written, Stevens's own language interfered with such a cure. Not only does he still think of the poet as someone who must *master* our lives (and who must be male), he also writes these ironically self-defeating words at the very point the "figure of the youth as a virile poet" supposedly speaks or finds his *own* voice: "*No longer do I believe that there is a mystic muse, sister of the Minotaur. This is another of the monsters I had for nurse, whom I have wasted. I am myself a part of what is real, and it is my own speech and the strength of it, this only, that I hear or ever shall"* (NA, 60, Stevens's emphasis). What is most provocative about this passage, especially since it is in such conflict with the semantic intent, is that even as he rejects the *"sister of the Minotaur"* at the supposed moment of self-identification, he reinstates the figure of the monster as a (presumably female) "nurse."[21]

However, we should note well that Stevens's struggle with this female metaphor for the imagination does not end with this monstrous figure but rather with an extremely complicated (even logically contradictory) evocation of that "virile poet" in conjunction with that *"sister of the Minotaur"* as the new, necessary figure for the imagination in the new era emerging under the pressure of war. The two concluding paragraphs of this essay, where such a complicated rhetorical gesture is made, are worthy of repeating here in their entirety:

> But genius is not our concern. We are trying to define what we mean by the imagination of life, and, in addition, by that special illumination, special abundance and severity of abundance, virtue in the midst of indulgence and *order in disorder that is involved in the idea of virility* [my emphasis]. We have been referring constantly to the simple figure of the youth, in his character of poet, as the virile poet. The reason for this is that if, for the poet, the imagination is paramount, and if he dwells apart in his imagination, as the philosopher dwells in his reason, and as the priest dwells in his belief, the masculine nature that we propose for one that must be the master of our lives will be lost as, for example, in the folds of the garments of the ghost or ghosts of Aristotle. As we say these things, there begins to develop, *in addition to the figure that has been seated in our midst* [that "virile poet"], composed, in the radiant and productive atmosphere with which we have surrounded him, *an intimation of what he is thinking as he reflects on the imagination of life, determined to be its master and ours* [my emphasis]. He is thinking of those facts of experience of which all of us have thought and which all of us have felt with such intensity, and he says:
>
> *Inexplicable sister of the Minotaur, enigma and mask, although I am part of what is real, hear me and recognize me as part of the unreal. I am the truth but the truth of that imagination of life in which with unfamiliar motion and manner you guide me in those exchanges of speech in which your words are mine, mine yours* [Stevens's emphasis]. (NA, 66–67)

The passage above that discusses in unison the imagined poet, philosopher, and priest also suggests in somewhat contradictory terms that the "virile poet" for whom the imagination is paramount will ironically be lost precisely if he dwells "apart in his imagination." However, this conundrum disappears if, in fact, Stevens is here rejecting the kind of "masculine" philosophical abstractions he clearly rejected the year before in the final numbered canto of "Notes toward a Supreme Fiction" as well as the "masculine" notions of aesthetic divinity he rejected in that same poem and even earlier, as in "Sunday Morning" and (however ironically) "A High-Toned Old Christian Woman," in which the limitations of Christianity are made parallel to the limits of abstract reasoning.

At the end of this extraordinary passage, Stevens clearly desires some kind of union of the metaphorically masculine and feminine parts of the imagination. He explicitly acknowledges the need for a poetic "voice" that will respond to actual "facts of experience" rather than one that will retreat into mere aesthetic or philosophical abstractions. As such, the conclusion of this essay represents the precise moment when Stevens's earlier derision of the "feminine" and his unexpected openness to it (or "her") during World War II has reached something of a crisis—a fact that I admittedly missed in earlier work on this subject.[22] In fact, this passage also suggests that Stevens is beginning to reject the kind of *masculine aesthetics* he had invoked in the actual composition and architecture of "Notes toward a Supreme Fiction." Reconsidered, these last two paragraphs move well beyond first-order reflections of the nature of the imagination in a time of war, or second-order reflections of the nature of that same imaginative force when considered as a future force compared to past manifestations, or even beyond third-order reflections, if indeed this uncanny figure is ultimately a critique of his own self-consciously masculine and virile aesthetics articulated the year before, to something genuinely "irrational." For however right the "*sister of the Minotaur*" feels in this passage and in the essay at large, "she" is genuinely beyond my own ability to rationally explicate. "Her" appearance seems here to move beyond a conscious or rational debate on Stevens's part about his configurations of male and female (even if in Jungian terms) to something of a "necessary angel," that is, an unpredictable textual eruption of expression previously repressed. As such, the "*sister of the Minotaur*" once again works on the order of a literary involucrum, forcing us to reevaluate Stevens's supposed commitment at this point in time to the "masculine nature" who would be, as he puts it in that same essay, the "master of our lives."

This crisis is overtly dramatized two years later in the third text I have chosen as representing singular touchstones in Stevens's evolving poetics, that is, an important section of the 1944 "Esthétique du Mal." In the tenth section of this clearly pivotal poem, which I have previously prescinded from discussion in chapter 4, Stevens distinguishes between two sets of female figures in his poetry, suggesting a conscious awareness of a problem in his figurations of women *after*, implicitly, introducing the possibility of resolution in an androgynous figure that could be regarded as the successful union of the "masculine" and "feminine" imaginations desired in the last two paragraphs of "The Figure of the Youth as a Virile Poet":

> He had studied the nostalgias. In these
> He sought the most grossly maternal, the creature
> Who most fecundly assuaged him, the softest
> Woman with a vague moustache and not the mauve
> *Maman*. His anima liked its animal
> And liked it unsubjugated, so that home
> Was a return to birth, . . .
>
> . . . .
>
> It is true there were other mothers, singular
> In form, lovers of heaven and earth, she-wolves
> And forest tigresses and women mixed
> With the sea. These were fantastic.
> (CP, 321)

These "other mothers," immediately troped in the text to the monstrous "she-wolves" and "tigresses," are the "fantastic" manifestations of his own feminine voice, or anima, repressed as we have seen throughout most of his early poetic career. For example, another effect of his earlier conscious repression of the feminine principle in "Life on a Battleship" (1939), where he appears to say good-bye to "her" while aligning himself with that ship *"The Masculine"* (OP, 106), was preceded by the extreme attention to "man number one" (CP, 166)—as in "The Man with the Blue Guitar" (1937)—with, however, a concurrent monstrous version of his poetic self that he largely tried to subjugate. It is both culturally and poetically predictable that whereas this "monster" in "The Man with the Blue Guitar" (the "lion in the lute / Before the lion locked in stone" [CP, 175]) *may* be male, in general the uncomposed and, therefore, potentially destructive aspect of his creative energy is perceived—or figured—by Stevens in his earliest work and, then again, in this section of "Esthétique du Mal" as a threatening woman. However, his desire to overcome such a distorting rift seems quite apparent in his Jungian evocation of an androgynous figure both in the poem and in the 1943 essay just remembered. It is therefore crucial to remember that this dynamic moment of change occurred as the violence of World War II was escalating exponentially, prompting Stevens to abandon his belief in the (masculine) poet's ability to "resist" the pressure of reality and to begin to register or record the widespread pain.

Finally, Stevens articulates this change directly in "Farewell without a Guitar," written in 1954, just one year before he died:

> Spring's bright paradise has come to this.
> Now the thousand-leaved green falls to the ground.
> Farewell, my days.
> . . . .
> 　　　　　The reflections and repetitions,
> The blows and buffets of fresh senses
> Of the rider that was,
>
> Are a final construction,
> Like glass and sun, of male reality
> And of that other and her desire.
> (OP, 125)

While the rather poignantly glossed "rider that was" refers to the failure of Stevens's attempt to create—and to become—the "Noble Rider" of 1941 (NA, 1–36), it is possible to say that from "To the One of Fictive Music" (1922) to the end of his life, much of Stevens's corpus was written in response to that significant "other." Yet *this* female figure, so nebulously and delicately evoked, is not the Elsie he largely dominated in his personal life or his mother (or a high-toned old Christian woman, for that matter) but precisely a part of himself that he could never fully come to know except as "she" was traced in his poetry and that appears to have emerged most poignantly under the "pressure of reality" of the Second World War.

If these touchstones demonstrate that Stevens did, in fact, wrestle with the "feminine" (metaphorically conceived) within himself and most acutely during World War II, they do not explain the more successful integration of that feminine principle in the late poems of his career or account for why those poems seem so amenable to feminist poets and critics. To explain this stage in Stevens's evolving poetics, I wish to examine here a few other poems written

during World War II and then, in the following chapter, to suggest why the
1945 publication of the illustrated *Esthétique du Mal* (which appeared *after*
he had written his more forward-looking poem "Description without Place")
may have provided a particular visual confirmation of Stevens's emerging
poetics. As we shall see, Stevens quickly recognized that the "normalcy" he
and so many others were already desiring in the spring of 1945 could not be
a return to an old, especially an old patriarchal, normalcy. Indeed, it would
demand an altogether new "normalcy," contingent on the dismantling of false
masculine rhetorics and on the emergence of new structures (both poetically
and politically conceived) open to that "feminine" expression held so long
in silence in the white space of Stevens's texts.

Specifically, after his obvious attempt to gain a unified "masculine" and
"feminine" voice in "The Figure of the Youth as a Virile Poet," Stevens becomes increasingly obsessed with what he would later call "the sound / Of
right joining," "[t]he final relation, the marriage of the rest" (CP, 464–65).
We see this desire anticipated in a 1940 letter, when he (perhaps surprisingly,
given his personal life) uses the pleasure that "a man and woman find in each
other's company" as an illustration of the "pleasure" of "[c]ross-reflections,
modifications, counter-balances, giving and taking" of the "various faculties
of the mind" (L, 368). Noticeably, in "Of Modern Poetry," written in 1940, and
later in "Burghers of Petty Death," written in 1946, we find men and women
together, successfully figured as equal representatives of humanity. "Modern
poetry," Stevens says,

> has to be living, to learn the speech of the place.
> It has to face the men of the time and to meet
> The women of the time.
> (CP, 240)

In the second poem, Stevens says:

> These are the small townsmen of death,
> A man and a woman, like two leaves
> That keep clinging to a tree,
> Before winter freezes and grows black.
> (CP, 362)

The women of these poems, equal in their humanness to the men, form
the clearest parentheses around a new moment achieved in World War II,

one in which "she" is not only validated but recognized both as a presence and as a human being rather than tracing, in either idealized or "monstrous" discourse, the path of failed signification and signifiers. [23] Psychologically speaking, it may be that the sheer, overwhelming, and uncontrollable violence of the Second World War reduced all human beings in Stevens's eyes to the supposedly passive position of "women," in the metaphorical sense of the word. In that case, we are "all" without power, not just "women," in this modern world, unable to control the world and possibly even our own lives.

Such a desire for intimacy as indicated by the simile of the two clinging leaves above reappears two years later (though still held only as a fiction) in the seventh section of "Notes toward a Supreme Fiction":

> Perhaps there are times of inherent excellence,
>
> As when the cock crows on the left and all
> Is well, incalculable balances,
>
> . . . .
>   not balances
> That we achieve but balances that happen,
>
> As a man and woman meet and love forthwith.
> (CP, 386)

Yet despite Stevens's efforts to achieve this balance in "Notes toward a Supreme Fiction," Nanzia Nunzio, for example, fails to achieve this promise, her erotic power being so contingent upon her willingness to be scripted or subjugated:

> Speak to me that, which spoken, will array me
> In its own only precious ornament.
> Set on me the spirit's diamond coronal.
> . . . .
> Clothe me entire in the final filament,
> So that I tremble with such love so known
> And myself am precious for your perfecting.
> (CP, 396)

The maiden Bawda and her captain perhaps fare better; at least they are both "love's characters come face to face" (CP, 401). Yet the last numbered section of the poem names the "[f]at girl" as the "irrational / Distortion," the "more than rational distortion" (CP, 406), phrases reminiscent of those used a year later to describe the *"sister of the Minotaur."* Although he is clearly invoking a more intimately experienced "her" during World War II, Stevens has not yet fully achieved communion with his interior paramour at this point.

Three years later, however, we see Stevens dismiss a figure of a "bright red woman" for (presumably) a real one in a poem intriguingly called "Debris of Life and Mind" (1945):

> She will think about them not quite able to sing.
> Besides, when the sky is so blue, things sing themselves,
>
> Even for her, already for her. She will listen
> And feel that her color is a meditation,
>
> The most gay and yet not so gay as it was.
> Stay here. Speak of familiar things for a while.
> (CP, 338)

The unexpected turn in the last line toward domestic intimacy, especially for such a previously "exotic" poet, enacts what is both a personal and poetic passage, a "fall," we might say, into the more fully human. Certainly his request, open to rejection, vulnerable, and wistful, is quite different in tone from the whole panoply of "hero" poems that preceded this poem and the earlier "rage to order."

And yet to return to "Description without Place," that poem that proves so crucial in his changing poetics, we should remember that it is in the first canto of that poem that Stevens, that most "masculine" and "virile" poet of the years before, privileges a female "mind" in ways that we have not seen before, a privileging far exceeding the merely rhetorical one of "The Idea of Order at Key West":

> Her green mind made the world around her green.
> The queen is an example . . . This green queen
>
> In the seeming of the summer of her sun
> By her own seeming made the summer change.
> (CP, 339)

Stevens even goes on to suggest that "[h]er time" actually "comes, / And seems to be on the saying of her name" (CP, 339), as opposed, specifically, to the "potential seemings, arrogant" of the "youngest poet's page" that wrongly imagines the "death of the soldier" (CP, 340–41), presumably in much the same way that the young and arrogant student of the sublime in "Esthétique du Mal" would misrepresent the death of actual soldiers. Written in the same year as "Debris of Life and Mind," "Description without Place" evokes the possibility of both a physical and psychic union not available to Stevens earlier in his career. In fact, taken together, "Debris" and "Description" clearly announce a new openness to the metaphorically feminine Stevens could not possibly have intended at the beginning of this horrific, and emasculating, war. In other words, despite his best ruminations, the "violence without" during World War II caused a fundamental change in Stevens's experience of that "violence from within," a change that began increasingly to dismantle the initial imperative for a "masculine violence" toward a burgeoning accep-tance of the "feminine" that would ultimately find its greatest expressions in the late poems of his career.

For example, in the 1947 poem "The Auroras of Autumn," Stevens meets his previously repressed self in an intense "rendezvous" that prepares the way for that later and most successful rendering of masculine and feminine intimacy found in "Final Soliloquy of the Interior Paramour." In a poem that repeatedly says "farewell" to several culturally reductive myths articu-lated specifically by a patriarchal voice within a largely patriarchal structure, Stevens shifts his ironic register of mere dismissal to one of welcoming:

This sense of the activity of fate—
The rendezvous, when she came alone,
By her coming became a freedom of the two,
An isolation which only the two could share.
(CP, 419)

As Frank Doggett and Dorothy Emerson have suggested, this "isolation" is an isolation only because it is the finally successful integration of his mas-culine and feminine selves.[24] What is most revealing about this description, however, is that within the poem it is simultaneously a "freedom of the two," a phrase that claims at least to have finally achieved what Stevens desired as early as "The Man with the Blue Guitar": reduction of the "monster to / Myself" so that he can "be, / Two things, the two together as one" (CP, 175).

It is also much to the point here that the "mother" in "Auroras" "who invites humanity to her house" (CP, 415) "has grown old" (CP, 413). Ultimately, she too is more vulnerable (and, therefore, human) than mythic, as is the woman in "Things of August" (1949), where "[s]he is exhausted and a little old" (CP, 496). In other words, toward the end of his career, Stevens increasingly articulated both male and female principles along ever increasingly human lines—quite in contrast to those mythic and "fantastic" lines of his early poetry.

Such an astonishing change is found most elegantly in "Angel Surrounded by Paysans" (1949), where we come across a supposedly masculine character, "a man / Of the mind" (CP, 497) who finally *speaks* with what I see as Stevens's previously repressed, though increasingly desired, feminine voice. There is no control, no mastering, no portioning of the night:

> Am I not,
> Myself, only half of a figure of a sort,
>
> A figure half seen, or seen for a moment, a man
> Of the mind, an apparition apparelled in
>
> Apparels of such lightest look that a turn
> Of my shoulder and quickly, too quickly, I am gone?
> (CP, 497)

The angel is, in fact, a "necessary angel," one who is questioning rather than "ordering," one who is, admittedly, too easily gone and subject to change—but, therefore, also a sign of our best and necessarily mutable linguistic orderings. Most importantly, he—she—is also finally heard *through* the door (instead of being held off beyond the portals), heard, even if only whispering. This poem, which ends the last volume of poetry that Stevens wrote before *The Rock*, achieves something of a resolution (emphasizing far more the "solution" or mixing than the earlier tone of "resolve"), which comes to find its greatest plenitude in the final lyrics of *The Rock*, including "Final Soliloquy of the Interior Paramour," among many other poems that we sometimes recognize as genuinely addressing this human condition.

In contrast to the 1934 poem "The Idea of Order at Key West," in Stevens's 1950 lyric "Final Soliloquy of the Interior Paramour" divisiveness in voice and in self is recognized rather than being "written over" or suppressed, just as in the interim years Stevens had learned to recognize, rather than repress, the actual and culturally realized emasculinization of a war's "evil." The divisiveness Stevens so eloquently inscribes in this late poem is explicitly held within the interior rather than being fallaciously described as a split between a dominating male poet/author/authority and a submitting, potentially chaotic feminine world, the fiction posited in the conclusion to "Notes toward a Supreme Fiction." As the word "paramour" suggests, there is a romance, even an intimacy/communion/communication, in this poem that is dependent upon "dif-ference" (to use Heidegger's term). The most telling sign of this is the plural pronoun "we" and that most feminine of garments, the "shawl," wrapped tightly round them since they "are poor":

> Light the first light of evening, as in a room
> In which we rest and, for small reason, think
> The world imagined is the ultimate good.
>
> This is, therefore, the intensest rendezvous.
> It is in that thought that we collect ourselves,
> Out of all the indifferences, into one thing:
>
> Within a single thing, a single shawl
> Wrapped tightly round us, since we are poor.
> (CP, 524)

Even though Stevens's characteristic tone of dominance is absent in this poem, the recognition and recovery of the feminine voice do not undermine his poetic authorship, as Stevens obviously feared it would in "Farewell to Florida." Instead, the recovery of this voice gives expression to what is beyond control, beyond order, beyond dominance in our actual lives and *thereby endows with significance* that little that we can order in words:

> Out of this same light, out of the central mind,
> We make a dwelling in the evening air,
> In which being together is enough.
> (CP, 524)

In this poem the thoroughly masculine "central mind" is consciously exposed *as a fiction*, most certainly not heralded as the "ideal realm" where the "new bourgeois man feels historically untouchable," as Frank Lentricchia has argued. [25] From the opening stanza, there is only "small reason" to "think / The word imagined is the ultimate good," a delicate disclaimer that quietly but continually dismantles the covert assumptions about and equations of reason, thinking, imagination, and essentially all Western (or at least Platonic) idealizations. But in submitting to the realization of the fictionality of our orderings, including the largely phallocentric privileging of the idea of order itself, *this* poem manages finally to be heard as fully human and humane. In this regard it might be fair to say, once again, that although Stevens would ultimately become a poet "of" his climate, he also at this time came to be again a poet "against" his climate, when "climate" means strictly that phallocentric logic privileging the poet as male, "virile," even "pounding"—particularly, the whole set of assumptions he bequeathed from the tradition of privileging the epic as the greatest of poetries.

In essence, the discovery here of the feminine voice, which was so silenced in his early poems, especially in *Harmonium*, opens up the space in Stevens for the magnificent tones and visions of his later years, ones heard, for example, in "Lebensweisheitspielerei," where he admits, in opposition to the "[p]ortentous enunciation" (CP, 43) of his earlier work, that

>   The proud and the strong
> Have departed.
>
> Those that are left are the unaccomplished,
> The finally human,
> Natives of a dwindled sphere

—but a sphere in which "[e]ach person completely touches *us*" (CP, 504–5, my emphasis). Admittedly, such a development as I have sketched here could appear itself reductive in a way. Certainly in "Madame La Fleurie," also a very late poem, we see the monstrous and bearded inversion of mother earth in the "bearded queen" who is devouring him (CP, 507). Similarly, the mother in "World without Peculiarity" becomes a hating "thing upon his breast" (CP, 454). Yet, in general, I think the development described above is accurate. As he says in "Artificial Populations," a poem written the year he died, "This artificial population [rosy men and women of the rose] is like / A healing-point in the sickness of the mind" (OP, 138).

This increasingly accepted and realized "feminine" part of Stevens's own voice changed his emerging "revolutionary poetics" in ways that ironically converge with a feminist politics of the sort articulated in Sara Ruddick's

Maternal Thinking or, somewhat differently, Sallie McFague's *The Body of God*.[26] Certainly, a feminist politics would initially seem to exclude the politics and poetics of Wallace Stevens, that poet so concerned at times with the "major man," the "thinker of the first idea," and abstraction in general. However, for this supposedly most "masculine poet" or "virile poet," it is especially important to remember that it is Wallace Stevens who wrote not only that the "earth is not a building but a body" (OP, 186) but also that "[p]oetry is a means of redemption" (OP, 186). While, once again, both of these lines could well hark back to Renaissance and medieval notions, taken together they also anticipate some of the best of recent feminist insights on the relation between the world and the power of words within it. In fact, our interest in Stevens in this regard must become heightened precisely because the "feminist presence" just described in these last chapters—and especially how that presence comes to be realized in his post–World War II work—is so unselfconscious, so artless, so much a part of how he would genuinely come to see the world that it becomes perhaps the most crucial moment in his changing poetics and politics. If, as he will finally conclude, "[n]ot one of those masculine myths we used to make" (CP, 518) is either true or ethical, Stevens's poetry at the end of and following World War II suggests that there is a "feminine reality" we must embrace.

In this regard, the seemingly inexplicable rearrangement of poems in the 1947 *Transport to Summer*, which places "Notes toward a Supreme Fiction" at the end of that volume, appears to signal a newfound faith in the power of words to create a new world of a different order—a faith totally different from the masculine bravado that initially informed that poem. Instead of valorizing a "virile" aesthetic resistance to World War II, "Notes toward a Supreme Fiction," as the closing poem of *Transport to Summer*, appears in its placement at the end of this volume to point truly forward to, or *toward*, a new world we have yet to create through future de-scriptions, with a newly felt conviction on Stevens's part for understanding both the necessity for and the power of words than he had originally held in 1942. As Stevens would write in an essay published the following year, "[T]he great poem of the earth remains to be written" (NA, 142). What Stevens means by this nearly epigrammatic statement is that the future world requires a new imagination, one that after the chaos of World War II will be able "to perceive the normal in the abnormal, the opposite of chaos in chaos" (NA, 153).

And yet this new imagination, as it is figured in the poems of Stevens's final years, exhibits a humility impossible to have anticipated from "The

Noble Rider and the Sound of Words." Perhaps the finest expression of this changed "voice" is found in "The Planet on the Table," in which (quite notably) poetry is recognized as fundamentally written, as well as poor, lacking altogether authorial bravado but poignantly related to "the planet of which they were part":

> Ariel was glad he had written his poems.
> They were of a remembered time
> Or of something seen that he liked.
>
> Other makings of the sun
> Were waste and welter
> And the ripe shrub writhed.
>
> His self and the sun were one
> And his poems, although makings of his self,
> Were no less makings of the sun.
>
> It was not important that they survive.
> What mattered was that they should bear
> Some lineament or character,
>
> Some affluence, if only half-perceived,
> In the poverty of their words,
> Of the planet of which they were part.
> (CP, 532–33)

As opposed to the bravado of his prewar poems, the tone of this poem—explicitly underscoring the written and nebulous nature of all poetry—accomplishes or perhaps even transcends genuine humility. Or, put differently, if after World War II Stevens would come to think that the missing part of "Notes toward a Supreme Fiction" would be a new section entitled "It Must Be Human" (L, 863–64), by the end of his life "human" definitely included "feminine."

CHAPTER SEVEN

PLANETS ON THE TABLE

By the early summer of 1945 Stevens had already penned and delivered "Description without Place." He was moving toward a period of new health and normalcy, and an Allied victory seemed imminent, facts that make the appearance of the illustrated volume *Esthétique du Mal* in July of that year both belated and ironic. Published before the volume *Transport to Summer* (in which the poem "Esthétique du Mal" would be included) but *after* the composition of "Description without Place," the chronological timing of the illustrated *Esthétique du Mal* initially frustrates our sense of Stevens's aesthetic and ethical development during this important period of his career. In fact, it may appear that we are stepping backward onto previously covered ground. However, even as he came to be more open to the "feminine," an openness that specifically coincided with a desire for a *new* normalcy rather than a mere return to an old one, Stevens also developed a new sense of *textuality*—even *intertextuality*—that I believe may have been codified for him by the appearance of the illustrated *Esthétique du Mal*. Put differently, even as Stevens was already moving on to yet another stage in his evolving aesthetic response to the Second World War, this volume—with its almost shocking illustrations—makes visual, and therefore all the more acute, the sense of language as having, quite literally, the power of "con-scription" that Stevens had begun to explore in the original version of 1944.

It is quite to the point that after World War II Stevens increasingly regarded poetry as being written rather than spoken. For a poet who had so loudly called for "The Noble Rider and the Sound of Words" in the early years of the war, it is markedly noticeable that his late poems bear titles such as "Page from a Tale," "Large Red Man Reading," "Long and Sluggish Lines," even "The Novel." These titles testify to the degree Stevens came to appreciate language as a *text* (or as essentially "written") rather than as an originating or ordering voice, thus anticipating by more than two decades the subsequent insights of Jacques Derrida and the entire deconstructionist movement. [1] It is hardly surprising that Stevens would become the deconstructionists' "dream poet," as Stevens's clear self-reflectiveness throughout his career became increasingly conjoined with the sense of language as written, arbitrary, and potentially con-scripting in its realized forms in the political world. [2] As chapter 6 demonstrates, one consequence of this intellectual shift on Stevens's part was to recognize the idea of "voice" and "origination" as precisely "male"—with numerous imbedded assumptions that finally supported structures of domination, even war—and to explore more earnestly what had been literally "glossed over" in that tradition, including the actual and the metaphorically "feminine." I suspect that the illustrated *Esthétique du Mal*, especially with the disturbing female figure on its title page, concretized for Stevens a shift that he had also just explored in depth in "Description without Place" only two months before and in ways that ultimately Stevens came to appreciate deeply.

While it is true that in a letter to Allen Tate on 2 May 1945 Stevens initially disparaged the drawings by Williams as something reducible to the advertisement of a movie of Dorian Gray as "Wilde and Weird" (L, 498), very quickly Stevens came to recognize these drawings as having added substance to his poem. Unfortunately, Joan Richardson minimizes this change in Stevens's reactions to the illustrations, saying,

> Stevens's liking for these more absent than present renderings is somehow surprising. It does not seem that the man who surrounded himself with paintings derived from the impressionist school would also see something in such an opposing style. Yet considered from our own abstract perspective, this taste for both the sensuous delight of colorful impressionistic canvases and the *edgy emptiness* of abstract line drawings perfectly reflects Stevens's movement up and down between two elements. [3]

Eleanor Cook finds this same doubled perspective within the poem itself. In addition to the poem's responding to actual war through the opening of a volcanic eruption, she also finds that canto 7, "How Red the Rose," is one that "makes sense" in his vacillations about the place of the sublime in a time of war. In fact, she concludes her summary of this poem by saying that the last canto (which ends with those "sensuous worlds") offers a "series with images of fertile, food-bearing land, a standard contrast with destructive volcanic fire in the literature of the sublime and elsewhere."[4] And yet, as I have already argued in chapter 4, it is the "panic in the face of the moon" from canto 9, or the statement later on that "[l]ife is a bitter aspic," that most encapsulates the sense of the poem.

Still, Cook does call attention to the fact that in a letter to John Crowe Ransom Stevens explained that when writing the poem he was "thinking of aesthetics as the equivalent of aperçus, which seems to have been the original meaning."[5] Although Cook focuses on a particular definition of "aesthetics" in the *Oxford English Dictionary* (with a headnote on Kant), I would like to point out that one of the meanings of aperçu is "sketch," so that it is not at all accidental but fundamental to understanding the book *Esthétique du Mal*— and specifically what Stevens came to appreciate about it—to consider, with the poetry, the drawings. "Sketches," with precisely an "edgy emptiness," seems to me to be the accurate word to describe the pen-and-ink drawings that illustrate Stevens's poem. Provided by Wightman Williams, the fifteen drawings, in addition to the title page illustration, that accompany the fifteen sections of Stevens's work all rather quickly suggest or hint at a sense of global confinement, cultural conscription, personal entrapment, and collapse.[6] Several of the sketches show a person—or the head of a person—enmeshed and entangled in abstract lines that closely resemble a web. In others the idea of a person is reduced simply to the sketch of an eye, again completely entrapped by crisscrossing lines that seem, in the progression of the volume, increasingly to engross and suffocate what we might euphemistically here call the human spirit. In the fourth sketch, which illustrates the section of the poem where "B. sat down at the piano," the artistic spirit—even art itself—appears to suffer the same fate. In that particular drawing, lines just resembling the raised lid of a grand piano and others evoking the piano strings and keys are overwhelmed by encroaching lines that appear to crush what was once an instrument, suggesting that the aesthetics of that student of the sublime are no longer viable in our modern violent world and its unrelenting "pressure of reality." Only the illustration accompanying canto 14 of the poem, the rather devastating section about "logical lunatics," has any sort of levity at all (a curious visual interpretation that alone seems to fail to capture the mood of its canto and of the poem in general). In the drawing for the final section, what was once the world spirit, or human spirit, or artistic spirit—or that "fertile" world many critics hear as the last "word" of the poem—appears totally prostrate, thoroughly and hopelessly entrapped by encroaching lines. These are not drawings—nor is the poem finally formed of sections—that testify to poetry's function as something "to help people live their lives." Instead, the sketches accurately highlight the overwhelming mood of the entire poem, that is, the feeling of being overwhelmed by the metaphorical Vesuvial and then actual "fulgurations" of war.

The fact that Stevens did not want the poem to be seen as one of levity or as one of those supposedly "sensuous worlds" of the last canto that he had ironically and consistently dismantled throughout the larger poem is made clear through his ongoing involvement with the publication of the illustrated volume and his eventual approval of the drawings. Although the editors of Cummington Press initially "wanted to use color to some extent," and although Stevens then sent them a copy of one of James Guthrie's books, "since green and blue were among the colors they were considering," Stevens noted in a letter of 18 October 1945 that, "[f]ortunately," the press "concluded to do the text in black," with only "initials and drawings in color" (L, 514–15). More importantly, despite his initial disparagement of the drawings, after its publication Stevens concluded that Williams's work "definitely adds to the text" (L, 514). It is precisely the visual display of textuality that is literally added to the text and, I would argue, to Stevens's own perception of the disturbing intersection of words and war. With the exception of the illustration accompanying the "logical lunatics" of canto 14 just noted, all of the illustrations Williams produced add to the text an acutely heightened sense of the increasingly con-textualized and con-scripted reality of this horrific period of time. Though it will be impossible to discuss each illustration here without turning this subject into a monograph of its own, I wish to concentrate in the remainder of this chapter on a few illustrations and their respective cantos in order to offer a literal "re-visionary" reading of this important poem, even beyond that given in the previous discussion of this poem in chapter 4. For it seems to me that this volume offers an unusually concrete bridge from the changes we have seen in Stevens's poetics in the previous chapters to those that would allow the great poem of his latest years.

Although the majority of the illustrations capture the theme and tone of the various sections, it is the title page illustration itself, the one that most specifically "addresses" the title of the poem, that proves most significant in understanding Stevens's poem and the fundamentally different direction his poetry would take in the future. Most of the other drawings (several of which will be reproduced below) present males as being impaled, trapped, crushed, and emasculated. The title page illustration, however, is clearly feminine. More than anything else, this figure evokes a Madonna-like figure in gesture and form with a feminized (emasculated) world that has been caught in her womb by the entrapping lines of war and words of the time. This is not to suggest that either Stevens or Williams thought that "she" is *the mal* (an old Western disfiguring poetic trope, to be sure) but rather that the literal signs of the times suggest an impoverished world in which what should have been nurturing, fruitful, even fertile is now entrapped by encroaching lines of fire and rhetoric—an unfortunate perversion of maternity and a concomitant reduction of the masculine principle to something close to distorted, if not aborted, infancy.

Rather than projecting a heroic, poetic, or aesthetic "resistance" to the overwhelming nature of world events at the time, the title page illustration exudes a sense of bearing an overwhelming burden. Specifically, the illustrated version of *Esthétique du Mal*, one curiously left unmentioned in Glen MacLeod's *Wallace Stevens and Modern Art*,[7] shows a Wallace Stevens whose poetic and aesthetic responses to a world at war are more clearly in line with the latent feminist protest of Elizabeth Bishop's poetry in "The Map" and *Geography III* as well as the overtly feminist/womanist protest of Adrienne Rich.[8] This illustration visually underscores something that Stevens appears to have already come to believe—that for a new "health" or "normalcy" there would be no "going back" to old orders. As he would put it later, the "strong and the proud have departed," meaning that traditional masculine myths have been defeated, leaving us in a radically changed world that would require new forms of community for any possibility of future healing for the "natives of a dwindled sphere" (CP, 504–5). In contrast to the very rational and controlled illustration for *Notes toward a Supreme Fiction* (see next figure), the illustrated title page of *Esthétique du Mal* suggests that there is nothing "normal" in our traditionally received notions of a female figure as either a nurturing or a demonic figure. All of those categories appear to have collapsed, and, if anything, we see "her" and the whole world "she" should be able to nurture (if freed herself) as entrapped victims, surrounded by the patriarchal lines (visually inscribed but also by traditional poetic lines such as "[o]f men and war I sing") that threaten to destroy

ESTHÉTIQUE DU MAL

A poem by WALLACE
STEVENS with pen &
ink drawings by Wightman
Williams; printed in July 1945 at
The Cummington Press, Cummington, Massachusetts.

3-22-54

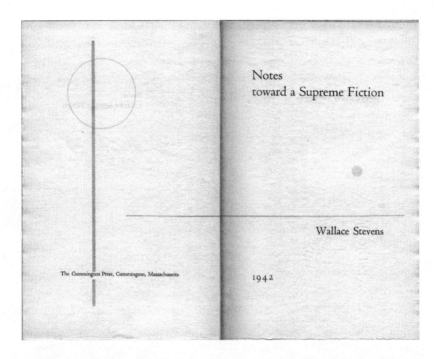

Notes
toward a Supreme Fiction

Wallace Stevens

The Cummington Press, Cummington, Massachusetts   1942

the future embryonic world as well or to "end civilization" (OP, 229) as we
know it.

In this context, the student of the sublime who opens canto 1 has a deeply
perverse desire to repeat patterns of the old:

He could describe
The terror of the sound because the sound
Was ancient. He tried to remember the phrases.

But, we should note, despite these rhetorical moves, the "volcano trembled
in another ether" (that is, reality and not the sublime of his remembered
aesthetics), just as "the body trembles at the end of life"—hardly a sublime
image at all, invoking, as it does, final death throes.[9] Against the pressing
reality of the situation described in canto 2, nothing provides a more enticing
image for the "student of the sublime" than a ruined landscape he wishes both
to discover and to recover. As such it is almost inevitable, as Stevens makes
clear, that this student (presumably educated in the way that the actual poet
had been in the years long before, even before the "Great War"—a "sublime"
nomenclature itself) would extend the image of a damaged but recovered

landscape to all aspects of his desire to recover and recuperate the past. It is logical that even in the midst of actual violence, this student, educated in a way that comes to be revealed as very limited, would think of previous texts and aesthetics—and think of them specifically as disinterred. In other words, for the student, the sublime in words is a "factual" reconstruction of what is revealed by Stevens in the course of the poem to be outmoded and even destructive aperçus.

However, for the poet understanding this student (both standing "under" him to present a past trope and standing "over" to criticize the deceptions of the past), the chaos and carnage of World War II cause the horrible suspicion that the literary past is itself an interment, a burial, and not just of a previous poetic position but a continuing force of interment operating on the present reality. Canto 2 then introduces the possibility of the student's almost re-alizing this inadequacy, with a consequent "intelligence of despair," and is accompanied in the illustrated version with a drawing that belies any notion of the student's reactionary desire for "freedom" or salvation postulated at the end of the same canto.

While the concluding lines of the second canto may appear to offer some kind of redemption to the despair with which the section begins, Wightman Williams's illustration captures what I believe to be the correct mood and thesis of the poem—the ultimate inefficacy and irony of such aesthetic con-solations in the face of the overwhelming pressure from a world at war—and thus serves as a better act of interpretation than we sometimes find in written discussions of this poem. Substituting the various noises and news of war for the "warblings" in the opening lines of the section, we find an ominous and overbearing din that comes quite literally from

>   too much the accents of
> Afflicted sleep, too much the syllables
> That would form themselves, in time, and communicate
> The intelligence of his despair.

Whereas later in the section the poem posits the fictional desire for some aesthetic distancing from this psychic pain (notably, "[t]he moon rose up *as if* it had escaped / His meditation" [my emphasis]), the drawing makes clear how thoroughly interconnected, interwoven everything is through visual lines that threaten to crush the anthropomorphic head figured in the illustration. In fact, it might not be going to far to say that the illustration suggests that the

At a town in which acacias grew, he lay
On his balcony at night. Warblings became
Too dark, too far, too much the accents of
Afflicted sleep, too much the syllables
That would form themselves, in time, and
   communicate
The intelligence of his despair, express
What meditation never quite achieved.

The moon rose up as if it had escaped
His meditation. It evaded his mind.
It was part of a supremacy always
Above him. The moon was always free from him,
As night was free from him. The shadow touched
Or merely seemed to touch him as he spoke
A kind of elegy he found in space:

It is pain that is indifferent to the sky
In spite of the yellow of the acacias, the scent
Of them in the air still hanging heavily
   In the hoary-hanging night. It does not regard
     This freedom, this supremacy, and in
      Its own hallucination
       never sees
       How that which rejects it
       saves it in the end.

"patriarchal lines," including the physical and verbal lines of war, are indeed crushing and silencing the human spirit in precisely the way that some recent feminist theorists such as Sherry Ortner have explained. [10] This suggestion is reinforced by the uncanny similarity of this particular drawing to a couple of illustrations by Paul Klee (Stevens's favorite artist) published many years before in *Broom* (an international journal to which Stevens was contributing in the 1920s), in which the drawings clearly convey the overwhelming and dispiriting pressure of the previous "Great War." [11] Far beyond the seeming deference to Baudelaire in its title or in its deliberate imitation of previous poetic imitations (including Stevens's own earlier imitation of Dante's *Divine Comedy* in "Notes toward a Supreme Fiction"), before the conclusion of *Esthétique du Mal* (in either its first version or illustrated one) this poem has become not only an acutely self-conscious inquisition of the "high poetry" that Stevens actually was taught and of his imagined student in the poem but also an inquisition of the very value and morality of civilization such high poetry purports to preserve and pass along.

Moreover, the illustration accompanying canto 2 of *Esthétique du Mal*, as well as the title page illustration, prepares us to see the awful and biting irony of that section of the poem some readers have interpreted as being largely supportive of war. In canto 7, the famous "How Red the Rose that Is the Soldier's Wound," Stevens exposes more acutely than anywhere else in the poem the cognitive disjunction between the need for the past to be a ground of present meaning and the fear that the past is not only meaningless within itself but also destructive to the present. The traditional valorization of "men and war," especially in the form of privileging the epic, is precisely the ideology of domination and destruction that this section of the poem seeks to subvert in its self-consciously parodic first line. Published separately in a book of war poems, canto 7 did indeed have "a life of its own" and has been interpreted more than once as indicating that Stevens and the editors who reprinted this poem regarded it as a "*pro*-war poem." [12] Berger, for example, regards this canto as an "outright elegy." [13] Similarly, Cook sees the canto as having a certain elegance, resulting in its being an "elegy" or a "hymn" in the Whitmanian tradition. Although she admits that the opening trope, which compares a wound to a rose, "can be offensive to modern ears," she (like many other critics) reads the canto as being affirmative, constructed by lines that are "smooth and calmed." [14] Yet, far from extolling war or the wounded, far from exuding a sense of peace and justification (that whole tradition of "dulce et decorum est" superficially evoked herein—that very tradition

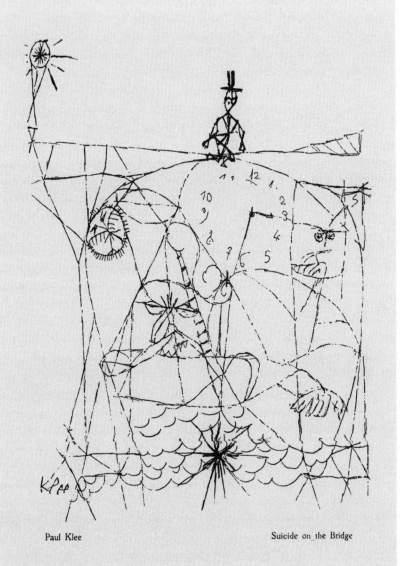

Paul Klee   Suicide on the Bridge

Hemingway had already derided in 1935),[15] this section of the poem, within the context of the whole work, once again exudes a sense of panic—of total entrapment—in face of a world that would *try* to cover up the real violence of war with such empty rhetorical platitudes as "[f]or the soldier of time, it breathes a summer sleep, / In which his wound is good because life was."

In contrast to canto 2, Wightman's illustration accompanying canto 7 has not even the remnants of an anthropomorphic figure (which was, apparently, being suffocated in the earlier drawing). Rather, the spherical shape on the bottom right-hand corner of the drawing, which repeats the world-as-womb shape from the cover, appears caught in an anonymous struggle carried out on a global scale against encroaching and conscripting lines. This particular canto does not posit the simple poetic consolation of "resistance" Stevens tried to create in "Notes toward a Supreme Fiction" or the "normalcy" he would try to create in the poems written after this one's original composition.[16] Rather, its overall mood anticipates the final canto, where the *poet* (as opposed to the student) clearly states the frustrating impasse the writer of poetry must reach when confronted with actual war: "Speech found the ear, for all the evil sound, / But the dark italics it could not propound" (canto 15). More relentlessly than the original "Esthétique du Mal" itself, because of the verbal and visual conjoinings, *Esthétique du Mal* debunks whole the "masculine" tradition of privileging war and war poetry, especially the epic.

Although canto 7 would be lifted out of the larger poem and reprinted in *War and the Poet* and again in *The War Poets*, it seems obvious that within the context of the original poem we are confronting one of Stevens's most satiric moments in his "revolutionary poetics," one deftly captured by Williams in the totally chaotic lines of the accompanying illustration. In his illustration of canto 7, Williams exaggerates the ominous lines of the title page illustration to where "she" is almost unrecognizable under the power of these new lines. In fact, the world as womb from the cover appears miscarried here at best. Thus, what the illustrated version of this poem "adds" to the text is a visual underscoring of the intense contradiction "buried" in this canto between the student's attempt to transform a body in pain through a "subliminal" poetic gesture into a rose (a standard trope that valorizes and falsifies war) and the actual poet's disgust with this gesture. Among Stevens's critics, only James Longenbach has been willing to suggest (although in carefully modified terms) that this canto may have been intended on Stevens's part "as an example of inadequate wartime rhetoric."[17]

How red the rose that is the soldier's wound,
The wounds of many soldiers, the wounds of all
The soldiers that have fallen, red in blood,
The soldier of time grown deathless in great
    size.

A mountain in which no ease is ever found,
Unless indifference to deeper death
Is ease, stands in the dark, a shadows' hill,
And there the soldier of time has deathless
    rest.

Concentric circles of shadows, motionless
Of their own part, yet moving on the wind,
Form mystical convolutions in the sleep
Of time's red soldier deathless on his bed.

The shadows of his fellows ring him round
In the high night, the summer breathes for them
Its fragrance, a heavy somnolence, and for him,
For the soldier of time, it breathes a summer sleep,

In which his wound is good because life was.
No part of him was ever part of death.
A woman smoothes her forehead with her hand
And the soldier of time lies calm beneath that stroke.

Of course, the fact that Stevens allowed this canto to be lifted out of the context of the larger poem of which it is a part and to be reprinted not once but twice may initially appear to undercut the interpretation of this canto I offer here. However, three facts mitigate against this dismissal of what I believe to be an instance of one of Stevens's most acerbic denigrations of the culturally received and rhetorical approbations of war. First, the rhetoric of this canto is precisely the rhetoric of the "sublime" the larger poem consistently seeks to disinherit. Second, lifted out of that context, this canto was reproduced in two volumes published in 1945, but, at least in the context of Oscar Williams's *The War Poets*, "How Red the Rose" would have been interpreted by many contemporary readers as an antiwar poem. As Malcolm Cowley notes with disgust in his 1945 review of that collection, for example, Williams has chosen only poems in which their authors "are opposed, not only to war in general, but also to fighting this particular war. He implies that any soldier who expresses a willingness to die for a cause or a country deludes himself and his readers."[18] Stevens's poem appears in the third section of his volume in which contemporary civilians write about war. Notably, that section garnered Cowley's most intense contempt for the supposedly unearned antipatriotic stance characteristic of all the poems in that section. Finally, even if the editors (both members of the military) of that other volume in which this canto was reprinted (*War and the Poet*) actually regarded "How Red the Rose" as a prowar poem, we should remember Stevens's unwavering decision *not* to correct the readers in their interpretations of his work. As he said in a letter to Hi Simons in 1940,

> A long time ago I made up my mind not to explain things, because most people have so little appreciation of poetry that once a poem has been explained it has been destroyed: that is to say, they are no longer able to seize the poem. Moreover, even in a case like your own, or in the case of any critic, I think that the critic is under obligation to base his remarks on what he has before him. It is not a question of what an author meant to say but of what he has said. In the case of a competent critic the author may well have a great deal to find out about himself and his work. This goes to the extent of saying that it would be legitimate for a critic to make statements respecting the purpose of an author's work that were altogether contrary to the intentions of the author. (L, 346)

Despite, then, its "separate life," canto 7 may well represent the most extreme instance of Stevens's disgust with the traditional valorization of war as "sung" by poets from Homer through the early British poets of World War I. It is a disgust that Wightman Williams genuinely captured in the illustration of this canto as well as in others. In fact, with the stifling lines accompanying each of the illustrations in mind, but most certainly with those accompanying "How Red the Rose that Is the Soldier's Wound," there can be little sense that such a fictional and healing movement as that described in the lines "[a] woman smoothes her forehead with her hand / And the soldier of time lies calm beneath that stroke" is even remotely possible. Instead, this section of the poem presents such poetic consolations as "how red the rose" (consolations typical of most war poetry before the middle of World War I) as utterly hypocritical, even nauseating.

This canto may well have been prompted by Yeats's trilogy of the Rose, written early in his career during his own time of civil unrest, leading me to conclude that canto 7 might best be called an *excoriation* in the deepest etymological sense.[19] Specifically, after "The Rose of the World," then "The Rose of Peace," Yeats concludes his trilogy with "The Rose of Battle," which he also calls "Rose of all Roses, Rose of all the World!":

Rose of all Roses, Rose of all the World!
. . . .
Danger no refuge holds, and war no peace,
For him who hears love sing and never cease,
Beside her clean-swept hearth, her quiet shade:
. . . .
Rose of all Roses, Rose of all the World!
You, too, have come where the dim tides are hurled
Upon the wharves of sorrow, and heard ring
The bell that calls us on; the sweet far thing.
Beauty grown sad with its eternity
Made you of us, and of the dim grey sea.
Our long ships loose thought-woven sails and wait,
For God has bid them share an equal fate;
And when at last, defeated in His wars,
They have gone down under the same white stars,
We shall no longer hear the little cry
Of our sad hearts, that may not live nor die.[20]

There is, then, in canto 7 of Stevens's poem a heavy surfeit of disgust drama-tized by the poet Stevens in the potent pairing of rose and wound. Through this verbal exaggeration of the traditional trope that venerates war and war poetry, Stevens arrests this poetic (and equally political) performance. By overloading the unquestioned valorizations of the soldier-poet's allegiance to war (and the clearly problematic displacement of women within the ethos accompanying this trope), Stevens makes sickeningly clear the cultural complicity between words, weapons, wounds, and actual war. As Stevens says elsewhere, "Not one of the masculine myths we used to make" proves reliable but rather results only in "a sound / Like the last muting of winter as it ends" (CP, 518–19).

From this perspective, we should look back and "re-invision" even "Dutch Graves in Bucks Country," discussed in chapter 4, in which Stevens had already made this point well—although mutedly—and without the overt mentioning of women (who are nonetheless the withheld counterpart to the opening "[a]ngry men and furious machines" of that poem). As in canto 7, just reinterpreted within its larger context, in the 1942 "Dutch Graves" Stevens makes a disturbing and arresting pronouncement:

> There are circles of weapons in the sun.
> The air attends the brightened guns,
> As if sounds were forming
> Out of themselves, a saying,
> An expressive on-dit, a profession.
>
> And you, my semblables, are doubly killed
> To be buried in desert and deserted earth.
> (CP, 290)

"Doubly killed," we might say, by the reality of war as a "profession" and by the profession of traditional tropes of war poetry (that "expressive on-dit") that would seek to hide actual destruction under sublime consolations.

Ultimately, so great is the weight of literary irony (including Stevens's own) that attends our adjustment in canto 7 from the student's presentation of the soldier's wound as "sublime" to the failure of this trope to meet, much less defeat, reality in the larger poem of which it is a part that we must conclude that such ironic density is a force of consciousness within Stevens himself about his own earlier relation to literary antecedents. It "makes sense," then, that after canto 7 and the next move to the "cold vacancy" of reality in canto 8 that canto 9 erupts precisely with panic—and panic "in the face of the moon" (that traditionally feminized object in space), "panic, because / The moon is no longer" any of our projected male myths and because "nothing is left but cosmic ugliness." The illustration that accompanies canto 9 visually recapitulates this disturbing conclusion. Once again, the student desires sounds of the sublime. Even if he must appeal to the sublime in nature rather than to that of ancient poetry, he still desperately wants to discover "another chant" that declares "[t]ruth's favors sonorously exhibited." The desperation here stems from his fear of hearing only "what one hears" and of seeing only "what one sees" in these actual and overwhelming times of war. To confront reality unabated in such times is to lose the artificial "paradise of meaning" and to find that the destitution of reality dissolves all verbal platitudes into personal and "cosmic ugliness."

Stevens continues to present the student's finally narcissistic desire for the poetic sublime and his own growing repulsion at that desire throughout the rest of the strophes of the poem. In fact, the very last stanza of the final canto of the poem concludes with the now recognizably naive (and even possibly immoral) desire of that student who would wish to make so "many sensuous worlds, / As if the air . . . was swarming / With the metaphysical changes that occur." Notably, the lines immediately above this last and delusionally "sublime" wish are framed and ultimately frustrated by this very "Esthétique":

> One might have thought of sight, but who could think
> Of what it sees, for all the ill it sees?
> Speech found the ear, for all the evil sound,
> But the dark italics it could not propound.

In ways that should be obvious with "Notes toward a Supreme Fiction" in mind, the aesthetic defeat the student experiences here replicates the growing distrust Stevens came to feel about his own earlier attempt at "formal resistance" or aesthetic consolations, even if he had attempted to replace the sublime of spiritual paradise at the end with a terrestrial one. Indeed, whatever intertextual accents we hear now sound clearly, though distressingly, different from those that had prompted the revision of Dante's *Divine Comedy* only a few years earlier.

For a poet who had initially said in 1939 that the United States should not enter the war "unless it does so with the idea of dominating the world that comes out it" and that the "responsibility of writers is a very theoretical thing" since "war is a military state of affairs, not a literary one,"[21] the change in Stevens's aesthetics from 1939 to 1945 is remarkable, radical,

Panic in the face of the moon—round effendi
Or the phosphored sleep in which he walks abroad
Or the majolica dish heaped up with phosphored fruit
That he sends ahead, out of the goodness of his heart,
To anyone that comes—panic, because
The moon is no longer these nor anything
And nothing is left but comic ugliness
Or a lustred nothingness. Effendi, he
That has lost the folly of the moon becomes
The prince of the proverbs of pure poverty.
To lose sensibility, to see what one sees,
As if sight had not its own miraculous thrift,
To hear only what one hears, one meaning
alone,
As if the paradise of meaning ceased
To be paradise, it is this to be destitute.
This is the sky divested of its fountains.
Here in the west indifferent crickets chant
Through our indifferent crises. Yet we require
Another chant, an incantation, as in
Another and later genesis, music
That buffets the shapes of its possible halcyon
Against the haggardie. . . A loud, large water
Bubbles up in the night and drowns the crickets' sound.
It is a declaration, a primitive ecstasy,
Truth's favors sonorously exhibited.

even "revolutionary" indeed. Gone is the "masculine" bravado of the early essays in *The Necessary Angel*, even the regret of the wartime poem "Girl in a Nightgown," which had figured "a tottering, a falling and an end" as an apocalyptic ending born of "[p]hrases . . . of fear and of fate" (CP, 214). Instead, by the war's conclusion, Stevens had come to recognize the awful power of words, whether propagandistic rhetoric or a poet's metaphors, in how we shape reality. However, it would be misleading to conclude that the illustrated *Esthétique du Mal* plunged Stevens back into a despair that he had begun to heal in the writing of "Description without Place." Instead, the illustrated *Esthétique du Mal* concretized that growing understanding Stevens had reached of the importance of *textuality*—that our words, which are never simply "objective," can be both limiting and liberating, "con-scripting" and "pre-scriptive," if (in the latter move toward health) earlier patriarchal lines, whether poetically or politically conceived, are "[c]leared of its stiff and stubborn, man-locked set" and opened to a "new text of the world" (CP, 497, 494).

Given his initial aesthetic argument with William Carlos Williams, Stevens's political positionings about the place and importance of poetry in the world may come to seem intensely ironic. It is Williams, after all, who would come to say,

> It is difficult
> to get the news from poems
> yet men die miserably every day
> for lack
> of what is found there.[22]

However, it is finally not ironic but consistent with the numerous ways in which Stevens's poetics changed during World War II that this critical insight would prove to be for Stevens his most deeply held conviction, with important ramifications that continue to extend well into our world today, as we desire—or require—a new "normalcy" for our own world. As Stevens himself wrote, in words that sound ironically very similar to those of Williams, "Poetry is a response to the daily necessity of getting the words right" (OP, 201).

To conclude with Stevens's own postwar reflections in the 1948 "Imagination as Value," he positions his comments in relation to war by saying, "Between the wars, we lived, it may be said, in an era when some attempt was made to apply the value of arts and letters to life" (NA, 148). As complicated as this subject must be, Stevens concludes, "My final point, then is that the imagination [that "irrepressible revolutionist" (NA, 152)] is the power that enables us to perceive the normal in the abnormal, the opposite of chaos in chaos" (NA, 153). Even more pointedly, in the 1951 essay "The Relations between Poetry and Painting," Stevens follows Simone Weil's *La Pesanteur et la grâce* by noting that she says that "decreation is making pass from the created to uncreated, but . . . destruction is making pass from the created to nothingness. Modern reality is a reality of decreation, in which our revelations are not revelations of belief, but the precious portents of our own powers" (NA, 174–75). Written toward the end of his life, Stevens's clear call here for "decreation"—what I have called "dismantling" but which we could easily call "deconstruction"—fully encapsulates the conclusion of the critical stages in his revolutionary poetics, announcing a vision that is certainly amenable to our most political feminist and postmodern poets and critics writing even now.[23]

CHAPTER EIGHT

MORE AND MORE HUMAN

Of the many poems Stevens wrote in the years immediately after the end of World War II that attempt to capture "the normal in the abnormal," "An Ordinary Evening in New Haven" (1949) and "The Rock" (1950) stand out exponentially, if only because their titles so clearly invoke and then deliberately deflate certain exalted, if not specifically Christological, expectations. If there is a tone of acceptance, as surely there is in these late poems, it is a tone at once open to the feminine, as we have seen, and one specifically responding to a new sense of textuality that would increasingly decry the bravado and certainly that persistent "rage to order" of his earlier years. As Stevens wrote in the 1948 "Imagination as Value," the imagination "is the irrepressible revolutionist" (NA, 152), a statement that hints at the kind of intersection between Stevens's politics and aesthetics that, at least for some time, Adrienne Rich found not only amenable but instrumental in teaching her what she calls a "revolutionary poetics."[1]

However, since I have borrowed Rich's own term for the title of this book, and since she ultimately rejects Stevens for failing to instantiate those "revolutionary poetics" in terms of racism, it is crucial to address this indictment of Stevens here in this final chapter. Put succinctly, the latest charge against Stevens for moral or ethical insufficiency, one voiced quite strongly by Mark

Halliday and Adrienne Rich and then echoed by Lisa DuRose and Rachel Blau DuPlessis, is that Stevens was unwaveringly racist throughout his poetic career—that there is no essential difference, for example, between Stevens's use of the word "darkies" in a 1916 poem and the use of the phrase "black men" in a poem of 1950.[2] At least as I interpret these critics' arguments and their various collections of supposedly racist references and slurs (including even for one critic the *blackbird* of "Thirteen Ways of Looking at a Black- bird" as representing "the rarity of black speech despite the strong presence of African-Americans in Stevens"),[3] any and all references to African Americans in his poetry are presumed to be condescending, with ramifications extending to his use of the tropics as settings for many poems and to darkness or merely the color black in other poems as a trope of racist desire and of dread.

For example, in what is a deliberately reductive form of argumentation, Mark Halliday asserts in a footnote accompanying the list he has made of Stevens's references to African Americans and black Africans that Stevens's "lazy-minded racism is a clear subject for an essay that could be written, an essay which I imagine as rather short and rather grim, since I doubt that there are interesting variations in Stevens's racism."[4] Adrienne Rich, it would seem, agrees. Although she announces her indebtedness to Wallace Stevens without qualification at the end of "Not How to Write Poetry, but Wherefore," in the next essay included in *What Is Found There* Rich attacks Stevens not only for being racist himself but also for representing the racism of the larger American poetic climate in the mid–twentieth century. After claiming to have learned in her youth her "revolutionary poetics" from Wallace Stevens, that "liberator" who told her "to face the men of the time and to meet / The women of the time," who urged her to

> Throw away the lights, the definitions
> And say of what you see in the dark
> That it is this or it is that,
> But do not use the rotted names,

Rich then abruptly and completely rejects Stevens upon her later reflec- tions as an adult: "Why . . . was that 'master' of my youth, that liberatory spokesman for the imagination, that mentor . . . so attracted and compelled by old, racist configurations? How . . . could he accept the stunting of his own imagination" by, among other things, his "compulsive reiterations of the word 'nigger'?"[5] (The total number of his use of this offensive word is actually limited to seven instances, and at least a few of these are moments in which he consciously exposes that word, as opposed to "black," as the derogatory slur that it is.) Rich goes on to say that she first tried to justify these moments of overtly "racial language" as "painful but encapsulated lesion[s] on the imagination, a momentary collapse of the poet's intelligence," but, she then stresses, later she realized that Stevens's racism was a *"key to the whole,"* one that explains not only the dynamics of Stevens's artistic work as well as his private life but also that of the entire poetic tradition she had been trying to embrace and to become a part of.[6]

Notably, in a recent essay, Stephen Burt says of this remark, "It is hard to imagine the lock that would fit such a key," citing a hostile review of Rich's collection of essays, *What Is Found There*, entitled "The Poet's Burden," in which David Bromwich "dismisses the idea."[7] Notwithstanding, in a subsequent essay published in 2000, " 'Darken Your Speech': Racialized Cultural Work of Modernist Poets," Rachel Blau DuPlessis makes an extensive case against Stevens in terms of racism, implying that the myriad instances she finds of denigrating references to blacks do indeed represent not only Stevens's own racist perspectives but also those of the more important white modernist poets in America.[8] Notably, DuPlessis does offer a convincing and disturbing reading of several of Stevens's poems as well as his 1916 play *Three Travelers at Sunrise*. She also provides many intriguing insights into the sometimes undeniable relationship between racism and the production of poetry by white writers. Yet DuPlessis seems to me to go too far in her derogatory interpretation of Stevens's corpus by overreading certain poems (such as "Thirteen Ways of Looking at a Blackbird") or by not reading certain poems involving black figurations at all, especially those written during and after World War II.

Nonetheless, DuPlessis's essay proves to be of critical interest here, for the vast majority of the poems she cites against Stevens in this regard are poems written very early in his career, at precisely the same point that we also find numerous instances of possible and sometimes unmistakable sexism in his verse (as discussed in chapter 6). And, notably, just as with the majority of the overtly sexist poems of his early period discussed in chapter 6, DuPlessis has culled the majority of the poems she discusses as exhibiting racism from *Opus Posthumous*. As she notes, the largest cluster of poems Stevens wrote referring to or incorporating blacks occurs between 1919 and 1922, concluding, "For Stevens, the buoyant black muse figures are male; the females are dangerous."[9] And yet as insightful as this remark may be, if the issue of race were withdrawn from this observation, DuPlessis's remark would also accurately describe Stevens's figurations of men and women in general during this time, regardless of race. Similarly, she notes, "Mainly, Stevens creates situations in which the white figures, instructing the speech of blacks, take both halves of the conversation," thereby preventing genuine dialogue and communication—a limitation that we have also seen largely characterizes his figurations of the "masculine" and the "feminine" in general, at least until World War II.[10] Finally, although DuPlessis covers a wide array of black figures in Stevens's poetry, convincingly concluding, for example, that the "negress" of "Virgin Carrying a Lantern" (1923) is a "sexual predator" when compared to the white virgin of the poem, there are several gaping holes in her coverage of Stevens's figurations of African Americans and black Africans.[11] She does not, for example, examine the only postwar instance of the word "negress," which occurs in "The Auroras of Autumn," where the word is clearly invoked by that patriarchal father whom Stevens is thoroughly criticizing and rejecting in the poem. Nor does she consider Stevens's meditations on the "black men" in the late poem "The Sick Man" (an important poem to which I will return momentarily). Most curiously, given that an entire section of her essay bears the heading "Owning Africa," DuPlessis does not examine Stevens's own self-conscious consideration of colonization in "The Greenest Continent." Had these and other poems been included, we might find that, just as was true of Stevens's problematic relation to the "feminine," over time and especially during and after World War II Stevens evolved a poetics increasingly open to ethical presentations of African Americans in poetry and in the actual world.

Admittedly, in a 1998 essay, "Racial Domain and the Imagination of Wallace Stevens," Lisa DuRose attempts a somewhat more sympathetic reading of Stevens and his struggle with racism. Noting, as did biographer Joan Richardson (as well as DuPlessis, who rejected this supposed identification with blacks), that Stevens at times expressed his alliance with blacks and his impatience with attitudes of white superiority, DuRose quickly modifies this supposed approbation by concluding that "his expressed alliance was often a troubling blend of support and stereotype."[12] She even goes on to assert that such rhetorical ambivalences were uttered by an "apolitical" poet largely unaware of the gap between ethical intentions and destructive ideologies: "That the poem, however [in a variety of poems and letters], expresses his views within a racist paradigm . . . suggests the difficulties even the *apolitical* Stevens had in overcoming the racial politics of his time; and it expresses a troubling symbiosis between sympathetic intentions and racist ideologies."[13]

Even when she turns to "The Sick Man," in which Stevens presents the "possibility of some symbiosis of black and white," DuRose dismisses the legitimacy of this possibility for being imagined by a man who is "somehow divorced from the outside world because of his sickness and isolation, solipsistically enjoying the idea of racial harmony but never really entering the song himself."[14]

As the preceding survey suggests, this latest charge against Stevens is being made by a growing number of very different kinds of readers and critics; at the same time, at least thus far, few critics have been genuinely willing to defend Stevens in this regard. A notable exception is Angus Cleghorn's *Wallace Stevens' Poetics: The Neglected Rhetoric*, published in 2000. Although the subject of racism is certainly not the subject of the entire book, his detailed discussion of "The Greenest Continent," a section of *Owl's Clover* published in 1936, proves invaluable for showing how early Stevens was committed to dismantling falsifying, reductive rhetorics, including specifically racist rhetoric. As Cleghorn notes, after completing "The Old Woman and the Statue" and "Mr. Burnshaw and the Statue," Stevens had expected to write the next three sections of *Owl's Clover* quite rapidly. But after three months he was still struggling with that section he initially called "The Statue in Africa" (but that he would eventually call "The Greenest Continent"): "I think I shall have to leave the STATUE IN AFRICA for a bit. I am head over heels in the thing. The specific subject is, I suppose, the white man in Africa. But it may be that no one will ever realize that. What I have been trying to do in the thing is to apply my own poetry to such a subject" (L, 307–8). Stevens's expressed fear that no one would understand the political subversions and ethical intentions in this section has, in fact, proved quite prophetic. And yet for a larger sense of the climate of which Stevens was a part, including his almost unexpected decision to write about the "white man in Africa," it might be quite fruitful to remember that this section of the poem and its exploration of white colonization in Africa was written in 1936 at almost exactly the same time as Ernest Hemingway's *Green Hills of Africa* (1935) and Isak Dinesen's *Out of Africa* (1937), both of which self-consciously critique the imposition of white colonial rule in pre–World War II Africa, including self-conscious exposures of the authors' own participation in this very imposition.[15] In this context, it may not finally be so surprising that, as Cleghorn demonstrates, in the "African" section of *Owl's Clover* Stevens "draws together bad measures made in Christian faith and colonization," offering a counterepistemology to this "destructive" and racist "missionary mindset," stretching the totalizing imposition of the statue from "The Old Woman" and "Mr. Burnshaw" to the African jungle. Placed there, the statue presents the imposition of European imperialism in Africa, much as in "Anecdote of the Jar" another seemingly innocuous object comes to present a similarly colonizing imposition in Tennessee.[16]

Within this context, what particularly interests me is the fact that following a canto in "The Greenest Continent" where Stevens has specifically asked, "[C]ould the statue stand in Africa?" (OP, 87), he concludes this most racially conscious section of *Owl's Clover* with a canto that includes, quite shockingly, that very word to which Rich so adamantly objects—and, I would add, to which Stevens objects as well. In contrast to his use of the word "blacks" earlier in the poem, the objectionable word intrudes in the last canto— precisely like a statue intruded into Africa—as a startling reminder of the crude and destructive consequences of European imperialism, colonization, appropriation, and denigration:

> He sees the angel in the nigger's mind
> And hears the nigger's prayer in motets, belched
> From pipes that swarm clerestory walls. The voice
> In the jungle is a voice in Fontainebleau.
> (OP, 90)

What this colonizer sees and hears is not the "black" who would "still / Be free to sing" (OP, 89) earlier in the poem had Africa been left alone at the end of the nineteenth century and early twentieth century during the period of Stevens's actual maturation or the "blacks" betrayed in an even earlier section of "The Greenest Continent" by the hypocritical intrusion of white colonists who, as self-described "angels," actually "come, armed, glorious to slay" (OP, 87). Much as in Elizabeth Bishop's "Brazil, January 1, 1502," the white colo- nizing of a continent reduces the actual people already living there to mere "voices"—perhaps to an undifferentiated single *"voice"* (i.e., precisely a racial *stereotype*)—ironically silenced through racist projections concomitant with actual political and personal domination.[17] While I disagree with Cleghorn's ultimate interpretation of this section of the poem (since he eventually finds the ending of "The Greenest Continent" quite disturbing), I do concur that in "The Greenest Continent" Stevens deliberately exposes the hypocrisy and unethical behavior of white colonists imposing their "world order" on and in Africa. As such, the "Statue in Africa" is in its most condensed form racist rhetoric itself that then justifies actual "con-scription" of lands and people in the actual world.

What finally troubles Cleghorn in this section is the figure/god Ananke, whom he regards as "the African alternative to the transposed Western Statue." Rather than considering that Stevens may be introducing yet another instance of white colonial rhetoric, Cleghorn interprets Ananke as the "intrusive exotic demonization" of an African presence.[18] In contrast, I find the "alternative" of Ananke to be no alternative at all but rather the flip side of that same imperialist "coin," that is, the projection of a supposedly appreciated aesthetic (but actually an equally reductive notion) of "primitivism" onto Africa and blacks. Such a projection is, in relation to the clearly derogatory word Stevens uses in this section, equally a culturally constructed "rhetoric" that justifies exploitation. And, we should note, it was a construction actually being projected, venerated, painted, even theatrically performed in Europe and in America in the immediate years surrounding the composition of this poem.[19] As such, there is ultimately a deeply ethical purpose in Stevens's very limited use of the word "nigger" in this poem—and in other poems as well—and certainly not one that he compulsively or reductively reiterated.

Admittedly, in the title of the 1935 poem "Like Decorations in a Nigger Cemetery," the racist epithet seems problematic, although we should also remember that Stevens is comparing the spontaneously proffered "decorations" there positively to his own seemingly unstructured series of poetic epigrams, which constitute the actual body of his poem. Certainly, in "Prelude to Objects" (1938), the objectionable word once again is being criticized by Stevens for demonstrating the kind of unethical and monolithic thinking that accompanies war (just as it demonstrated the type of totalizing and reductive rhetoric that accompanied colonization in "The Greenest Continent"):

Granted each picture is a glass,
That the walls are mirrors multiplied,
That the marbles are gluey pastiches, the stairs
The sweep of an impossible elegance,
And the notorious views from the windows
Wax wasted, monarchies beyond
The S.S. *Normandie*, granted
One is always seeing and feeling oneself,
That's not by chance. It comes to this:

>That the guerilla I should be booked
>And bound. Its nigger mystics should change
>Foolscap for wigs. Academies
>As of a tragic science should rise.
>(CP, 195)

The offensive word appears three times in one of Stevens's earliest World War II poems: "The News and the Weather" (1941). Once again, Stevens's inclusion of the word in this poem demonstrates that the public rhetoric accompanying a monolithic and uncritical support of war almost inevitably includes unthinking racist rhetoric as well. The poem opens with "[t]he blue sun in his red cockade / Walked the United States today" (CP, 264), undoubtedly a figure being derided here by Stevens. Later in the poem, after "quoting" the disturbing lines, the "nigger tree . . . with a nigger name," Stevens reveals those words as being from an imaginary "Solange" who would be a "euphonious bone" (an ironic nomenclature for a person uttering such lines). The poem then closes with "a poison at winter's end," clearly criticizing both the opening rhetoric of war and its concluding racist rhetoric (CP, 265). Thus, if Stevens has indeed "reiterated" this racist term, at least in these instances (which constitute, in fact, all the occurrences of the word in both his collected and posthumous poems), he has done so not compulsively but deliberately and with an ethical perspective that the preceding chapters may encourage us finally to recognize.

In fact, just as Stevens would come to invoke both "men" and "women" with an implied sense of equality during World War II, during this same period Stevens came to invoke a greater respect for African Americans. In "Contrary Theses (II)," for example, Stevens notes that the "negroes were playing football in the park" with no more derision than he notes the "wide-moving swans" or the "leaves" that "were falling like notes from a piano" (CP, 270). In this poem, which was published in *Parts of a World*, we hear a tone regarding racial configurations with a very different register from the "dark-ies" of the very early "Two at Norfolk" or the "negress" in "Virgin Carrying a Lantern." At the same time, in contrast to the numerous instances when Stevens employs various figurations of blacks during the early 1920s, after World War II Stevens largely forgoes his earlier attempts to render or appro-priate black experiences. Gone, along with that "masculine" (and presumably white) figure he had once privileged, is the deluding self as "Sambo" that he had once been willing to inscribe in both letters and poems of his early years.[20] Of course, it could be argued that the few appearances of black characters in his later poetry testify to an increased myopia or discrimination on Stevens's part. However, I find the lack of black characters in his later verse, as opposed to their frequently disturbing presence in the poems composed before World War II, to be a register of Stevens's growing sense of the *textuality* of words, that is, his recognition that language can be, even if not initially intended so, powerfully "con-scripting," and of his subsequent decision not to repeat cultural stereotypes as an easy prompting for poetic production.

Thus, whereas the escalating racist rhetoric in Europe during World War II led Stevens to pen the title "Less and Less Human, O Savage Spirit," his subsequent decisions about if and when and certainly how to represent our own most victimized ethnic group in America point to a "more and more human" spirit on Stevens's part. From this perspective, it is quite significant that in the late poem "The Sick Man," written in 1950, Stevens does overtly examine the disturbing remnants of racism within the larger culture (and possibly within himself as well) in what I regard to be one of his most courageous poems (cited in full below):

Bands of black men seem to be drifting in the air,
In the South, bands of thousands of black men,
Playing mouth-organs in the night or, now, guitars.

Here in the North, late, late, there are voices of men,
Voices in chorus, singing without words, remote and deep,
Drifting choirs, long movements and turnings of sounds.

And in a bed in one room, alone, a listener
Waits for the unison of the music of the drifting bands
And the dissolving chorals, waits for it and imagines

The words of winter in which these two will come together,
In the ceiling of the distant room, in which he lies,
The listener, listening to the shadows, seeing them,

Choosing out of himself, out of everything within him,
Speech for the quiet, good hail of himself, good hail, good hail,
The peaceful, blissful words, well-tuned, well-sung, well-spoken.
(OP, 118)

It might be possible, initially, to interpret this poem as espousing continued racism on Stevens's part, since the (presumably white) men in the North have "voices," whereas the "bands of thousands of black men" in the South are "[p]laying mouth-organs." However, the poem immediately tropes the mouth organs to "guitars"—and, quite notably, from "The Man with the Blue Guitar" to "Of Modern Poetry" and elsewhere, guitars are associated positively by Stevens with artistic production, even with the poet himself. More importantly, Stevens presents the segregation configured in the poem as "sick." The lone listener, who seems to me quite healthy in spirit, desires and "[w]aits for the unison of the music of the drifting bands / And the dissolving chorals." He imagines a time "in which these two will come to-gether" in a future world, as yet unrealized, of peace and health. It is not, to my mind, inconsequential that the word "nigger" is *not* used in this poem: as in "The Greenest Continent," the word "black" is used by Stevens here as a signal of his respect for African Americans, specifically positioned against the larger cultural (and reductive) rhetoric of the very racism he had, admit-tedly at times, uttered in his earlier years. If, indeed, the poem is in some ways an admission of racism articulated intermittently by Stevens himself, he clearly admits that in uttering previously such racist rhetoric, he himself was a "sick man."

It is possible that, once again, Stevens's personal and poetic development registers something of the larger political climate of his time. In an issue of the *New Republic* in the spring of 1950, for example, William Gardner Smith pub-lished a review of three books on African Americans (Lillian Smith's *Killers of the Dream*, Maurice R. Davies's *Negroes in American Society*, and Arnold M. Rose's *The Negro's Morale*), thus indicating a growing concern with the fate of blacks in America after World War II, well in advance of the actual civil rights movement looming but as yet unseen on the horizon.[21] Consequently, I think it is more than likely that Stevens may have also intended the "sick man" of this 1950 poem to refer to the country itself, one that after the chaos of World War II had yet to heal within itself the kind of ethnic divisiveness that had, though with very different ethnic groups in Europe and elsewhere, so clearly helped to fuel the war. Far from indicating the kind of solipsistic thinking that DuRose finds, the last lines in which the listener is "[c]hoosing out of himself" words that are "peaceful, . . . well-tuned, well-sung, well-spoken" resonate with the kind of impassioned responsibility Stevens had come to see as necessary not only for the poet but for the public in our future world.

As Stevens had noted at the end of "Imagination as Value" only two years earlier, the "problems of any artist," as for anyone, "are the problems of the normal and that he needs, in order to solve them, everything that the imagination has to give" (NA, 156). Rather than reiterating his earlier "rage to order," this conclusion evokes a poet vulnerable precisely to the gifts of a new collective imagination—a "necessary angel," as it were, that might resolve the problems still clearly plaguing our polis and cosmos-polis. Here Stevens no longer posits that "masculine voice" that he once cherished as a mask for himself but instead appeals to an imagined collective that will write the "new text of the world," specifically, "a text that *we* shall be needing" (CP, 494–95, my emphasis). In one of his *Adagia* Stevens inscribed what seems to me to be the concomitant desire "[t]o live in the world, but outside existing conceptions of it" (OP, 190)—a cryptic line that, at the beginning of this study, could most assuredly have sounded socially irresponsible. Instead, what I think Stevens means here is precisely the need for the intersection between the private and public imaginations to bring into being a future world we have not yet conceived but that could, or at least should, be a place where we all could truly live. As I interpret it, "The Sick Man" implies that in such a possible world, one born of new conceptions though very much still of this earth, racist rhetoric and the racism it both represents and simultaneously helps to create will have dissolved in a new "unison." If, as DuRose notes, the listener in this poem never enters the song of racial harmony itself, it is because Stevens recognizes that such a song has yet to be sung in reality while clearly desiring that his own words might help to bring into being such a truly communal "revolution."

At the end of this study, I would like to say that the various changes in Stevens's relationship to aesthetics and politics genuinely converge in his late poetry, so that certain resonant poems of his final years can be legitimately read through various critical lenses. Whether biographical, formalist, historicist, feminist, racially concerned, textually focused, or even economically aware, all of them allow us to see the consistency with which Stevens continued to abandon those "masculine myths" he once reified if not deified. The most remarkable poem in these terms is the rarely discussed poem of 1952, "The Hermitage at the Center," a poem that simultaneously *interbraids* (rather than merely substituting) a new vision clearly ethical in both its structure and theme. It appears in the volume *The Rock*, immediately after "Lebensweisheitspielerei," another late poem that specifically asserts that "the proud and the strong have departed," that

Those that are left are the unaccomplished,
The finally human,
Natives of a dwindled sphere.
(CP, 504)

But, as "The Hermitage at the Center" makes clear, the loss of the masculine rhetoric and structures that characterized the first half of the twentieth
century is finally not a dwindling but rather an opening to "future portents"
of a very different ethical structure:

The leaves on the macadam make a noise—
    How soft the grass on which the desired
    Reclines in the temperature of heaven—

Like tales that were told the day before yesterday—
    Sleek in a natural nakedness,
    She attends the tintinnabula—

And the wind sways like a great thing tottering—
    Of birds called up by more than the sun,
    Birds of more wit, that substitute—

Which suddenly is all dissolved and gone—
    Their intelligible twittering
    For unintelligible thought.

And yet this end and this beginning are one,
    And one last look at the ducks is a look
    At lucent children round her in a ring.
(CP, 505–6)

What is most fascinating about this poem is that precisely at the moment
that Stevens imagines the total dismantling of any "center," including authorial domination in the form of that "great thing tottering" that he had
regretted in "Girl in a Nightgown," Stevens produces a new poetic line and
structure that have no other counterpart in the rest of his work. As opposed
to the impasse Stevens encountered in his 1934 poem, "A Rabbit as King
of the Ghosts" (a sociopolitical allegory in which Stevens merely inverted a

hierarchical structure, making the previous "hunted," or oppressed, the new "hunter," or dominating force),[22] here the "last look at the ducks" is finally not at a center or even a look at "her" but rather a look at those "intelligible" and "lucent children *round her in a ring*" (my emphasis). It is not accidental that these "[b]irds of more wit" can "substitute" what Stevens calls "[t]heir intelligible twittering / For [a heretofore] unintelligible thought." As Stevens says in *The Necessary Angel*, it seems to be "one of the peculiarities of the imagination that it is always at the end of an era" (NA, 22), implicitly decreating the existing structures so as to imagine a new and more creative future. Indeed, "this end and this beginning are one"—but only in the sense of a magical, redemptive moment of new creation, certainly not a reinstitution of monolithic singularity.

The poem's doubly entwined structure therefore supports the new sociopolitical narrative that the poem foretells, that is, the "end" of a monumentalizing structure built on a totalizing (and therefore reductive) rhetoric. Yet Stevens refuses here merely to invert the relative positions of the dominant and the dominated, whether sexually, racially, or perhaps even economically conceived. As opposed to "A Rabbit as King of the Ghosts" and its failure to articulate truly "something new under the moon," in "The Hermitage at the Center" not a single bird but multiple birds are "called up by more than the sun" (with a pun on "son"). Even if there were a temptation to impose his own "authorial I" here, as there appears to have been in his 1930s volume *Ideas of Order*, in this poem Stevens clearly wishes that voice and other monumental "rage[s] to order" to collapse altogether in order to reinvent themselves as a far more communal ring embracing polyphonic voices.

Over time, Stevens increasingly recognized the need for a new language, specifically, a communal language, to create a new reality for our modern world—a possibility Stevens well describes in the poem he chose to conclude his *Collected Poems*, "Not Ideas about the Thing but the Thing Itself":

> At the earliest ending of winter,
> In March, a scrawny cry from outside
> Seemed like a sound in his mind.
>
> . . . .
>
> That scrawny cry—it was
> A chorister whose c preceded the choir.
> It was part of the colossal sun,

Surrounded by its choral rings,
Still far away. It was like
A new knowledge of reality.
(CP, 534)

The "chorister" here, who may remind us of that "one tireless chorister" of "a single phrase" in "Notes toward a Supreme Fiction" (CP, 394), is clearly able to utter only a "scrawny cry" in isolation. However, "Not Ideas" assures us that *this* chorister is part of a choir, implying again a new sense on Stevens's part of the necessity of polyphony. Quite provocatively, the old "colossal sun" yields, as in "Hermitage," to a dependence on multiplicity, surrounded, as it is, by "choral rings." Even the textual self-consciousness in the poem is of a different order from that found in his earlier poems, readily dissolving here into a sense of community. Specifically recalling that hyper self-conscious state of textuality in the early "The Comedian as the Letter C," the "chorister" of this final poem, "whose c preceded the choir," heralds (or hopes for), with both its aural and visual puns, something we will soon be both "seeing" and hearing—something revisionary, revolutionary.

Finally, although Stevens is clearly aware here that he can imagine and articulate something *"like* / A new knowledge of reality" (my emphasis), he no longer believes he can or even wishes to try to usher that reality into being through some "rage to order." Rather, it is much to Stevens's credit that over the course of his life he came to realize that the very "violence from within" that he once thought could be a morally justified gesture against a "violence without" (a violence that increased, in its actual political crises, through the most formative years of his career) was itself not only a response to but also an integral and even causal part of that very chaos he had hoped poetry could assuage. Beginning in his early years with a genuinely aesthetic response to other poetries of his time that he found intellectually naive in their allegiance to objectivism, through many subsequent changes, including the need to resist, then register the pain of his times, followed by an awareness of the need for an altogether new normalcy quite different from any historical or poetic structures he had seen before, Stevens's corpus records a remarkable evolution from one of our most private poets to one of the most ethical and visionary poets writing in America during the twentieth century. Although he obviously would not have wished it, the actual emergency of a second world war was precisely the "pressure" that allowed his most revolutionary poetics finally to emerge in forms often quite different from the "antiobjectivist" stance with which he began and with ever-expanding ramifications in ethical and social concerns that remain acutely important to us today in our own politically torn world. As opposed to any naive opposition to "objectivism," certainly as opposed to some ivory-tower privileging of a detached imagination, Stevens's poetics became increasingly committed to the genuinely revolutionary idea summarized in one of his *Adagia*, that is, that "[r]eality is the object seen in its greatest common sense" (OP, 202), where "common sense" appeals to our collective desire for health rather than to a mere cliché. If, in fact, as he himself noted in his early dismissal of Williams, we are never interested in a poet until we are convinced he or she has something to say, the previous study demonstrates that all along, and ever increasingly, Stevens had more to say than we have easily or readily recognized. Nearly fifty years after his death, perhaps we are finally coming close to hearing, and to seeing, the genuinely revolutionary import of his words.

NOTES

PREFACE

1. I am indebted to Adrienne Rich for this term, which I am borrowing from *What Is Found There* (194).

INTRODUCTION

1. See my *Part of the Climate* and "The 'Founding Mother,'" 248–66.
2. Conte, *Unending Design*, 7. Among my favorites in a truly staggering proliferation of publications on the subject noted in the text is Von Hallberg, *Politics and Poetic Value*, which draws largely on essays published in *Critical Inquiry* 13, no. 3 (1987).
3. See, for example, Levinson and Mailloux, eds., *Interpreting Law and Literature*. For an excellent work devoted specifically to Stevens, poetry, and law, see Grey, *The Wallace Stevens Case*.
4. For excellent works in this regard, see Lane, "The Poetics of Legal Interpretation," 269–84; and Rasula, "The Politics of, the Politics In," 315–22.
5. Note that although written in 1821 in response to Thomas Love Peacock's *The Four Ages of Poetry*, the "Defence" was not published until 1840.
6. Shelley, "A Defence of Poetry," 1073, my emphasis.
7. Ibid., 1074.

8. For a succinct but excellent summary of this moment of literary history, see Whittemoore, *Little Magazines*, 33.
9. See, for example, Lauter, *Canons and Context*.
10. Litz makes this point about Stevens's poetry in "Introduction," 83–84.
11. Dickie, *Lyric Contingencies*, 75, 2.
12. Moramarco, "Stevens, Rich, and Merrill," 3–4.
13. As early as 1940 Brooks (accurately) noted that "probably none [of the poets] . . . in our time has had to face so continually the charge that his work was precious—obvious ivory-tower ware" (Untitled statement, 29).
14. Armstrong, "Major Man and His Muses," 747.
15. Dickie, *Lyric Contingencies*, 145. An especially helpful discussion of Stevens's complicated responses to Communism (including his earlier appreciation of it) is to be found in Cleghorn, *Wallace Stevens' Poetics*. In addition, Richardson offers a much-needed discussion of Stevens's subsequent rejection of Communism in *Wallace Stevens: The Later Years*.
16. Bishop, from "Crusoe in England," in *Elizabeth Bishop*, 162.

1. POEMS AGAINST HIS CLIMATE

1. This particular word is taken from "The Irrational Element in Poetry," reprinted in OP, 230.
2. The earliest parameters of this debate were first summarized in Riddel's "The Climate of Our Poems," discussed at length in my *Stevens and Simile* and traced in great detail in Schaum's *Wallace Stevens and the Critical Schools*.
3. See Mills, "Wallace Stevens: The Image of the Rock," in which he discusses the "transfer of the generative power from the divine Logos" to "the human spirit" achieved in these lines (100).
4. Though deconstructive approaches to language have been a commonplace for over three decades, it is still useful to see Derrida, "Structure, Sign, and Play," perhaps the earliest and clearest statement of this position (first given as a paper in 1966).
5. Riddel, *The Clairvoyant Eye*, 154, 65.
6. Bloom, *Wallace Stevens: The Poems of Our Climate*, 150, 140–41.
7. For example, William Carlos Williams had published his *Collected Poems: 1921–1931* as well as *An Early Martyr and Other Poems* immediately prior to the period we are examining here—in 1934 and 1935, respectively.
8. See MacLeod, *Wallace Stevens and Company*, esp. chap. 6; Heinzelman, "Williams and Stevens," 85–113; and Strom, "The Uneasy Friendship," 291–98.
9. Reprinted in OP, 254–57.
10. Heinzelman, "Williams and Stevens," 95; Williams cited in MacLeod, *Wallace Stevens and Company*, 90.

11. Walker, *The Transparent Lyric*, xii. Walker convincingly demonstrates that Stevens and Williams cannot be critically distinguished as "polar opposites" (ix). Yet despite the similarities that we may be able to perceive in the lyrics of each poet, Stevens still placed himself in opposition to Williams's poetry. It is this ironic "source" with which I am concerned here.

12. Greene, *The Light in Troy*, 18.

13. As Albert Cook points out in *Figural Choice in Poetry and Art*, "perfection" is one of Williams's favorite words (137).

14. With regard to the inherently ironic "reflective" nature of consciousness and language, see DeMan's discussion of the "conscious dialectic" of "reflective poetic consciousness" in "Intentional Structure of the Romantic Image," 65–77. It is worth noting that Stevens challenges the idea of "perfection" in a number of poems during this period, including "Of Bright & Blue Birds & the Gala Sun" (1940):

> It is there, being imperfect, and with these things
> And erudite in happiness, with nothing learned
> That we are joyously ourselves.
>
> (CP, 248)

15. Among the more amusing of the "sub-texts" to Stevens's poems is the relation of Williams's 1937 review of *The Man with the Blue Guitar and Other Poems* to Stevens's preface for Williams. In each, the one accuses the other of having aged. For a lively discussion of the lengthy "dialogue" between these two poets, see Heinzelman, "Williams and Stevens."

16. "Canonica," *Southern Review* 4 (1938): 382–95.

17. See MacLeod, *Wallace Stevens and Modern Art*, 95, as well as the larger discussion of this group of poems (79–102).

18. See Williams, "Against the Weather," 196–218. Interestingly, Williams notes that "Dante was the agent of art facing a time and place and enforcement which were his 'weather.' Taking this weather as his starting point, as an artist, he had to deal with it to affirm that which to him was greater than it. By his structure he shows his struggle" (205).

19. In this regard we might also consider *For Whom the Bell Tolls*, a novel published immediately after the actual onset of a war that, like Wallace Stevens, Ernest Hemingway did not want us to join. Although Robert Jordan of Hemingway's novel may be highly romanticized, both as the hero and as a lover, the overall tone of the novel is finally quite grim, almost passionately antiwar, as Hemingway ruthlessly exposes the absurdities and atrocities of both political camps (Fascists and Communists) that not only occurred in reality in Spain but also would be enacted (as Hemingway prophesied) in the atrocious powers and alignments of World War II. See, in particular, Hemingway, "A Program for U.S.

Realism," written from Spain. Put in this context, the lines cited above from the 1939 "Forces, the Will & the Weather" virtually summarize the moral quandary of Hemingway's novel.

20. Perhaps Stevens is even referring to those stinging prophecies Hemingway had written for and published in *Esquire* in the late 1930s, not only of the next world war, which he saw as the next stage of Spain's "civil" war, but also of Japan's involvement to come, of the civil war looming on the horizon in China, and of continued European expansion and concomitant warfare in Africa. See "Notes on the Next War," 205–12.

21. I am, of course, alluding to Perloff's well-known essay "Revolving in Crystal," 41–63.

2. A CRITICAL MISPRISION

1. The most famous of the early criticisms against Stevens for lacking social awareness is Winters, "Wallace Stevens, or the Hedonist's Progress," 88–119. However, the negative evaluation of Stevens's lack of social relevance had wide currency among Stevens's contemporaries.

2. See Burnshaw, "Turmoil in the Middle Ground," 41–42; and Perloff, "Revolving in Crystal," 41–63. To be fair, Burnshaw's critique of Stevens is not as negative as our critical tradition has represented it. And Perloff's essay, which raises the important question about the value of humanistic ideals in our technological and violent world, represents Stevens as responding to the Second World War in his poetry and his politics but in deeply disturbing ways. Nevertheless, the charge that Stevens's work was "obvious ivory-tower ware" has continued to be leveled against Stevens over the subsequent decades. Among the earliest of critics who have made an argument for Stevens's poetry having a specifically political content are Riddel, " 'Poets' Politics,' " 118–32, and his "Wallace Stevens' *Ideas of Order*," 328–51; Howard, "Wallace Stevens and Politics," 52–75; and the larger argument of Pearce, whose *Continuity of American Poetry* laid the early groundwork for political readings of Stevens. The best of recent critics in this regard includes Berger, *Forms of Farewell*; Lentricchia, *Ariel and the Police*; Cook, *Poetry, Word-Play, and Word-War*; Filreis, *Wallace Stevens and the Actual World*; Longenbach, *Wallace Stevens: The Plain Sense of Things*; and Cleghorn, *Wallace Stevens' Poetics*.

3. Perloff, "Revolving in Crystal," 47, 43.

4. The reference is to the title of Perloff's essay "Revolving in Crystal," which is itself borrowed from Stevens's "Notes toward a Supreme Fiction." It would be possible to add to Stevens's place, or lack of place, in history at this moment by noting not only that he published "Variations on a Summer Day" in the *Kenyon Review* 2 (winter 1940): 72–75, during World War II but also that he wrote that

he had deliberately "excluded" any genuine thinking about the war in that poem (L, 346). However, as he also makes clear in the same letter to Hi Simons, his "own main objective" during that time "is to do" the "kind of thinking" that, for someone sitting under the Maginot Line, would "make the situation reasonable, inevitable and free from question" (L, 346). I find this markedly different from his earlier stance, as in his 1935 marginalia written in a copy of Marianne Moore's poetry, where he specifically praises her for not having any people in her work. On the inside back flap, Stevens writes, "There are no people in this book. Thank God. This is a great relief. On the other hand, there are more animals than there are in Barnum & Bailey's big show" (see her *Selected Poems*, currently held at the Huntington Library). Certainly, thinking about the Maginot Line in 1940 is markedly different from that earlier 1935 stance.

5. Again, we could buttress this interpretation of Stevens by noting that in his *Adagia* he writes, "Money is a kind of poetry" (OP, 191).

6. Holly Stevens identifies this review as Jean Wahl's review of John Crowe Ransom's *Selected Poems*.

7. The quotations in the text are taken from two successive articles entitled "The Situation in American Writing" that appeared in the the summer 1939 and fall 1939 issues of *Partisan Review* (PR). Admittedly, not all the writers responded with such aesthetic detachment as those cited in the text. Even so, Harold Rosenberg's one-line answer to what the writer's social obligation should be in war creates, with its ironic tone, something of the very detachment that the semantic content of his answer attempts to belie: "In time of war the writer has at least the obligation *not to find the 'good side' of it*" (PR, 49).

8. PR, 125–26. This article, which takes the form of a letter signed by the League for Culture, Freedom, and Socialism, argues that while "[w]ar has become *the* issue," still, "[o]nly the German people can free themselves of the fascist yoke. The American masses can best help them by fighting *at home* to keep their own liberties." It then calls upon "all American artists, writers and professional workers to join" in a "statement of implacable opposition to this dance of war in which Wall Street joins with the Roosevelt administration." In this regard it is especially provocative to note Frese's observation in "Poetic Prowess in *Brunanburh* and *Maldon*" that another critic, Traugott Lawlor, traces in *The Battle of Brunanburh* ways in which the "art of war and weapon-making" are linked "to the craft of making books and poems, all of it joined on the intersection of words and weapons that produce a carving of history" (85).

9. One such "repression" can be seen in the combination of the introduction to Stevens that Vendler wrote for the new *Harper American Literature* anthology (where she writes that those of his poems that attempted to "treat social issues, including the war in Ethiopia and World War II . . . achieved no real stylistic

success," that Stevens "remained, for the rest of his career, preeminently a poet of the inner life") and her choice of poems to be included in the anthology (a choice that notably excludes all but one of the poems I will discuss here) (2: 1528). In fact, the only poems reprinted in that collection from this remarkably productive period of Stevens's career are "Arrival at the Waldorf" and "No Possum, No Sop, No Taters," the latter of which I will discuss briefly.

10. Interestingly, as early as 20 September 1939 (the date upon which this letter was written) Stevens conveyed his own understanding that a second war with Germany would affect everyone in all places: "I hope that this war will not involve you in your far-off home, but even in Ceylon you are bound to feel some of the effects of this unbelievable catastrophe" (L, 342–43).

11. Pratt, "What Can We Defend?" 267 (24 February 1941).

12. I have borrowed this phrase from Bloom, *Wallace Stevens: The Poems of Our Climate:* "A poem begins because there is an absence. An image must be given, for a beginning, and so that absence is ironically called a presence. Or, a poem begins because there is too strong a presence, which needs to be imaged as an absence, if there is to be any imaging at all" (79).

13. However, following Stevens when discussing the omnipresent importance of language or rhetoric as actual politics before its "failure" in the form of war, Schaum notes, "In its most basic sense, the theatre of war has always been a 'theatre of trope'" ("Views of the Political," 177).

14. These two poems were first published as "Two Theoretic Poems," *Hika* 6, no. 7 (May 1940): 6–7.

15. Filreis notes that William Van O'Connor asserts that in "A Dish of Peaches in Russia" Stevens is "attacking 'the unnaturalness of attempting to give one's allegiance to an abstract system'" (*Wallace Stevens and the Actual World,* 274), an interpretation that both Filreis and I regard as reductive. See O'Connor, "The Politics of a Poet," 205. Among most Stevens critics, this poem is rarely mentioned.

16. "Illustrations of the Poetic as a Sense" appeared in *Poetry* 54, no. 4 (July 1939): 177–83.

17. Originally a Latinate word meaning the membranous coverings of rosette flowers, involucrum has been extended by Riffaterre to mean a noticeable textual aberration that requires a "double-reading" to understand its full complexity. See Riffaterre, *Semiotics of Poetry.*

18. Frese, *An Ars Legendi,* 94, citing Riffaterre, *Semiotics of Poetry,* 2.

19. See Filreis, *Wallace Stevens and the Actual World,* 6–10.

20. Compare Stevens's sense of the "fatal unity of war" with an article published in the *New Republic* entitled "Global Strategy": whereas in World War I "a common Allied front was a reality," "[t]oday the Allied fronts are separated by thousands of miles and the goal of unified strategy is to coordinate the several

fronts" (40 [12 January 1942]). As this article suggests, one of the more confusing and catastrophic facts of the Second World War was that there was no longer an identifiable "front" but instead a "fatal unity" involving many fronts, at many places, all at one time.

21. Note that in addition to other writers mentioned in the preceding chapter and in addition to Hemingway's warnings against U.S. involvement in several essays written before the war (see chapter 1, note 19), by June 1941 Charles Lindbergh was announcing that the British had already lost the war and that at that time "college students were holding 'peace' rallies and strikes against participation in a foreign war" on U.S. university campuses (Reynolds, *Hemingway: The Final Years*, 41).

22. See Berger, *Forms of Farewell*, 35ff.; Perloff, "Revolving in Crystal," 42–48. Something of a similar dilemma in interpreting Stevens can be found even in his annotations and markings in other books. For instance, the marginalia of Arnold's *Essays in Criticism*, now held at the Huntington, reveals Stevens's interest in very *disinterested* criticism, since he has marked Arnold's assertion that "[c]riticism must maintain its independence of the practical spirit and its aims" (34); yet it also shows Stevens's interest in the political function of the "creative power," since he has also marked the passage in which Arnold praises Burke for bringing "thought to bear upon politics" (14).

23. Mauron, *Aesthetics and Psychology*, 25. Stevens's personal and heavily marked copy of this book is held at the Huntington Library.

24. My specific context for initially describing the larger historical context surrounding Stevens's verse is the *New Republic*, which the letter addressed to José Rodríguez Feo, cited in the preceding chapter, indicates that Stevens was reading and which he seems to have been in the habit of reading for some time (see L, 184–85).

25. In "Call Japan's Bluff!" Bisson notes that at least from the perspective of Japan, "Greater East Asia" must now be, for economic and pragmatic reasons, "carved from territories now held by China, Britain, Holland, the United States and the Soviet Union" (579 [3 November 1941]). However, the use of the word "Asia" to mean the equivalence of "Japan" is even more specifically indicated in "What Next in Asia?" an article singly focused on "What Sort of War" might happen between the United States and Japan in the "deadlock" at which the two countries had "arrived" (750 [8 December 1941]) following Japan's own use of the word in its propagandistic slogan "Asians for Asia." Ironically, the date of this issue of the *New Republic* was one day after Japan had actually bombed Pearl Harbor, since, as with many of our current journals, it had gone to press before the announced newsstand date.

26. In addition to Bisson's article above, see Hale, "Hold the Pacific!" 394–96 (29 September 1941); and the editorial "Stay Tough with Japan," 323 (15 September

1941). However, in the first edition of the *New Republic* to be printed after the bombing of Pearl Harbor, the editorial entitled "Our War" makes the point: "It is being widely said now that we must not forget that our real enemy is not Japan but Hitler. That is not true. Our real enemy is the coalition arrayed against us" (812 [15 December 1941]).

27. In what I have found to be possibly the most bitterly ironic publication of this period in time, the *New Republic* of 8 December 1941 (again, the issue that had gone to press before the catastrophic events of 7 December 1941) contains a special section of several contemporary "Writers under Thirty." For a nation that was in reality hearing of the bombing of Pearl Harbor over the radio and that was declaring war against the Japanese on the actual date of this publication, Barker's "Notes from the Largest Imaginary Empire" must not have been perceived with the irony I think he intended: "[N]o one could understand the Japanese without knowledge of the fact that they gestated for only six months in the womb. This . . . is why, when they travel in trains, first they remove their shoes, then they curl up on the seat in the posture of the embryo. . . . It also explains the public acts of urination and defecation. . . . And most of all it explains the fundamental sense of inferiority that vents itself in militarism, the cultivation of supercilious silences and the invention of tortures" (794). In a similar fashion, at the end of the war, one week after the atomic bombs had been dropped on Hiroshima and Nagasaki, the *New Republic* was advertising a book by John F. Embree entitled *The Japanese Nation* (Farrar and Rinehart) this way: "It tells where the Japanese came from; why the Japanese regard themselves as descendants of God; why the Japanese are one of the most regimented people on earth; why the Japanese are able to regard themselves as liberators, not aggressors." In bold type the advertisement asks, "Are they [the Japanese] capable of democracy?" (195 [13 August 1945]). In addition, see Fussell, *Wartime*, esp. chap. 9, "Typecasting," 115–29, for an excellent discussion of the way in which the Japanese were typecast during this period as animals, such as bats "of an especially dwarfish but vicious species" (120).

28. The racial slur included in this poem—and Stevens's criticism of that slur and racism itself—is discussed in the final chapter, "More and More Human."

29. Hale, "After Pearl Harbor," 816–17 (15 December 1941), my emphasis.

30. See Bevis, *Mind of Winter*, whose entire work explores the possible relation of Stevens's thought to Buddhist thought.

31. See Cornell, "From the Lighthouse," 1687–1714. Consider, in addition, that less than a month after Pearl Harbor, Quincey Howe blamed authors and publishers as well as the military for America's unpreparedness on 7 December 1941: "Our books and authors as well as the people who publish and share them bear their share of responsibility" for not being alert to the actual danger that ensued ("Books about the War," *New Republic*, 25 [5 January 1942]). Within this

context, "Notes toward a Supreme Fiction"—and the imperatives it declaims as a "must"—indicates the degree to which Stevens once again was waging his own fight against what he considered to be a naive and finally wrong sense of the responsibility of the writer in a time of war.

32. See Nakashima, "Concentration Camp: U.S. Style," 822–23 (15 June 1942).

33. See the editorial "Bombing Civilians in Europe," 494 (19 April 1943).

34. Auden, "The Poet and the City," 178.

35. The "shift / Of realities" that "could be wrong," which Stevens had earlier anticipated in "Forces, the Will & the Weather," is made especially clear in this instance by comparing "Bombing Is a Quiet Business," written by a London reporter in 1941, to another London report, "Life under the Robot Bombs," written in 1944. In the first, John Strachey gives a very eerie picture in which the bombing of London is not only peculiarly quiet—he writes that the bombs falling through the air make more noise than when they detonate on the ground—but that in general the unaffected go on about their normal business (617–19 [10 November 1941]). In the second, however, Michael Young exposes the dehumanization of "Life under the Robot Bombs" by reporting that glass is the biggest danger in bombing. Quoting another article from the *New Statesman*, he writes, "Powdered glass may be driven deep into you; doctors tell me that you may literally have to have your face cut right away to save your life" (271 [4 September 1944]).

3. FORMAL RESISTANCE

1. The relation of Dante's formal structure to the violent civil strife surrounding him is a commonplace in Dante criticism. An excellent summary of that connection is found in Quinones, "Foundation Sacrifice and Florentine History," 10–19.

2. In this regard, it seems quite to the point that Fussell has noted that the year 1942, when "all looked black" for the Allies (including America)—the year in which Stevens composed "Notes toward a Supreme Fiction"—was "thus the moment of the greatest need" for "uplifting" literature; see *Wartime*, 235.

3. Greene, *The Light in Troy*, 4–5.

4. Ibid., 5.

5. Williams, "Against the Weather." Interestingly, in this essay Williams uses Dante as an example of a poet's finding a structural form to match his beliefs.

6. See Richardson, *Wallace Stevens: The Early Years*, 472–73.

7. See L, 26, 44, 101, 822. Richardson also discusses these facts in her biography, concluding that Stevens had an "epic desire to rival Dante's *Divine Comedy*," a desire most manifested in the "attitude of the comedian" (*Wallace Stevens: The Early Years*, 29).

8. See Richardson's discussion of "The Comedian as the Letter C" (*Wallace Stevens: The Early Years*, 518); Wentersdorf, "Wallace Stevens, Dante Alighieri and the Emperor," 197–204; and Cook, *Poetry, Word-Play, and Word-War*, 202–5, 273–76, 311, respectively. Somewhat surprisingly, Cook does mention Dante in relation to "Notes" but only in passing (*Poetry, Word-Play, and Word-War*, 215, 219).

9. Cook, in particular, reads "Notes" in relation to Genesis, though she incorporates other anterior texts as well (*Poetry, Word-Play, and Word-War*, 217ff.). In *Wallace Stevens: The Poems of Our Climate* Bloom links "Notes" to all the authors listed in the text above as well as to Nietzsche, Schopenhauer, and Pierce (167ff.).

10. Greene, *The Light in Troy*, 51.

11. Riddel, *The Clairvoyant Eye*, 167–68, my emphasis.

12. Cited in Lensing, *Wallace Stevens: A Poet's Growth*, 141.

13. Richardson, *Wallace Stevens: The Later Years*, 212.

14. Perloff, "Revolving in Crystal," 47. I should clarify that while she calls attention to the aesthetic arrangement of this poem, as noted in the previous chapter Perloff finds Stevens's preoccupation with the form of the poem—and with how it would be literally printed—somewhat alarming during a time of such catastrophic violence. It is worth noting that she reads the number of lines differently from Riddel, who finds 659 lines by including the coda. Finally, Richardson implies that in general Stevens's use of tercets is an adaptation of Dante's *Divine Comedy* (*Wallace Stevens: The Later Years*, 100).

15. The introduction, prosodically different from the rest of the text in being comprised of eight unseparated lines, is to be distinguished from the rest of the text for an additional reason to be discussed below. Note that while Stevens was normally quite "loose" about the organization of his longer poems, according to Lensing, "The distribution of parts and stanzas in 'Notes toward a Supreme Fiction' was to be much more symmetrical than was usually the case" (*Wallace Stevens: A Poet's Growth*, 142–45). In fact, the symmetry of the poem (which roughly parallels that of Dante) remained exact, with the exception of "a sort of epilogue" (L, 407), which constitutes the final, unnumbered canto of the poem.

16. See Cook, *Poetry, Word-Play, and Word-War*, 267–94.

17. Note that Cook sees "An Ordinary Evening in New Haven" as beginning with the phrase "heaven-haven," as found in Gerard Manley Hopkins (ibid., 12–13).

18. In canto 18 of the *Paradiso*, Dante and Beatrice directly face each other. Thereafter, Beatrice shows Dante further wonders of Paradise, which include actual letters of the alphabet shaped in the heavenly skies by flying birds. (They spell out "diligite justitiam" and "qui judicatis terram.")

19. The contemporaneous concern with form may be seen in Focillon's *The Life of Forms in Art*, a work notably translated into English the year Stevens was writing the poem with which we are concerned (1942). In fact, as Leggett notes,

Stevens read the book carefully, making heavy annotations, and provided his own index of the book's contents, which includes this intriguing line: "Form is a mobile life in a changing world 5" (*Wallace Stevens and Poetic Theory*, 149). Also, as MacAllister notes in the introduction to the well-known translation of the *Inferno* by John Ciardi, "That Dante had ample reason to feel that the political chaos of his day was a prime menace to man's pursuit of happiness should be quite apparent. It should also be understandable that he used the *Comedy* to protest this evil and to suggest a remedy" (xx). Surely the same could be said of Wallace Stevens.

20. However, I must stress that Stevens's appeal to the "abstract" here is neither a glib or simple reversal of Dante's use of the historically concrete nor finally an expression of an aesthetics deliberately indifferent to the actual world. As Stevens writes in his *Adagia*, "Abstraction is part of idealism. It is in that sense that it is ugly," and "[i]n poetry at least the imagination must not detach itself from reality" (OP, 187).

21. See Arensberg, *The Cryptography of Dante*, esp. 55–114, where he finds a number of convincing (and a number of dubious) "signatures" by Dante in his poem.

22. Actually, if Stevens *did* inscribe his whole name, Wallace Stevens, this very fact could still be a witty subversion on his part. Whereas Arensberg finds "Dante Poeta" in many lines of the *Comedy* (with attention to his "divine" vocation and without his earthly designated "last name"), Stevens perhaps decided deliberately to "encrypt" precisely his secular or terrestrial label, the earthly "Wallace Stevens."

23. Rosenthal and Gall, *The Modern Poetic Sequence*, 363.

24. This controversial account of Stevens's late conversion is recorded in Brazeau, *Parts of a World*, 294–96.

25. Elizabeth Bishop, "At the Fishhouses," in Bishop, *Elizabeth Bishop: The Complete Poems*, 66.

4. THE POET IN/UNDER HISTORY

1. Focillon, *The Life of Forms in Art*, 1.
2. Cook, *Poetry, Word-Play, and Word-War*, 215.
3. Stevens, *Transport to Summer*.
4. We should note, however, that despite the formal resistance to war that Stevens attempted to create in "Notes toward a Supreme Fiction," the possible irony he intended with a poem so effusively titled as "God Is Good. It Is a Beautiful Night" is supported by the fact that he also wrote "Of Bright & Blue Birds & the Gala Sun" in the same year he wrote "Of Modern Poetry" (1940), just as he also wrote "Holiday in Reality" in the same year he wrote "Esthétique du Mal" (1944), his most bitter poem.

5. Altieri, *Painterly Abstraction*, 331.

6. In this regard, Lentricchia's reading of "Anecdote of the Jar" as signaling basically the background of imperialistic attitudes in the West is particularly provocative; see *Ariel and the Police*, 3–27.

7. See Frank Doggett's discussion of this poem in *Stevens' Poetry of Thought*, 65–66, especially in conjunction with Dorothy Emerson's "Wallace Stevens' Sky that Thinks" (71–84).

8. Straight, "Hitler's Guerillas over Here," 481–83 (13 April 1942).

9. Notably, in a letter written to Stevens on 14 October 1941, Van Geyzel says, "One can't be very enthusiastic about Roosevelt-Churchill, but at least it will be better than Hitler. No wonder most people are so stupid about this war, when all our fighting is over a choice of evils" (letter held at the Huntington Library).

10. Cook, *Poetry, Word-Play, and Word-War*, 200.

11. In an earlier edition of the *New Republic*, one editorial explains that Hitler was managing to conquer Europe successfully because no one could take seriously Hitler's stated intention to eliminate the Jewish people and to "grade" the remaining conquered peoples according to race and blood, precisely because such an intention was so appalling. See "Germany's Plan for Japan," 392 (29 September 1941). However, the editorial entitled "Hitler's Speech" (8 March 1943) not only announces that Hitler is, in fact, fulfilling that intention but that he intends to extend this practice of "elimination" to all the peoples of Europe who stand in his way of gaining total domination (300).

12. See "The New Zionism," 304 (8 March 1943).

13. See the editorial "Bombing Civilians in Europe," 494 (19 April 1943).

14. See Dickie, *Lyric Contingencies*, 145.

15. In this regard Stevens's sympathy with Communist ideas of equality as opposed to actual domination, whether by class or individuals, is almost exactly the same as that of Ernest Hemingway at approximately the same time. In fact, both men leaned toward Communism as opposed to Fascism. But, just as Hemingway would come to show in *For Whom the Bell Tolls* the equally corrupt or exaggerated use of ideological rhetoric and the consequence of abuse of power in reality for both sides, Stevens too would reject the monolithic rhetoric of Communism during the same period. In fact, Hemingway himself had been criticized in 1936 in reviews of *Farewell to Arms* for not "being more concerned for the working class" (much as Stevens had been criticized as well)—notably, the same year that Stevens and Hemingway had the well-known but dubiously described "boxing match" at Key West (see Reynolds, *Hemingway: The 1930s*, 220–21). Despite this altercation, it is important to note that both writers respected each other and both would subsequently praise each other—precisely for being great poets. As Stevens wrote to José Rodríguez Feo on 26 November 1945, "No one can read more than a few pages of Hemingway without becoming

very much aware of the fact that he is a poet" (L, 520). Stevens went so far as to say in a 1945 letter to Van Geyzel that he thought "it likely that he [Hemingway] will write a kind of poetry in which the consciousness of reality will produce an extraordinary effect" (L, 500).

Nonetheless, by 1938, and given his growing disgust with Fascism as being "a lie," Hemingway, at least briefly, committed himself to the Communist rebellion (the Republic) in Spain: "Hemingway, after years of insisting upon his political disinterest, was now publicly committed to antifascism, if not to communism itself" (see Reynolds, *Hemingway: The 1930s*, 38; Hemingway, "Fascism Is a Lie," 4 [22 June 1937]). Even so, after first donating and raising money for the Republican side of the Spanish civil war, Hemingway would eventually come to reject both sides of the war in his novel written after actually seeing and covering the war itself and would then go on to urge the United States to avoid entering into the next world war that he predicted as coming.

16. See Frese, "Poetic Prowess in *Brunanburh* and *Maldon*," as discussed in chapter 2, note 8.

17. Cook, *Poetry, Word-Play, and Word-War*, 182.

18. In fact, "Gigantomachia" first appeared in Boggs, ed., *American Decade* (1943), within a panoply of poems written by poets such as Elizabeth Bishop, John Ciardi, Langston Hughes, Robinson Jeffers, Muriel Rukeyser, and William Carlos Williams, among others, suggesting that either for Stevens or the editor, this poem has a certain importance in his overall work of the decade.

19. Although working with Stevens in a very different context, "perspectivist reaction against the reality-imagination dichotomy" is one of the many competing theoretical positions that Grey finds in Stevens's poetry (*The Wallace Stevens Case*, 69).

20. As a critical term for interpretation, *excoriation* will be explained and explored at length in chapter 7, most particularly with regard to canto 7 of this poem, "How Red the Rose that Is the Soldier's Wound."

21. As Kern and Fussell have variously demonstrated, soldiers fighting in the wars of this century have felt themselves to be essentially passive and emasculated victims. In less gendered terms, Hemingway had warned that fighting in a coming second world war would be futile—that it would be experienced as being "enslaved," with the sure consequence of death, given our new technological developments: "They wrote in the old days that it is sweet and fitting to die for one's country. But in modern war there is nothing sweet nor fitting in you dying. You will die like a dog for no good reason" ("Notes on the Next War" [September 1935], reprinted in White, ed., *By-Line*, 209). Such rhetoric as that of those "old days" is specifically decried by Stevens in his 1945 poem "Description without Place" as "arrogant" seemings "on the youngest poet's page," false seemings that glorify the "death of a soldier" as the "more

than human commonplace of blood" (CP, 340–41). This is a critical change in our heroic tradition, with many important psychological consequences that Stevens appears here to be fully capable of imagining, even if far removed from the actual experience of combat. In essence, this change is the ironic defeat, at least for Stevens, during this period of political chaos and collapse, of the epic tradition of poetry that "sings of man and war." As he had said in 1940, even if what we need is a "new belief," the world in general was passing during World War II into "a stage in which the primary sense is a sense of helplessness" (L, 350)—a metaphorically "feminine" stage, to be discussed at greater length in the following chapters.

22. Filreis, *Wallace Stevens and the Actual World*, 46–48.

23. Ibid., 48.

24. Richardson, *Wallace Stevens: The Later Years*, 230.

25. Riddel, *The Clairvoyant Eye*, 202.

26. In terms of this clearly New Critical reading (a position that, of course, Riddel would come to abandon), it is interesting to note that Reynolds has argued that even as early as December 1940, "Modernism" (perhaps as typified by James Joyce's *Portrait of the Artist as a Young Man*) "had become a historical period, and what would follow was not yet written," a fact that haunted Hemingway's writings as well (*Hemingway: The Final Years*, 36). Note that Berger does later discuss this poem in relation to World War II in *Forms of Farewell* but also in relation to other poems such as "The Auroras of Autumn" that I think represent a very different and subsequent stage in Stevens's changing aesthetics.

27. See respective discussions of this poem in these various works, though most particularly in Longenbach, *Wallace Stevens: The Plain Sense of Things*, 239.

28. Hemingway, "Voyage to Victory" (22 July 1944), reprinted in White, ed., *By-Line*, 355.

29. Riddel, *The Clairvoyant Eye*, 204, cited in Cook, *Poetry, Word-Play, and Word-War*, 191.

30. Cook, *Poetry, Word-Play, and Word-War*, 192.

31. Ibid., 213.

32. Ibid., 211–12.

33. Ibid., 195–96.

34. Ibid., 197. Others, including Longenbach and Filreis, have recognized the subversive relation of this canto to Dante.

35. It is also uncannily similar, I should add, to one of the imagined and horrible ways of dying in a second world war that Hemingway included in this 1936 warning against joining the impending war. Projecting that the coming war will begin in Africa as European powers battle over space for commerce and domination, Hemingway warns, "What happens to a man, once he is dead, is of little matter, but the carrion birds of Africa will hit a wounded man. . . . The

first thing an *Italian soldier* [my emphasis, given the setting of the poem at hand] should be told" (though Hemingway insists that the following is precisely what a propagandistic leader *will not* tell his soldiers) "is to roll over on his face if he is hit and cannot keep moving. There is a man alive today who did not know that rule. . . . While he was unconscious the vultures got his eyes and he woke in the stabbing blinding pain with the stinking, feathered shuffle over him and, beating at them, rolled onto his face in time to save half of it" ("Notes on the Next War" [September 1935], reprinted in White, ed., *By-Line*, 209–10).

5. A SLOW (RE)TURN

1. See Norris, "Germany after Defeat," 703 (22 May 1944), in which he also says, "I think that it ought to be said that what I say about Germany, with certain modifications necessary under the differences in conditions, should serve as a model for both Japan and Italy."
2. Special section of the *New Republic* (unnumbered), 27 March 1944, 427.
3. William Carlos Williams's "All the Fancy Things," in *Collected Poems*. In this regard it is interesting to compare Stevens's late "The Green Plant" (CP, 506) and the "barbarous green / Of the harsh reality of which it is part."
4. Picasso, "Conversation avec Picasso," 173, cited in Weston, "The Artist as Guitarist," 115. See also Steiner, *The Colors of Rhetoric*, 180–83.
5. See Derrida, *Of Grammatology*, 46–47.
6. As T. R. B.'s "After the Charter Is Ratified" (102–3 [23 July 1945]) makes clear, the expectation of calamity was in the air during the summer of 1945. But as he also writes in "Atomic Anxieties" (20 August 1945), not only was "the revelation" more shocking "than anyone had expected," but "[i]n a short week man learned that he had at last found how to blow himself up. . . . The next big war may very well blow us out of the solar system. At any rate, we now have our choice" (222).
7. "Poland, Russia, and America," 35–37 (8 January 1945); ibid., map, 37.
8. *More Poems for Liadoff* appeared in the *Quarterly Review of Literature* 3, no. 2 (fall 1946): 105–13.
9. Although he interprets the poem somewhat differently, Frankenberg suggestively asks of this poem, "Do we repeat, *in mass disaster*, the tragic inspiration of the artist?" in a critical study published only four years after the end of World War II ("Variations on Wallace Stevens," 254, my emphasis). Interestingly, the metaphor of the atomic bomb as a "firecracker" had been established, almost immediately after the bombs were dropped, in an article published in the *New Republic*; this will be discussed in the text below.
10. Among the other poems obviously concerned with war in this series are "A Woman Sings a Song for a Soldier Come Home," "Mountain Covered with

Cats," and "Extraordinary References." The series ends, notably, with "Attempt to Discover Life," a poem that points to Stevens's later postwar mentality that poetry must somehow now return to the "normal."

11. "Words about Death" is taken from page 7 of the handwritten manuscript entitled *From Pieces of Paper* (dated 1955 by the Huntington Library), a page that also bears the title of the obviously political poem, "Asides on the Oboe." The other two titles are taken from pages 10 and 12, respectively, of the same manuscript. Quoted with permission. George S. Lensing transcribes one of these phrases (which I transcribe as "Why the Poet Doesn't Smile") as "Why the Past Doesn't Smile" in his edition of *From Pieces of Paper* included in *Wallace Stevens: A Poet's Growth*, 180.

12. See Jaffe, "How the Bomb Came to Be," esp. 347 (17 September 1945).

13. T. R. B., "Atomic Anxieties," 222 (20 August 1945). In this article, the writer notes with something of a horror that only one month before he had concluded that the "'evolution of destructiveness is still accelerating, and the Japanese have something to learn'" (cited from "After the Charter Is Ratified," 103 [23 July 1945]). He then states that "the revelation, when it came was incomparably greater than anyone had expected" (222). The piercing irony of what this writer experienced, in reflecting upon his own words, seems to me very similar to what Stevens must have felt in remembering of his letter of 25 June 1945 (also discussed in the text above).

14. Bliven, "The Bomb and the Future," 210–12 (20 August 1945). Note that this issue begins with the editorial "The Perils of Victory," which announces that instead of experiencing exultation at the end of the war, Americans were "strangely dazed": "Gladness for the safety of loved ones in the armed services, hopes for a more normal mode of living, did not quite shut out a sense that some of the greatest implications of the event had not yet become clear" (203).

15. In Berger's *Forms of Farewell*, "The Auroras of Autumn" is interpreted precisely as a response to the explosion of the atomic bomb (34–80), an interpretation that Richardson enthusiastically supports as well in the second volume of her own biography of Stevens.

16. See Berger, *Forms of Farewell*, 81–110.

17. Southard, "Escape to Reality," 136–37.

18. Williams, "Against the Weather," 199.

6. OPENING THE FIELD

1. *The Rock*, of course, is the concluding book of poetry that appears for the first time as the last book in the 1954 volume, *Collected Poems*.

2. See the entirety of Schaum, ed., *Wallace Stevens and the Feminine*.

3. Gelpi, "The Transfiguration of the Body," 8–11, 17–18. For Rich's indebtedness to and complaints about Stevens, see her *What Is Found There*, esp. 190–205.

4. Jarrell, "The Collected Poems," 55–73. There he says of Stevens, "There is about him, under the translucent glazes, a Dutch solidity and weight; he sits surrounded by all the good things of this earth, with rosy cheeks and fresh clear blue eyes, eyes not going out at you but shining in their place, like fixed stars" (67). A similar sense of Stevens's magnanimity is found in Moore's review of *Harmonium* ("Well Moused, Lion," 84–91) and Monroe's review of the same volume ("A Cavalier of Beauty," 322–27).

5. See Brazeau, *Parts of a World*, in which Naaman Corn says not only that "Mr. Stevens was very dominating" and that "[n]o one dictated anything else but Mr. Stevens" but that he also caused his wife to "quit talking" by "snapping" at her whenever she spoke (248). With regard to Stevens's "scripting" of Elsie, see Richardson, *Wallace Stevens: The Early Years*, esp. chap. 5.

6. Halliday, "Stevens and Heterosexual Love," 135–55.

7. Bates has handled these and other facts about Stevens's relationship with his wife with great tact in *Wallace Stevens: A Mythology of Self* and in "Stevens in Love," 231–55.

8. This phrase is taken from Gilbert and Gubar, *The Madwoman in the Attic*. See all of chapter 2, "Infection in the Sentence," for a lengthy discussion of the "ill" consequences of our largely phallocentric language (45–92).

9. With regard to Stevens's attitude toward "A High-Toned Old Christian Woman," see Lensing's remark: "She is never permitted to present her side in the poem, though the speaker ironically pretends to represent that side for her" ("'A High-Toned Old Christian Woman,'" 46).

10. The first edition of *Ideas of Order* opened with "Sailing after Lunch," a poem that makes the possible spiritual content and intent of the first edition much more obvious. However, just as the first edition (1935) was being published, Stevens suffered several well-known critical attacks, most of which condemned his lack of social awareness. (The most famous of these is Stanley Burnshaw's review of *Ideas of Order*, "Turmoil in the Middle Ground.") The second edition (1936), which begins with a new poem written after these reviews ("Farewell to Florida"), might correctly be seen as Stevens's attempt to make his poetry somewhat more socially relevant.

11. John Serio has suggested to me that the speaker of this poem is a female, though I find the possibility of the speaker's being male much more consistent with the rest of his verse. As an interesting parallel, consider Frank Lentricchia's (I think) faulty analysis of Stevens's early sketch in which a young man opens a picture of his sweetheart only to find it is an image of himself as an act in which the feminine image is "empathetically assumed," not "trivialized in macho perspective" (*Ariel and the Police*, 222). Despite Lentricchia's dismissal of

Gilbert and Gubar, I do not think that these critics would interpret this sketch in such a sympathetic way. The replacement of the female with the male image would rightly, I believe, signal an instance of total phallocentric mastery. Similarly, if the speaker of "Two Figures" *were* a female, we would have a poem of extreme empathy rather than of male mastering. However, the other possibility, in which the female presence is silenced by masculine ruminations, seems much more consistent with the poetry of Stevens discussed thus far.

12. Walsh, *Concordance to Wallace Stevens*. It is also interesting that, combined, forms of speaking and forms of voice appear 285 times in Stevens's corpus. Conversely, and very curiously, words for Stevens are almost never "written"— a mere twenty times, in fact. However, the idea of poetry as *written* rather than *spoken* involves a later sense of textualization, even conscription on Stevens's part, to be explored in chapter 7.

13. As an amusing point of comparison for the climate of the times, see the journal *Others: The Spectric School* 3, no. 5 (1917): 10–11, which contains a number of poems by Elizah Hay, including "Spectrum of Mrs. X," "Of Mrs. Y," "Of Mrs. Z," and "Of Mrs. & So Forth," that are similar in tone to those by Stevens I am discussing here, albeit in a well-known hoax parodying various poetic and artistic "schools" of the time.

14. While there are many critics who have discussed "The Idea of Order at Key West" in such positive terms, see in particular Borroff, "Wallace Stevens: The World and the Poet," 9; Mizejewski, "Images of Woman," 13–21.

15. Baker, "Wallace Stevens and Other Poets," 373–96. Frank Doggett and Susan Weston have both called attention to the influence of Jung on Stevens; see Doggett, *Stevens' Poetry of Thought*, 38–45; Weston, *Wallace Stevens: An Introduction to the Poetry*.

16. I have discussed this aspect of "The Idea of Order at Key West" at length in "Elizabeth Bishop: Perversity as Voice," 31–49.

17. An interesting point of comparison here is William Carlos Williams's essay "For a New Magazine," in which he says that new literature should be "the machine of women and men," thereby not only mentioning women as authors but putting them first. However, he goes on, much like Stevens, to say, "Poetry is thus everything that a man of the greatest power could wish to encompass" (30–32 [March 1929]). Similarly, George Oppen asserts that Ezra Pound was, at least in the early years, "caught in the idea of being 'macho' though the word didn't exist at that time. He was going to be the pounding poet, the masculine poet" (cited in Hatlen and Mandel, "Poetry and Politics," 27).

18. Cited in Reynolds, *Hemingway: The 1930s*, 4, my emphasis.

19. Richardson, *Wallace Stevens: The Later Years*, 167.

20. In this regard, Kessler finds that Crispin of "The Comedian as the Letter C" accepts his "masculine and feminine natures" late in the poem. He also argues

that the androgynous nature of the "creative imagination" also informs the invocation of "Le Monocle de Mon Oncle" (*Images of Wallace Stevens*, 66, 238n15). In contrast, Lentricchia interprets the possibly androgynous nature of the speaker in "Final Soliloquy of the Interior Paramour" as something much more suspect: "a self-sustaining bisexual unity" that is specifically *not* an "enhanced" individuation (*Ariel and the Police*, 222–23).

21. Curiously enough, Morrison has noted in the chapter on Hemingway entitled "Disturbing Nurses and the Kindness of Sharks" that a consistent preoccupation with nurses (whether male or female) figures throughout his corpus (*Playing in the Dark*, 61–91).

22. Cleghorn rightly notes that my earlier work on this subject misinterpreted or, more rightly, ignored the ending of Stevens's essay (*Wallace Stevens' Poetics*, 173).

23. In this regard, Arensberg discusses the usual figuration of the female in Stevens as an *absence* (" 'Golden Vacancies,' " 36–41).

24. I am indebted to Frank Doggett and Dorothy Emerson for this observation.

25. Lentricchia, *Ariel and the Police*, 217.

26. Ruddick, *Maternal Thinking*; McFague, *The Body of God*.

7. PLANETS ON THE TABLE

1. Actually, it was a mere eleven years after Stevens's death that Derrida would first announce in his 1966 paper, "Structure, Sign, and Play," what he called a monumental "event" of changed consciousness.

2. See Schaum, *Stevens and the Critical Schools*, for an excellent summary of how Stevens's poetry, once thought of as successfully joining reality and the imagination among several major critics, rapidly became interpreted as demonstrating numerous tenets of deconstruction.

3. Richardson, *Wallace Stevens: The Later Years*, 313, my emphasis.

4. Cook, *Poetry, Word-Play, and Word-War*, 209.

5. L, 469, cited in Cook, *Poetry, Word-Play, and Word-War*, 189.

6. For a succinct summary of these illustrations and Stevens's reactions to them, see MacLeod's recent catalog, *Painting in Poetry/Poetry in Painting: Wallace Stevens and Modern Art*. There MacLeod summarizes the illustrations as seeming "to show a figure weaving at a loom who becomes increasingly entangled in the web until eventually he or she is inextricably interwoven with it (as on the title page)" (37). While I concur with the sense of weaving on the title page illustration, I would say that other illustrations—if, indeed, they continue the theme of weaving—suggest that the chaos of the world is "weaving" or entrapping various males and females. In sum, the chaos of World War II is engulfing individual identity—this is the "Esthétique du Mal." I should also clarify here that although certain letters by Stevens might make it

appear that he did not initially care for the illustrations, MacLeod's discussion in the catalog makes it clear that Williams's illustrations were indeed a particular selling point for Stevens with Cummington Press: "'The illustrations were part of a package intended to snare the poem, to attract Stevens's proposal'" (37; MacLeod is citing Harry Duncan, founder of the press). In addition, Stevens eventually found the published book, with illustrations, "marvelous" (L, 515).

Perhaps more germane here is the fact that Williams illustrated the work of several other poets with drawings that are distinctly different in style and tone from those he used for Stevens's poem. For example, his illustration for the cover of William Carlos Williams's *The Wedge* specifically uses somewhat balanced and pleasingly circular lines to capture the "undulations" and "physicality" William Carlos Williams associated with poetry rather than the highly rigid and encroaching lines of *Esthétique du Mal*, which are, in turn, reminiscent of certain drawings of Paul Klee, one of Stevens's favorite artists. I am indebted to Jeffrey Peterson for his insights into the cover illustration for *The Wedge* and am paraphrasing particulars from a letter to me dated 30 October 1994.

7. I should clarify that subsequent to my giving the paper on which this essay is based, Glen MacLeod did introduce the illustrated *Esthétique du Mal* in his art exhibit noted above. There he succinctly notes, "Countering critics who read *Esthétique du Mal* as an attempt to escape from or transcend the pain of life, Brogan interprets the poem as Stevens's recognition of 'the inefficacy of aesthetic consolation in time of war'" (42n142). MacLeod's own description of the illustrations, noted above, would seem to concur with my interpretation that these illustrations and the poem they accompany reflect pain, not resistance.

8. I have discussed this unlikely connection at length in "Planets on the Table."

9. As a humorous aside, I should note that Cleghorn says this "student" of "Esthétique du Mal" could well be Hemingway (*Wallace Stevens' Poetics*, 138), though as a "student of the sublime" I can hardly agree that Hemingway is a real possibility in this lyrical plot.

10. Although such a tenet is clearly implied in the various works of Hélène Cixous, among others, a particularly accessible essay in this regard is Ortner's, "Is Female to Male as Nature Is to Culture?"

11. Specifically, the abstract lines of Paul Klee's *Suicide on the Bridge* and *Murder* (reprinted in *Broom* 4, no. 3 [1923]) show the crushing power of time, in the form of clocks, on the individual body and spirit in much the same way that Kern has related the imposition of World Standard Time in 1912 to the global anonymity of the Great War (*The Culture of Time and Space*). The similarity in style of Klee's drawings to those of Wightman Williams when illustrating this

particular poem (written at the height of World War II) as opposed to other illustrations seems intentional, as noted above.

12. As Filreis rightly notes, " 'How Red the Rose' was indeed plucked from the other cantos [of *Esthétique du Mal*] and hailed as a 'war poem' in the professional sense, and set out on a career all its own" (*Wallace Stevens and the Actual World*, 137). Specifically, it appeared in Eberhart and Rodman, eds., *War and the Poet*, and again in Williams, ed., *The War Poets*. Yet as Filreis implies, this canto has a more biting and satirical edge when placed in the context of its larger poem, a fact that is even more pronounced when seen in the illustrated version.

13. Berger, *Forms of Farewell*, 17.

14. Cook, *Poetry, Word-Play, and Word-War*, 204.

15. See, again, Hemingway's "Notes on the Next War," (September 1935), reprinted in White, ed., *By-Line*, 205–12.

16. I am here summarizing the overall thesis of Cook's entire chapter on this poem, "War and Normal Sublime," 189–213, as a point of contrast for my own interpretation.

17. Longenbach, *Wallace Stevens: The Plain Sense of Things*, 240.

18. Cowley, "War and the Poets," 258–60.

19. I am indebted to Professor Dolores Warwick Frese, who suggested this specific term as a way to describe the ironic component and intention of this canto. Although "excoriate" literally means to remove the skin from, the convergence of that term, with the obvious pun on "cord-" as "heart," is particularly salutary in this instance as well as in Yeats's "The Lover Tells of the Rose in His Heart" (*The Collected Poems*, 54). I find it of particular interest that Longenbach would compare "Esthétique du Mal" to Yeats's "Nineteen Hundred and Nineteen" (*Wallace Stevens: The Plain Sense of Things*, 241). In that poem, written at the close of World War I, Yeats had himself come to challenge his own previous poetic consolations about and valorizations of war in a very similar way that I am asserting Stevens came to do during World War II. In addition, Cook finds that canto 14 of *Esthétique du Mal*, the one about the "logical lunatics," is indebted to Yeats's "Easter 1916," in which hearts have become stone from rigid commitments to a political side (*Poetry, Word-Play, and Word-War*, 210).

20. Yeats, *The Collected Poems*, 36–37, emphasis in original.

21. PR, 40.

22. William Carlos Williams, "Asphodel, that Greeny Flower," in Rosenthal, ed., *The William Carlos Williams Reader*, 74.

23. I have discussed the uncanny similarity of Stevens's sense of *textuality* to Elizabeth Bishop, June Jordan, and Adrienne Rich in "Planets on the Table," 255–78.

8. MORE AND MORE HUMAN

1. The phrase in quotations marks is taken from Rich, *What Is Found There*, 194.
2. See Halliday, *Stevens and the Interpersonal*; DuRose, "Racial Domain and the Imagination of Wallace Stevens," 3–22; and DuPlessis, " 'Darken Your Speech,' " 43–83.
3. For DuPlessis's reading of the *blackbird*, see " 'Darken Your Speech,' " 55; however, the entire section on Stevens (48–62) is unusually harsh in her reading of racist slurs. Admittedly, certain moments in Stevens (such as his infamous use of the words "coons" and "darkies") are more than problematic and finally irresolvable other than being instances of racist slurs. However, I do not think that every instance of Stevens's use of the words "dark" and "black" has racial (or racist) connotations any more than I think that every instance of his setting a poem in the Caribbean is an instance of what DuPlessis calls "a site in which whiteness can be gathered" (51).
4. Halliday, *Stevens and the Interpersonal*, 182n29.
5. Rich, *What Is Found There*, 196, 201–2, 204.
6. Ibid., 204–5, Rich's emphasis.
7. See Burt, "Charles Baxter, August Kleinzahler, Adrienne Rich," 121, referring to Bromwich, "The Poet's Burden," 33–37.
8. Among the many poets DuPlessis covers in this regard are Ezra Pound, Gertrude Stein, Mina Loy, E. E. Cummings, and William Carlos Williams.
9. DuPlessis, " 'Darken Your Speech,' " 51, 50.
10. Ibid., 56.
11. Ibid., 50.
12. DuRose, "Racial Domain and the Imagination of Wallace Stevens," 5.
13. Ibid., 5, my emphasis.
14. Ibid., 19.
15. See *Green Hills of Africa* (1935) and *Out of Africa* (1937). While Hemingway has also been indicted for being racist (specifically by Morrison in *Playing in the Dark*), consider the following remarkably similar passages about the inappropriate imposition of white European and/or American colonizers in Africa as counterparts to what Stevens was doing in "The Statue in Africa." In his 1935 "fictional memoir" *Green Hills of Africa*, Hemingway laments that a "continent ages quickly once we come. The natives live in harmony with it. But the foreigner destroys, cuts down the trees, drains the water, so that the water supply is altered and in a short time the soil, once the sod is turned under, is cropped out and, next, it starts to blow away as it has blown away in every old country" (284). In her 1937 memoir, *Out of Africa* (which Hemingway once called the best book on Africa he had read), Isak Dinesen (Baroness Von Blixen) writes, "It is more than their land that you take away from the people [of

Africa], whose Native land you take. It is their past as well, their roots and their identity," adding that "not very long ago, at a time that could still be remembered, the Natives of the country had held their land undisputed, and had never heard of the white men and their laws. Within the general insecurity of their existence the land to them was still steadfast" (359, 361).

Since Hemingway will undoubtedly be accused again of racism with the recent publication of the posthumous *True at First Light*, it is worth noting that in that work, late in his life, Hemingway still incorporated similar insights into the damage white colonizers were causing: "The old days [in Africa] were supposed to have been simpler but they were not; they were only rougher. The Reservation was rougher than the Shamba. Maybe not. I did not really know but I did know that the white people always took the other people's lands away from them and put them on a reservation where they could go to hell and be destroyed as though they were in a concentration camp. Here they called the reservations the Reserves and there was much do-gooding about how the natives, now called the Africans, were administered" (209). It seems obvious that Hemingway is criticizing precisely the construction of "Africanism" (with a devastating allusion and/or comparison to the "concentration camps" of World War II) that Morrison accuses him of consciously perpetuating (*Playing in the Dark*, 63–91). While I have defended Hemingway against this charge in "*True at First Light*: A New Look at Hemingway and Race," 199–224, I am asserting here that Stevens, writing of Africa in the 1930s as well, has been similarly misunderstood as perpetuating if not condoning racism.

16. Cleghorn, *Wallace Stevens' Poetics*, 119. Cleghorn makes this comparison of the statue in this poem with the jar in "Anecdote of the Jar" (131), but he is clearly referring to the well-known argument first made by Lentricchia in *Critical Enquiry* and then reprinted in *Ariel and the Police*.

17. Similarly, in terms of the ethical dimensions of Stevens's *Esthétique du Mal*, I have argued in "Planets on the Table" that in "Brazil, January 1, 1502," Bishop, as "with Adrienne Rich after her[,] . . . unmasks the destructive and totalizing power of language—of cliché—as something that fabricates or weaves over or suffocates the world in a way similar to what Stevens does" in his bleakest of wartime poems (269).

18. Cleghorn, *Wallace Stevens' Poetics*, 126–27.

19. "Primitivism" might be said to have begun with certain of Picasso's sculptures and cubist paintings as early as 1908, though the ethical stance of his art has been recently called into question in terms quite similar to the point I am making here about the reductive nature of primitivism. By the 1920s, however, from the real-life figure of Josephine Baker to any number of appearances of primitivism in both the verbal and visual arts as something erotically charged and fetishized, the supposed aesthetic appreciation of "primitivism" was being

called into question on both sides of the Atlantic. I am suggesting that Stevens was aware of that questioning and was bringing it to bear on the fetishized Ananke that I believe whites, not blacks, would project as a self-justifying alternative to their use of the word we find so offensive. In this regard, see Stovall, *Paris Noir.*

20. That Stevens had been willing to sign early letters to his wife (1908) with "Sambo" is a well-known fact that Richardson, DuPlessis, and DuRose (among others) have reported.

21. Smith, "Status of the Negro," 27–28.

22. I have developed the contrast between "A Rabbit as King of the Ghosts" and "The Hermitage at the Center" at greater length in "Wrestling with Those 'Rotted Names,'" 19–39.

BIBLIOGRAPHY

Altieri, Charles. *Painterly Abstraction in Modernist American Poetry.* Cambridge: Cambridge University Press, 1989.

Arensberg, Mary. " 'Golden Vacancies': Wallace Stevens' Problematics of Place and Presence." *Wallace Stevens Journal* 10, no. 1 (1986): 36–41.

Arensberg, Walter. *The Cryptography of Dante.* New York: Knopf, 1921.

Armstrong, Tim. "Major Man and His Muses." *Times Literary Supplement,* 10 July 1987, 747.

Arnold, Matthew. *Essays in Criticism.* New York: Macmillan, 1865.

Auden, W. H. "The Poet and the City." In James Scully, ed., *Modern Poetics,* 167–82. New York: McGraw-Hill, 1965.

Baker, Howard. "Wallace Stevens and Other Poets." *Southern Review* 1 (fall 1935): 373–96.

Barker, George. "Notes from the Largest Imaginary Empire." *New Republic* 105, no. 23 (8 December 1941): 791–94.

Bates, Milton. "Stevens in Love: The Woman Won, the Woman Lost." *ELH* 48, no. 1 (spring 1981): 231–55.

———. *Wallace Stevens: A Mythology of Self.* Berkeley: University of California Press, 1985.

Berger, Charles. *Forms of Farewell: The Late Poetry of Wallace Stevens.* Madison: University of Wisconsin Press, 1985.

Bevis, William W. *Mind of Winter: Wallace Stevens, Meditation, and Literature.* Pittsburgh, Pa.: University of Pittsburgh Press, 1989.

Bishop, Elizabeth. *Elizabeth Bishop: The Complete Poems, 1927–1979.* New York: Farrar, Straus and Giroux, 1984.

Bisson, T. A. "Call Japan's Bluff!" *New Republic* 105, no. 18 (3 November 1941): 579–81.

Bliven, Bruce. "The Bomb and the Future." *New Republic* 113, no. 8 (20 August 1945): 210–12.

Bloom, Harold. *Wallace Stevens: The Poems of Our Climate.* Ithaca, N.Y.: Cornell University Press, 1976.

Boggs, Tom, ed. *American Decade.* New York: Cummington Press, 1943.

"Bombing Civilians in Europe." *New Republic* 108, no. 16 (19 April 1943): 494.

Borroff, Marie. "Wallace Stevens: The World and the Poet." In Marie Borroff, ed., *Wallace Stevens: A Collection of Critical Essays,* 1–20. Englewood Cliffs, N.J.: Prentice-Hall, 1963.

Brazeau, Peter. *Parts of a World: Wallace Stevens Remembered.* New York: Random House, 1983.

Brogan, Jacqueline Vaught. "Elizabeth Bishop: Perversity as Voice." *American Poetry* 7, no. 2 (1990): 31–49.

———. "The 'Founding Mother': Gertrude Stein and the Cubist Phenomenon." In Joyce W. Warren and Margaret Dickie, eds., *Challenging Boundaries: Gender and Periodization,* 248–66. Athens: University of Georgia Press, 2000.

———. *Part of the Climate: American Cubist Poetry.* Berkeley: University of California Press, 1991.

———. "Planets on the Table: From Wallace Stevens and Elizabeth Bishop to Adrienne Rich and June Jordan." *Wallace Stevens Journal* 19, no. 2 (1995): 255–78.

———. *Stevens and Simile: A Theory of Language.* Princeton, N.J.: Princeton University Press, 1986.

———. "*True at First Light:* A New Look at Hemingway and Race." *North Dakota Quarterly* 68, nos. 2–3 (2001): 199–224.

———. "Wrestling with Those 'Rotted Names': Wallace Stevens' and Adrienne Rich's Revolutionary Poetics." *Wallace Stevens Journal* 25, no. 1 (2001): 19–39.

Bromwich, David. "The Poet's Burden." *New Republic* 209, no. 8 (8 November 1993): 33–37.

Brooks, Cleanth. Untitled statement. *Harvard Advocate* 127, no. 3 (December 1940): 29.

Burnshaw, Stanley. "Turmoil in the Middle Ground." *New Masses* 17 (1 October 1935): 41–42.

Burt, Stephen. "Charles Baxter, August Kleinzahler, Adrienne Rich: Contemporary Stevensians and the Problem of 'Other Lives.'" *Wallace Stevens Journal* 24, no. 2 (2000): 115–34.

Cleghorn, Angus. *Wallace Stevens' Poetics: The Neglected Rhetoric.* New York: Palgrave, 2000.

Conte, Joseph M. *Unending Design: The Forms of Postmodern Poetry.* Ithaca, N.Y.: Cornell University Press, 1991.

Cook, Albert. *Figural Choice in Poetry and Art.* Hanover, N.H.: University Press of New England for Brown University, 1985.

Cook, Eleanor. *Poetry, Word-Play, and Word-War in Wallace Stevens.* Princeton, N.J.: Princeton University Press, 1988.

Cornell, Drucilla. "From the Lighthouse: The Promise of Redemption and the Possibility of Legal Interpretation." *Cardozo Law Review* 11, nos. 5–6 (1990): 1687–1714.

Cowley, Malcolm. "War and the Poets." Review of *The War Poets: An Anthology of War Poetry of the Twentieth Century,* edited by Oscar Williams. *New Republic* 113, no. 9 (27 August 1945): 258–60.

DeMan, Paul. "Intentional Structure of the Romantic Image." In Harold Bloom, ed., *Romanticism and Consciousness,* 65–77. New York: W. W. Norton, 1970.

Derrida, Jacques. *Of Grammatology.* Trans. Gayatri Chakravorty Spivak. Baltimore, Md.: Johns Hopkins University Press, 1976.

———. "Structure, Sign, and Play in the Discourse of the Human Sciences." In Richard Macksey and Eugenio Donato, eds., *The Structuralist Controversy: The Languages of Criticism and the Sciences of Man,* 247–72. Baltimore, Md.: Johns Hopkins University Press, 1972.

Dickie, Margaret. *Lyric Contingencies: Emily Dickinson and Wallace Stevens.* Philadelphia: University of Pennsylvania Press, 1991.

Dinesen, Isak. *Out of Africa* (1937). New York: Vintage, 1987.

Doggett, Frank. *Stevens' Poetry of Thought.* Baltimore, Md.: Johns Hopkins Press, 1966.

DuPlessis, Rachel Blau. " 'Darken Your Speech': Racialized Cultural Work of Modernist Poets." In Aldon Lynn Nielsen, ed., *Reading Race in American Poetry,* 43–83. Urbana: University of Illinois Press, 2000.

DuRose, Lisa. "Racial Domain and the Imagination of Wallace Stevens." *Wallace Stevens Journal* 22, no. 1 (spring 1998): 3–22.

Eberhart, Lt. Comdr. Richard, and M. Sgt. Selden Rodman, eds. *War and the Poet.* New York: Devin-Adair, 1945.

Emerson, Dorothy. "Wallace Stevens' Sky that Thinks." *Wallace Stevens Journal* 9, no. 2 (1985): 71–84.

Filreis, Alan. *Wallace Stevens and the Actual World.* Princeton, N.J.: Princeton University Press, 1991.

Focillon, Henri. *The Life of Forms in Art.* Trans. C. Beeches Hogan and George Kulber. New Haven, Conn.: Yale University Press, 1942.

Frankenberg, Lloyd. "Variations on Wallace Stevens." In Lloyd Frankenberg,

Pleasure Dome: On Reading Modern Poetry, 197–267. Boston: Houghton Mifflin, 1949.

Frese, Dolores Warwick. *An Ars Legendi for Chaucer's Canterbury Tales: Re-Constructive Reading.* Gainesville: University of Florida Press, 1991.

———. "Poetic Prowess in *Brunanburh* and *Maldon:* Winning, Losing and Literary Outcome." In Phyllis Rugg Brown et al., eds., *Modes of Interpretation in Old English Literature*, 83–99. Toronto: University of Toronto Press, 1986.

Fussell, Paul. *Wartime: Understanding and Behavior in the Second World War.* New York: Oxford University Press, 1989.

Gelpi, Albert. "The Transfiguration of the Body: Adrienne Rich's Witness." *Wallace Stevens Journal* 25, no. 1 (spring 2001): 7–18.

"Germany's Plan for Japan." *New Republic* 105, no. 13 (29 September 1941): 392.

Gilbert, Sandra M., and Susan Gubar. *The Madwoman in the Attic: The Woman Writer and the Nineteenth-Century Imagination.* New Haven, Conn.: Yale University Press, 1979.

"Global Strategy." *New Republic* 106, no. 2 (12 January 1942): 40.

Greene, Thomas. *The Light in Troy: Imitation and Discovery in Renaissance Poetry.* New Haven, Conn.: Yale University Press, 1982.

Grey, Thomas C. *The Wallace Stevens Case: Law and the Practice of Poetry.* Cambridge, Mass.: Harvard University Press, 1991.

Hale, William Harlan. "After Pearl Harbor." *New Republic* 105, no. 24 (15 December 1941): 816–17.

———. "Hold the Pacific!" *New Republic* 105, no. 13 (29 September 1941): 394–96.

Halliday, Mark. "Stevens and Heterosexual Love." *Essays in Literature* 13, no. 1 (spring 1986): 133–55.

———. *Stevens and the Interpersonal.* Princeton, N.J.: Princeton University Press, 1991.

Hatlen, Burton, and Tom Mandel. "Poetry and Politics: A Conversation with George and Mary Oppen." In Burton Hatlen, ed., *George Oppen: Man and Poet*, 23–50. Orono: University of Maine, 1981.

Heinzelman, Kurt. "Williams and Stevens: The Vanishing-Point of Resemblance." In Dave Oliphant and Thomas Zigal, eds., *WCW and Others*, 85–113. Austin: Humanities Research Center, 1985.

Hemingway, Ernest. "Fascism Is a Lie." *New Masses*, 22 June 1937, 4.

———. *Green Hills of Africa* (1935). New York: Touchstone, 1996.

———. "Notes on the Next War: A Serious Topical Letter." *Esquire* (September 1935). Reprinted in William White, ed., *By-Line: Ernest Hemingway*, 205–12. New York: Simon and Schuster, 1998.

———. "A Program for U.S. Realism." *Ken* 2, no. 4 (1938). Reprinted in William White, ed., *By-Line: Ernest Hemingway*, 290–93. New York: Simon and Schuster, 1998.

————. *True at First Light*. New York: Scribner's, 1999.

————. "Voyage to Victory." *Collier's*, 22 July 1944. Reprinted in William White, ed., *By-Line: Ernest Hemingway*, 340–55. New York: Simon and Schuster, 1998.

————. "Wings Always over Africa: An Ornithological Letter." *Esquire* (January 1936). Reprinted in William White, ed., *By-Line: Ernest Hemingway*, 229–35. New York: Simon and Schuster, 1998.

"Hitler's Speech." *New Republic* 108, no. 10 (8 March 1943): 300.

Howard, David. "Wallace Stevens and Politics." *Renaissance and Modern Studies* 21 (1977): 52–75.

Howe, Quincey. "Books about the War." *New Republic* 106, no. 1 (5 January 1942): 25–26.

Kern, Stephen. *The Culture of Time and Space, 1880–1918*. Cambridge, Mass.: Harvard University Press, 1983.

Kessler, Edward. *Images of Wallace Stevens*. New Brunswick, N.J.: Rutgers University Press, 1972.

Jaffe, Bernard. "How the Bomb Came to Be." *New Republic* 113, no. 12 (17 September 1945): 344–47.

Jarrell, Randall. "The Collected Poems of Wallace Stevens." In Randall Jarrell, *The Third Book of Criticism*, 55–73. New York: Farrar, Straus and Giroux, 1969. First published in *Yale Review* 44 (March 1955): 340–53.

Lane, Jessica. "The Poetics of Legal Interpretation." In Sanford Levinson and Steven Mailloux, eds., *Interpreting Law and Literature: A Hermeneutic Reader*, 269–94. Evanston, Ill.: Northwestern University Press, 1988.

Lauter, Paul. *Canons and Context*. New York: Oxford University Press, 1991.

Leggett, B. J. *Wallace Stevens and Poetic Theory: Conceiving the Supreme Fiction*. Chapel Hill: University of North Carolina Press, 1987.

Lensing, George S. "'A High-Toned Old Christian Woman': Wallace Stevens' Parable of the Supreme Fiction." *Notre Dame English Journal* 8, no. 1 (fall 1972): 43–49.

————. *Wallace Stevens: A Poet's Growth*. Baton Rouge: Louisiana State University Press, 1986.

Lentricchia, Frank. *Ariel and the Police: Michel Foucault, William James, and Wallace Stevens*. Madison: University of Wisconsin Press, 1988.

Levinson, Sanford, and Steven Mailloux, eds. *Interpreting Law and Literature: A Hermeneutic Reader*. Evanston, Ill.: Northwestern University Press, 1988.

Litz, Walton A. "Introduction." *Wallace Stevens Journal* 13, no. 2 (1989): 83–84. Special issue: *Stevens and Politics*.

Longenbach, James. *Wallace Stevens: The Plain Sense of Things*. New York: Oxford University Press, 1991.

MacAllister, Archibald T. "Introduction." In Dante Alighieri, *Inferno*, xiii–xxvi. Trans. John Ciardi. New York: New American Library, 1954.

MacLeod, Glen. *Painting in Poetry/Poetry in Painting: Wallace Stevens and Modern Art* (catalog). Sidney Mishkin Gallery, Baruch College, 17 March–27 April 1995.

————. *Wallace Stevens and Company: The Harmonium Years, 1913–1923*. Ann Arbor: UMI Research Press, 1983.

————. *Wallace Stevens and Modern Art: From the Armory Show to Abstract Expressionism*. New Haven, Conn.: Yale University Press, 1993.

Mauron, Charles. *Aesthetics and Psychology*. Trans. Roger Fry and Katherine John. London: Leonard and Virginia Woolf, Hogarth Press, 1935.

McFague, Sallie. *The Body of God*. Minneapolis: Fortress Press, 1993.

Mills, Ralph J., Jr. "Wallace Stevens: The Image of the Rock." In Marie Borroff, ed., *Wallace Stevens: A Collection of Critical Essays*, 96–110. Englewood Cliffs, N.J.: Prentice Hall, 1963.

Mizejewski, Linda. "Images of Woman in Wallace Stevens." *Thoth* 14 (1973–74): 13–21.

Monroe, Harriet. "A Cavalier of Beauty." *Poetry* 23, no. 6 (March 1924): 322–27.

Moore, Marianne. *Selected Poems*. New York: Macmillan, 1935.

————. "Well Moused, Lion." *Dial* 76 (January 1924): 84–91.

Moramarco, Fred. "Stevens, Rich, and Merrill: An Introduction." *Wallace Stevens Journal* 25, no. 1 (2001): 3–6.

Morrison, Toni. *Playing in the Dark: Whiteness and Literary Imagination*. Cambridge, Mass.: Harvard University Press, 1992.

Nakashima, Ted. "Concentration Camp: U.S. Style." *New Republic* 106, no. 24 (15 June 1942): 822–23.

"The New Zionism." *New Republic* 108, no. 10 (8 March 1943): 303–4.

Norris, George W. "Germany after Defeat." *New Republic* 110, no. 21 (22 May 1944): 703–5.

O'Connor, William Van. "The Politics of a Poet." *Perspective* 1, no. 4 (1948): 204–7.

Ortner, Sherry. "Is Female to Male as Nature Is to Culture?" In Michelle Zimbalist Rosaldo, ed., *Woman, Culture, and Society*, 67–87. Stanford, Calif.: Stanford University Press, 1974.

"Our War." *New Republic* 105, no. 24 (15 December 1941): 811–12.

Pearce, Roy Harvey. *Continuity of American Poetry*. Princeton, N.J.: Princeton University Press, 1961.

"The Perils of Victory." *New Republic* 113, no. 8 (20 August 1945): 203–7.

Perloff, Marjorie. "Revolving in Crystal: The Supreme Fiction and the Impasse of Modernist Lyric." In Albert Gelpi, ed., *Wallace Stevens: The Poetics of Modernism*, 41–64. New York: Cambridge University Press, 1985.

Picasso, Pablo. "Conversation avec Picasso." Ed. Christian Zervos. *Cahiers d'Art* 10 (1935): 173.

"Poland, Russia, and America." *New Republic* 112, no. 2 (8 January 1945): 35–37.

Pratt, Fletcher. "What Can We Defend?" *New Republic* 104, no. 8 (24 February 1941): 267–69.

Quinones, Ricardo. "Foundation Sacrifice and Florentine History." *Lectura Dantis* 4 (1989): 10–19.

Ransom, John Crowe. *Selected Poems.* New York: Knopf, 1945.

Rasula, Jed. "The Politics of, the Politics In." In Robert Von Hallberg, ed., *Politics and Poetic Value,* 315–22. Chicago: University of Chicago Press, 1997.

Reynolds, Michael. *Hemingway: The Final Years.* New York: Norton, 1999.

———. *Hemingway: The 1930s.* New York: Norton, 1997.

Rich, Adrienne. *What Is Found There: Notebooks on Poetry and Politics.* New York: Norton, 1993.

Richardson, Joan. *Wallace Stevens: The Early Years, 1879–1923.* New York: William Morrow, 1986.

———. *Wallace Stevens: The Later Years, 1923–1955.* New York: Beech Tree, 1988.

Riddel, Joseph N. *The Clairvoyant Eye: The Poetry and Poetics of Wallace Stevens.* Baton Rouge: Louisiana State University Press, 1965.

———. "The Climate of Our Poems." *Wallace Stevens Journal* 7, no. 2 (fall 1983): 59–75.

———. " 'Poets' Politics'—Wallace Stevens' *Owl's Clover." Modern Philology* 56 (1958): 118–32.

———. "Wallace Stevens' *Ideas of Order:* The Rhetoric of Politics and the Rhetoric of Poetry." *New England Quarterly* 34 (1961): 328–51.

Riffaterre, Michael. *Semiotics of Poetry.* Bloomington: Indiana University Press, 1984.

Rosenthal, M. L., ed. *The William Carlos Williams Reader.* New York: New Directions, 1966.

Rosenthal, M. L., and Sally M. Gall. *The Modern Poetic Sequence: The Genius of Modern Poetry.* New York: Oxford University Press, 1983.

Ruddick, Sara. *Maternal Thinking: Toward a Politics of Peace.* Boston: Beacon Press, 1989.

Schaum, Melita. "Views of the Political in the Poetics of Wallace Stevens and H. D." In Melita Schaum, ed., *Wallace Stevens and the Feminine,* 171–89. Tuscaloosa: University of Alabama Press, 1993.

———. *Wallace Stevens and the Critical Schools.* Tuscaloosa: University of Alabama Press, 1988.

———, ed. *Wallace Stevens and the Feminine.* Tuscaloosa: University of Alabama Press, 1993.

Shelley, Percy Bysshe. "A Defence of Poetry." In David Perkins, ed., *English Romantic Writers,* 1131–46. New York: International Thomas Publishing, 1967.

"The Situation in American Writing." *Partisan Review* 6, no. 4 (summer 1939): 25–51; 6, no. 5 (fall 1939): 103–22.

Smith, William Gardner. "Status of the Negro." *New Republic* 122, no. 16 (17 April 1950): 27–28.

Southard, W. P. "Escape to Reality." *Kenyon Review* 8, no. 1 (winter 1946): 136–39.

"Stay Tough with Japan." *New Republic* 105, no. 11 (15 September 1941): 323.

Steiner, Wendy. *The Colors of Rhetoric*. Chicago: University of Chicago Press, 1982.

Stevens, Wallace. *Collected Poems*. New York: Alfred A. Knopf, 1954.

————. *Esthétique du Mal*. Illustrations by Wightman Williams. Cummington, Mass.: Cummington Press, 1945.

————. *Letters of Wallace Stevens*. New York: Alfred A. Knopf, 1966.

————. *The Man with the Blue Guitar and Other Poems*. New York: Knopf, 1937.

————. *The Necessary Angel: Essays on Reality and the Imagination*. New York: Alfred A. Knopf, 1951.

————. *Notes toward a Supreme Fiction*. New York: Cummington Press, 1942.

————. *Opus Posthumous*. Ed. Milton Bates. New York: Alfred A. Knopf, 1989.

————. *Parts of a World*. New York: Alfred A. Knopf, 1942.

————. *Transport to Summer*. New York: Alfred A. Knopf, 1947.

Stovall, Tyler. *Paris Noir: African Americans in the City of Light*. Boston: Houghton Mifflin, 1996.

Strachey, John. "Bombing Is a Quiet Business." *New Republic* 105, no. 19 (10 November 1941): 617–19.

Straight, Michael. "Hitler's Guerillas over Here." *New Republic* 106, no. 45 (13 April 1942): 481–83.

Strom, Martha Helen. "The Uneasy Friendship of William Carlos Williams and Wallace Stevens." *Journal of Modern Literature* 11, no. 2 (July 1984): 291–98.

T. R. B. "After the Charter Is Ratified." *New Republic* 113, no. 4 (23 July 1945): 102–3.

————. "Atomic Anxieties." *New Republic* 113, no. 8 (20 August 1945): 222.

Vendler, Helen. "Introduction." In Helen Vendler, ed., *Harper American Literature*, 2 vols., 2: 1527–30. New York: Harper and Row, 1987.

Von Hallberg, Robert, ed. *Politics and Poetic Value*. Chicago: University of Chicago Press, 1987.

Wahl, Jean. Review of *Selected Poems*, by John Crowe Ransom. *New Republic* 113, no. 7 (13 August 1945): 196–98.

Walker, David. *The Transparent Lyric: Reading and Meaning in the Poetry of Stevens and Williams*. Princeton, N.J.: Princeton University Press, 1984.

Walsh, Thomas. *Concordance to Wallace Stevens*. University Park: Pennsylvania State University Press, 1963.

Wentersdorf, Karl P. "Wallace Stevens, Dante Alighieri and the Emperor." *Twentieth Century Literature* 13, no. 4 (1968): 197–204.

Weston, Susan B. "The Artist as Guitarist: Stevens and Picasso." *Criticism* 17 (1975): 111–20.

————. *Wallace Stevens: An Introduction to the Poetry*. New York: Columbia University Press, 1977.

"What Next in Asia?" *New Republic* 105, no. 23 (8 December 1941): 750–51.

Whittemoore, Reed. *Little Magazines.* University of Minnesota Pamphlets on
   American Writers, no. 32. Minneapolis: University of Minnesota Press, 1963.
Williams, Oscar, ed. *The War Poets.* New York: John Day, 1945.
Williams, William Carlos. "Against the Weather: A Study of the Artist" (1939).
   Reprinted in William Carlos Williams, *Selected Essays of William Carlos
   Williams,* 196–218. New York: Random House, 1954.
———. *Collected Poems: 1921–1931.* New York: Objectivist Press, 1934.
———. *An Early Martyr and Other Poems.* New York: Alcestis, 1935.
———. "For a New Magazine." *Blues* 1, no. 2 (March 1929): 30–32.
———. Review of *The Man with the Blue Guitar and Other Poems,* by Wallace
   Stevens. *New Republic* 93, no. 1198 (17 November 1937): 50.
Winters, Yvor. "Wallace Stevens, or the Hedonist's Progress." In Yvor Winters, *The
   Anatomy of Nonsense,* 88–119. Norfolk, Conn.: New Directions, 1943.
Yeats, W. B. *The Collected Poems of W. B. Yeats.* New York: Macmillan, 1950.
Young, Michael. "Life under the Robot Bombs." *New Republic* 111, no. 10
   (4 September 1944): 271–72.

INDEX

Page references to illustrations are given in italics.

conversion to, 54; and sexism, rejection
of, 106–19 *passim*; and temptation to
despair during WWII, 60–70 *passim*,
74–78, 80–82, 89; and *textuality*, 121–22,
139–40; and theories of language, 9–10;
and war anthologies, 132–135; and Yeats,
135–36. *See also individual titles of works.*
Strachey, John, on life in London during
war, 165 (n. 35)
Structuralism, 3
"Study of Two Pears" (Stevens), 17
"Suicide on the Bridge" (Klee), 131
"Sunday Morning" (Stevens), 15, 31, 34,
63–64, 68, 82, 101, 109
Supplement to the *Oxford English Dictionary*, 31
Surrealism, 17

Tate, Allen, 28, 47, 122
Textuality, 121, 139, 177 (n. 23)
Theater, changes in meaning of, 31
"Things of August" (Stevens), 116
"Thirteen Ways of Looking at a Blackbird"
(Stevens), 142, 143
"This Is Just to Say" (W. Williams), 18,
33–35
"Thought Revolved, A" (Stevens), 100, 101
Three Travelers at Sunrise (Stevens), 143
"To a Solitary Disciple" (W. Williams), 17
"To the One of Fictive Music" (Stevens),
104, 111
Toynbee, Arnold, 3
Transport to Summer (Stevens), 7, 57,
58–60, 64, 69, 81, 93, 119, 121
T. R. B., 171 (n. 6), 172 (n. 13)
Trilling, Lionel, 28
"Two at Norfolk" (Stevens), 148
"Two Figures in Dense Violet Night"
(Stevens), 100
"Two Tales of Liadoff" (Stevens), 87–88
"Two Theoretic Poems" (Stevens), 31

Van Geyzel, Leonard, 61, 168 (n. 9), 169
(n. 15)
"Variations on a Summer Day" (Stevens),
11, 160 (n. 4)

Vendler, Helen, on poetry in anthologies,
161 (n. 9)
Vesuvius, 72
Vietnam War, 2
"Virgin Carrying a Lantern" (Stevens), 144,
148
Von Hallberg, Robert, 157 (n. 2)

Wahl, Jean, 27
War and the Poet (Eberhart and Rodman),
132, 134, 177 (n. 12)
War Poets, The (O. Williams), 177 (n. 12)
Wedge, The (W. Williams), 176 (n. 6)
Weil, Simone, on "decreation," 140
Weston, Susan, 174 (n. 15)
"What Can We Defend?" (Pratt), 30
"What Next in Asia?" 38, 163 (n. 25)
Whitman, Walt, 3, 46
Whitmanian tradition, 130
Whittemoore, Reed, 158 (introduction,
n. 8)
Williams, Oscar, and war anthologies, 26,
82, 134
Williams, Wightman, 122–23, 128, 135,
176 (nn. 6, 11); *Esthétique du Mal*
illustrations, 126, 129, 133, 138
Williams, William Carlos: on Dante and
structural form, 165 (n. 5); illustrations
for *The Wedge*, 176 (n. 6); review of
Stevens's *The Man with the Blue Guitar
and Other Poems*, 159 (n. 15); Stevens's
concord with, 139; Stevens's reactions
against, 9, 11–19, 83, 85, 171 (n. 3);
mentioned, viii, 1, 5, 8, 82, 95, 106, 169
(n. 18), 174 (n. 17), 176 (n. 6), 177 (n. 22),
178 (n. 8). *See also individual titles of
works.*
Winters, Yvor, early criticism of Stevens's
poetry, 160 (n. 1)
Wister, Owen, praising Hemingway's
masculine voice, 106–7
"Woman Sings a Song for a Solider Come
Home, A" (Stevens), 171 (n. 10)
"Woman Who Blamed Life on a Spaniard,
The" (Stevens), 104
Women's suffrage, 105